KU-482-289

Contents

Acknowledgements

MARY ROBINSON AND I were first elected to Seanad Eireann on the same day in 1969. It was a special pleasure, therefore, to interview her in June 1997 for this book. It was an interview in which her qualities of self-confidence, compassion and good humour were especially evident, and in which she spoke with her customary frankness about her life in Irish politics and some of the key events in her career.

This interview was one of a number carried out for this book. Many of them were with friends and key contemporaries of Mary Robinson, whose insights and recollections have been incorporated into the text generally – and at their request – without direct attribution. My own records of my period in the Parliamentary Labour Party were a primary source for this critically important period in the evolution of Mary Robinson's politics, and additional research was carried out in Oireachtas records and newspaper archives. A number of earlier books, including those by Fergus Finlay, Deirdre McQuillan, Emily O'Reilly and Michael O'Sullivan are fully identified where appropriate in the footnotes rather than in an orthodox bibliography.

At the O'Brien Press, Fran Power and the team performed miracles in producing this book in an extraordinarily short period of time. I am also indebted to Desmond Fisher, who first edited my copy in 1962 and still has a few lessons to teach me. And throughout all this, the encouragement and support of my wife, Mary Jones, and my family, for an enterprise which made its own intense demands on them, deserves my very special acknowledgement and thanks.

Do
Mhná na hÉireann

MARY ROBINSON

JOHN HORGAN lectures in journalism at Dublin City University, and writes for the *Irish Times* and international periodicals as well as contributing to current affairs programmes on Irish and British radio and television. He has been a member of both the Dáil and the Senate, to which he was elected in 1969 on the same day as Mary Robinson. He has published a number of books, including *Labour: The Price of Power* and a biography of Seán Lemass.

MARY ROBINSON

AN INDEPENDENT VOICE

John Horgan

THE O'BRIEN PRESS

DUBLIN

First published 1997 by The O'Brien Press Ltd.,
20 Victoria Road, Rathgar, Dublin 6, Ireland.

© for text – John Horgan
© for layout, cover design – The O'Brien Press Ltd.

ISBN 0-86278-540-5

British Library Cataloguing-in-Publication Data
Cataloguing information for this title is available from the British Library

1 2 3 4 5 6 7 8 9 10
97 98 99 00 01 02 03 04 05 06

The O'Brien Press receives assistance from The Arts Council/An Chomhairle Ealaíon

Typesetting, editing, layout, design: The O'Brien Press Ltd.
Indexing: Helen Litton
Cover photograph: Conor Horgan
Cover separations: Lithoset Ltd
Printing: Hartnolls Ltd

Introduction

THE LAST TIME there was a woman in power in the Park was nearly a century ago. The woman was Queen Victoria, who was on an official visit to Ireland in April 1900, 'in all the decrepitude of her eighty-one years', as the nationalist revolutionary Maud Gonne put it pugnaciously, to boost Irish recruitment to the British forces for the Boer War. One afternoon during her visit, the approach roads to the Vice-Regal Lodge in the Phoenix Park were thronged with carriages. The carriages were bringing some 5,000 children – dressed in the height of fashion and carefully selected from Dublin's most loyal families – who had been invited by the Lord Lieutenant of Ireland to a garden party in honour of the Queen.

Elsewhere in Dublin, a city that contained some of the most foetid slums in Europe, a number of young nationalist women had other ideas. They decided that the Queen, and her administration in Ireland, should be pointedly reminded that they did not have any monopoly on patriotism. There and then they founded a new organisation – Inghinidhe na hÉireann or Daughters of Ireland – through which nationalist women such as Maud Gonne, Constance Markievicz and many others were to give forceful expression to a new women's consciousness in political, social and economic affairs. For the next two months, Maud Gonne and her helpers organised, street by street, a Patriotic Children's Treat which brought an astonishing 30,000 children from the other Ireland to festivities in the Phoenix Park, just outside the gates of the Vice-Regal Lodge where Victoria had entertained the loyal children of the bourgeoisie.

Nine decades later in 1990 the iron gates of the Vice-Regal Lodge, now the official residence of the President of Ireland, were thrown open – from the inside – by an Irish woman, to Irish children and adults of all social classes and every political allegiance. Mary Robinson, Ireland's first woman president, was in the process of turning an institution that had become virtually fossilised and politically irrelevant into a powerful symbol of the Ireland that had shaped her and a new generation of confident, talented and outward-looking young Irish men and women.

Mary Robinson, like Maud Gonne, is a profound believer in things Irish and a passionate supporter of social justice. The similarities between her and Maud Gonne, however, should not be overdrawn. The woman who became President of Ireland in 1990 is a constitutional lawyer: Maud Gonne was a firebrand, dedicated to overthrowing the constitutional link that bound

Ireland to Britain, a woman for whom W.B. Yeats conceived a fatal attraction, and a relentless opponent of compromise and of Britain.

More significant than these accidents of history is the fact that the women who came together to organise that patriotic garden party for the poor of Dublin in 1900 realised after the event that the momentum they had built up was precious and should not be dissipated. Inghinidhe na hÉireann flourished for a decade or more before it was absorbed into – and to some extent domesticated by – Cumann na mBan, the women's arm of the Irish Volunteers. Ninety years later, Mná na hÉireann, the women of Ireland, emerged from the same sort of process as an unstructured but powerful vehicle that helped to propel Mary Robinson into the presidency.

Mary Robinson shared the burning sense of the need for justice of those early campaigners, but worked in a different era and in different ways. She won an election campaign that seemed at the outset as hopeless a cause as any of their crusades, but that succeeded in focusing the hopes and aspirations of the Irish people as a whole on objectives and ideals characterised by inclusiveness and by a rare sensitivity to the marginalised and the forgotten.

She could not have done any of this without an unusual degree of political skill: a sense of humanity alone is rarely enough for success in this much-contested field. And the political skills which Mary Robinson brought to the presidency on her election in 1990 had been honed in the rough and tumble of institutions which show little mercy to the unprepared and the neophyte: the courts of justice and the Irish democratic political system.

She had a childhood and upbringing that was by any Irish standards comfortable, even privileged. She was the child of professionals, both doctors, she received the best private education available before being sent to Trinity College Dublin to study law. Throughout her university career, she garnered first class honours with deceptive ease, but the social conscience which was to flower later did not really appear publicly until after a sojourn at the Harvard Law School in the late 1960s. Here, American student radicalism and Irish idealism combined to provide the launching pad for an extraordinary politico-legal career.

It was a career that started with a huge sense of promise, but which seemed almost to go off the rails at mid-point, taking twists and turns which showed that she was not entirely in control of its direction or speed. She was elected to the Senate on her first attempt in 1969, at the age of twenty-five. Her early years there were characterised by the development of a form of political guerrilla warfare, in which – despite the fact that she could rarely count on more than a handful of senators to support some of her legislative initiatives – she focused public attention on the Senate itself and on the issues she raised to a hitherto unknown degree.

Some of the issues had for years been taboo in Irish society – or at least in the legislature. Family planning had been banned for more than thirty years: she was to embarrass all the major political parties with her insistent demands for change. Discrimination against married couples of different religions who wanted to adopt children was another area in which she cheerfully took on the powerful interests of the Catholic Church. Divorce, which had been dropped like a hot potato by an Irish prime minister four years before her election, was to be addressed as well. And behind these issues relating to family and reproduction, she focused on other issues connected with equality: equal pay for women in the workplace, equal social welfare rights, equal pension rights.

Side by side with this developed a legal career which was to make her an increasingly familiar figure in the Irish Supreme Court and, eventually, the European Court of Justice. When the legislature remained obdurate, judges could sometimes be persuaded to change the law on the basis of specific cases: the family's rights to marital privacy; a woman's right to legal aid to fight her estranged husband in court; a married couple's right to fair tax treatment – all these provided landmark cases where her forensic skills led eventually to changes in Irish legislation through the medium of the courts.

Some seven years into this career, a deepening commitment led her to join the Labour Party. She remained a member for nine years, but it was a period during which the initial sense of party commitment gave way all too rapidly to a sense of frustration at the slowness of progress. The possibility of attaining executive power as a member of an Irish Cabinet receded with two successive defeats in Dáil elections (she retained her Senate seat), and vanished completely in 1984 when she was passed over for the post of Attorney-General. A year later she had resigned from the Labour Party – not on this issue, but on an issue connected with Northern Ireland – and had returned to her original independent status.

In 1987 she fought her last general election. Shortly afterwards, she announced that she would no longer seek elective office. With her husband, the lawyer Nicholas Robinson, she set up the Centre for European Law in her old university, Trinity College, and prepared for an orderly withdrawal from the world of democratic politics she had inhabited for almost twenty years.

At the beginning of 1990, however, the leader of the Labour Party, Dick Spring, began actively canvassing the idea that the presidency, due to become vacant at the end of the same year, should be the subject of a contested election instead of merely being filled by a non-controversial candidate agreed between the parties. By February, Mary Robinson's name was being discussed as a candidate. Still determined to maintain her independence, she declined to rejoin the party as the price of securing the nomination, and that was nearly that. But the party decided to go ahead on her terms and she was nominated. In December 1990 she was elected after one of the most unusual election campaigns in Irish political history, in which she came from behind to turn what her supporters had hoped would be, at best, a modest moral victory into a triumph.

In the following seven years, she pioneered – as she had promised she would during her election campaign – a new kind of presidency: open, interactive, participatory and inclusive. A new relationship had to be hammered out between president and government and the process did not take place without intermittent pain, misunderstanding, and even suspicion. There was a new sense of openness to the North, both nationalist and unionist. Groups in Irish society which had been, at best, brushed under the carpet or, at worst, reviled, found a welcome in the Phoenix Park: travellers, gays, people with disabilities. The minorities which had helped to propel her into the presidency were now, in effect, part of a national coalition. And, linking that coalition together, women of all classes and ages responded to her leadership, just as she had tapped their political potential.

At the end of her presidency, with an approval rating from the Irish electorate that was consistently higher than that won by any elected leader in Europe (or perhaps anywhere), she had achieved a moral authority which stood almost in inverse relationship to the highly circumscribed set of functions and powers allotted to her under the Constitution. She could have had a second seven-year term for the asking. Instead, she looked outwards, towards the United Nations, where a chance vacancy in the key High Commissionership for Human Rights suddenly offered the prospect of doing the sort of work to which she was most committed, at an international level where it could be particularly effective. In June 1997 she was confirmed as the UN Secretary-General's nominee for the position by the UN General Assembly and the next phase in a truly remarkable career was about to begin for her at the age of fifty-three. With her track record, it would be unwise to predict that it would be the last.

This book is essentially an examination of the politics of Mary Robinson's career, now spanning almost three decades of one of the most formative and tumultuous times in modern Irish history, as she leaves to take up what she herself describes as 'the worst job in the world, but the one I really want'. It is, therefore, the story of a remarkable Irish woman, of her contribution to the politics and public life of the country which elected her against the odds as its president, and to which she gave so much of herself.

CHAPTER 1

The Beginning: Bright Hopes

MARY BOURKE WAS BORN in Ballina, Co. Mayo, on 21 May 1944, to parents who were both medical doctors. The young Mary Bourke benefited not only from a warm and supportive family environment but from every possible advantage that her parents could provide. Her father is Aubrey Bourke, whose family had links to the British colonial service, combining a certain genteel Anglo-Irishry with a sense of stock that had been firmly planted in the Mayo soil for generations. Her mother was Tessa O'Donnell from Co. Donegal, a keen sportswoman who was not known for hiding her opinions. Both parents were Catholic but their forebears were of Protestant and Anglo-Norman stock who had been in Mayo since the thirteenth century. Through inter-marriage, some branches of the family, such as the branch that produced Mary Bourke, had become Catholics. In some cases, all the children of mixed marriages were brought up as Catholics, often despite the wishes of the Protestant partner; in others, the sons were brought up in the religion of the father, the daughters in the religion of the mother.

In political terms, the family would be assumed locally to have had Fine Gael sympathies, although it firmly eschewed overt political allegiances. Indeed, had Mary opted for that party in later life, she could, from a base in Mayo – the extended family probably mustered enough votes for a quota all on its own – have realistically expected a Dáil seat for as long as she wanted it, in all probability a Cabinet position, and a seat for the Connaught constituency in the European Parliament to round off a distinguished legal and political career.

Her position in the family provides a significant pointer to her future development. She was the only girl, sandwiched between two older and two younger brothers. It was a family of high achievers, in which intellectual rough and tumble was the order of the day and in which Mary's competitiveness was honed by sibling rivalry, as it was polished by sibling affection, until it shone.

Her brother Adrian remembers that she was always eager to prove her abilities *vis-à-vis* those of other members of her family.[1]

Commonsense suggests also that her position in the family as the only daughter, and the child of a mother who not only had strong opinions of her own but who was also a doctor, strongly influenced her intellectual development. 'A family isn't complete', her mother said before her daughter's birth, 'until there's a Mary in it.' High achievers, psychologists know, almost invariably hold special family positions, in that they have been treated as special by the family as a whole, or by key members of it, early in their development. Nor is the middle position in the family the disadvantage it is usually described to be: middle children accounted for 15% of US presidents and a quarter of all British prime ministers up to 1980.[2]

Sandwiched between two sets of brothers and the only daughter, it is not difficult to see that Mary Robinson was in some important respects, right from the beginning, the jewel in the crown. Her two older brothers, Aubrey and Oliver, both followed their parents into medicine (Aubrey was to die of cancer in 1984 at the age of forty-one). And it is certainly significant that her two younger brothers, Henry and Adrian, followed their older sister into law. Role models can cross gender boundaries, too.

Mary Bourke was educated first at a small private school in Ballina, run by a Miss Claire Ruddy, an independent-minded woman with strong nationalist views. Middle-class parents in towns like Ballina often supported, or even started, such establishments, to prepare their children for boarding school in Dublin or elsewhere. If the object of such an education was to maintain social divisions, however, it conspicuously did not have this effect on the young Mary Bourke, who found that Claire Ruddy's nationalism and her own father's social conscience combined to produce a permanent and deeply personal sense of justice that was to provide much of the motivating force for an astonishing career.

'I had, I think, a sense of human rights from the age of about seven,' she recalled in an interview for this book. 'It was that sense of wanting to achieve greater equality. I used to walk the beach at Enniscrone and say to myself: "When I grow up I'm going to change this."

'It all happened in our house, because the surgery was in our house and I was very observant. My father had very poor people coming in every day or was visiting them on calls. I don't fully understand it, but I think I had a huge, very formative period in the back of my father's car, going on calls. I loved going with him – I loved being an adult with him at the age of six, seven and eight – one to one. I loved his company.'

She was subsequently sent to school in Mount Anville in Dublin, then one of Ireland's smallest and strictest convent boarding schools, at the age of ten. She stayed there from 1954 to 1961, where her intelligence and self-confidence were enhanced, if, indeed, this was necessary. One of her contemporaries remembers a 'lanky, slightly awkward, freckled young Ballina girl arriving, full of brains and sporting prowess, almost irritating in her all-round excellence'.[3] This was followed by a year in a finishing school in Paris at the quaintly named 'Madame Anita's'. Although to be at finishing school in Paris was a privilege few Irish girls of her age would have experienced, Mary Bourke was not living in the lap of luxury. There were times when she had to walk across the city, acquiring a close acquaintance with its cobblestones and alleyways, in order to save the Metro fare. Many years later, on a State visit as President of Ireland, the Avenue des Champs-Élysées was closed off in her honour and her official limousine preceded by serried ranks of the Garde Republicaine. The contrast was not lost on the President.

One of her brothers, Henry Bourke, said later that the year in Paris completed the metamorphosis from tomboy to young woman. 'I still have a crystal-clear memory of the moment when it occurred to me that this distinctly feminine creature who spoke fluent French along with some Italian or Spanish, who could intelligently discuss art and literature and current affairs, was lost forever as Batman . . . or Robin!'

She won a scholarship in 1963 to Trinity College, Dublin (TCD), where, as a Catholic, she was a member of a minority. Most Catholic university students in Dublin attended University College, Dublin (UCD), a constituent college of the National University of Ireland (NUI), which enjoyed the approval of the Catholic bishops. Many years previously the Catholic hierarchy had instituted, and still maintained, a ban on Catholics attending Trinity, which the bishops thought would be injurious to their faith: the college had been established by Queen Elizabeth I in 1591 as a Protestant foundation for the 'banishment of barbarism, tumults and disorderly living'. As recently as 1954 the bishops' warning had been solemnly reiterated from Maynooth: one of its effects was to ensure the continued dominance of Protestants, many of them from Northern Ireland, among the student body. In the 1950s, only about a third of students were from the country's majority religion.

The fact that there were that many Catholics at TCD bespoke a somewhat casual attitude to episcopal warnings. The task of monitoring the ban was entrusted to the Archbishop of Dublin, who was in 1963 (and had been since 1940) John Charles McQuaid, an awesomely powerful cleric who negotiated with government ministers from a position of strength and who reiterated the hierarchy's ban in his annual Lenten regulations for the archdiocese. In theory, he was the only bishop who could decide when and under what conditions Catholics could attend the college. In practice, many other Irish bishops gave informal permission with increasing frequency to parents, among them Mary Bourke's, and other parents risked eternal damnation by making up their own minds. The bishops, after considering the matter intermittently at their meetings over five years, finally abolished the ban in 1970.

Mary and her four brothers all went to Trinity. Their mother, Tessa, decided at an early stage that there was no point in struggling with an endless series of apartments or other forms of rented accommodation and bought a house at 21 Westland Row, a small and somewhat dilapidated street just behind Trinity. The house was actually the birthplace of Oscar Wilde – a blue plaque on the wall notes the event – and the Wilde family lived there for a short time after his birth before moving a hundred yards or so to much grander accommodation on the corner of Merrion Square.

Tessa installed there Ann Coyne, better known as 'Nan', a Mayo woman of boundless energy and enormous home-making talents, who created a home from home for all the Robinson children during their period at university. This house – later bought by Trinity as part of its expansion plans – was to be the nerve-centre of Mary Bourke's campaign for the Senate in 1969.

Her academic career was marked at a very early stage by evidence of extraordinary ability. She won a scholarship to the university's Law School in 1965, and was in the thick of things almost immediately. The law school was something of an enclave within an enclave, tucked away inside a university that was only just beginning to be accessible to the Irish population as a whole. It was unusual in having a female professor, Fanny Moran, but the majority of the lecturers were somewhat staid part-timers with substantial careers elsewhere. Two exceptions were Max Abrahamson, a lively young Jewish solicitor with a taste for liberal causes, and Kadar Asmal, a South African of Indian origin who had made his base in Dublin where he was a lynch-pin of the Irish Anti-Apartheid Association. A long-time member of the African National Congress, he returned to South Africa as apartheid ended and became a minister in Nelson Mandela's first government.

Even in the mid-sixties, Mary Bourke stood out to some extent from the crowd – partly because she had little time for the student uniform of the day and favoured fairly restrained and unexceptional attire. She established a strong relationship with a fellow law student, Nicholas Robinson, who also had a talent as a cartoonist, and who – by his own account – used to sit at the back of the class drawing caricatures of the lecturers while Mary was sitting in the front row taking notes. A later cartoon, drawn to reassure Mary on the eve of her first public lecture as Reid Professor of Constitutional and Criminal Law in 1969, is of Mary herself, academic gown swirling, making an impassioned address to an empty lecture hall on 'Crowd Control and the Criminal Law'.

Although there were two universities in Dublin in the 1960s, there was little contact between them and it was to be late in the decade before a pushy Minister for Education, Donogh O'Malley, announced a scheme (which never finally materialised) to yoke the two institutions together. Law students, however, shared a professional training scheme and relationships were closer between the two law schools than in other areas. In the winter of 1965, for instance, Mary Bourke co-edited with Fergus Armstrong, a UCD law student, an issue of the *Irish Student Law Review*. For her contribution to the review, Mary chose to interview John A. Costello, a former Fine Gael Taoiseach (1948-51 and 1954-57) on his fifty years at the Irish Bar. Nick Robinson contributed some airy cartoons and a not entirely serious examination of the licensing laws. Members of the editorial board included Niall Connolly, later a Dublin solicitor and Labour Party stalwart who was to oversee one of Mary Robinson's unsuccessful Dáil election campaigns, and Harry Whelehan, who was Attorney-General in the Haughey and Reynolds Fianna Fáil governments in the period immediately after Mary Robinson's election as President and whose appointment as president of the High Court in 1994 precipitated one of the most gripping political crises the country has ever experienced.

Mary Bourke was awarded an LL.B and BL (both with first class honours) in 1967. She was called to the Bar in the same year. The next step was post-graduate study. Her profile had attracted the attention of some Harvard law professors, who suggested that she spend a year there studying for an LL.M. She replied cheerfully that she'd love to, if funding could be arranged. Harvard found money for her and she headed off for Cambridge. Fergus Armstrong was the other Irish post-graduate student at Harvard Law School in the same year.

Cambridge, Mass., in 1967-68, was a ferment of political as well as legal ideas. The young Irish graduate student found herself exposed not just to the raging controversies about civil rights which were at their peak towards the end of the Johnson era but to a sense of public service among her peers which at once surprised and strongly influenced her.

In the Harvard Law School, and not only in the LL.M class, were students from intensely privileged backgrounds who were becoming more and more politically involved in social and political causes, in some cases abandoning or certainly postponing lucrative careers in order to do so. Her classmates also formed a core group of lawyers from a wide range of countries: Italy, Brazil, Finland, Japan, Australia, Canada and France. Her key classes were in International Legal Processes (Abe Chayes), European Community Law (Henry Shiner) and in US Constitutional Law (Paul Freund). Her thesis, prefiguring an area of law which was to become a permanent passion, was on part of the Treaty of Rome – the Treaty that established the European Economic Community (EEC) and its associated institutions, including the European Court of Justice. Nor did this exhaust her interests: like other Harvard Law School students, she had the right to 'audit' (attend without taking examinations) other courses she was interested in, and during this eye-opening year she also sat at the feet of Alan Dershowitz, still today one of the best known criminal lawyers in America, and Archibald Cox, who later came to prominence as the independent counsel who helped to seal Richard Nixon's fate.

What was probably even more important than what she learned at Harvard, however, was the way that she learned it. In both the Dublin universities at that time, law lecturing was for the most part the preserve of lawyers whose view of their body of knowledge was highly systematic. The law was to be found in books and in reported judgements; it could be applied, in an almost Euclidean sense, to the solution of problems. The business of students was to learn the system and to apply it in line with the norms which had also been inculcated in the lecture halls.

In the major law schools in the United States in the late 1960s, however – not least because of the involvement of young US lawyers in the broiling politics of the day – the teaching of law had become more Socratic in its methodology. It had not yet reached the point at which law schools everywhere would break down into mutually suspicious camps, peopled by the proponents of critical legal studies on one hand and legal conservatism on the other. But the fashion was definitely changing.

'It was not so much that it put an old-fashioned notion of law out of my head,' Mary Robinson remembers, 'it was that it showed me the potential of law. The Law School at Trinity was a reasonably good school; classes were reasonably small; we were reasonably well taught by Irish standards, but we were *taught* law, and then suddenly I went to Harvard and it was a *learning together*. And don't forget it was the time of all that questioning about the war, about Vietnam, about civil rights. I learned that law is an instrument for social change. That's the phrase; I've used it a lot since. It's not a fixed point. You use it or abuse it as you wish, but it has a huge potential if you understand how to use it.'

For any young Irish law student, this was a fascinating experience. It could also be an intimidating one. The Harvard class did not have a separate corporate existence: under the modular system, its members (many of whom were international students and very few of whom were female) attended lectures with many of the undergraduates, depending on which courses they were taking. The process of dialogue and disputation, therefore, took place in large lecture halls where any student could be called on at any time by a lecturer to defend a position or advance an argument or a solution to a problem. Preparation was everything: if you went to class ill-prepared, there were no short-cuts and no way out. It tested Mary Bourke, as it tested many students; and her ability to rise to the challenge attracted a certain admiration from her contemporaries, not least because she was one of the few women in any of her courses.

It was a formative experience in very many ways, but the Mary Bourke being formed was more than just an academic high-flyer; she was also, as she recalled later very much the Irish girl a long way from home. In spite of the fact that she knew she was away only for a fixed period and would definitely be returning, the sense of distance could not be ignored.

'I was a student, away from home and homesick for my family and friends. I walked out one evening and happened to go into a Boston newsagent's shop. There, just at the back of the news stand, almost to my disbelief, was *The Western People*. I will never forget the joy with which I bought it and took it back with me and found, of course, that the river Moy was still there and the cathedral was still standing. I remember the hunger with which I read the news from home.'[4]

In all these circumstances, it is hardly surprising that she developed a desire to relate her American experiences to her work in Ireland when she got home – to fuse law and politics into 'an instrument for social change'. In 1968 she wrote an article on 'Urban Law Studies' for the *Dublin University Law Review* which put her American experience into a nutshell. She argued against undue concentration on the minutiae of legal precedents and in favour of an extension to Ireland of the 'Neighbourhood Law Offices' which, in the US, provided free legal services in slum areas. The shape of the future Free Legal Aid Centres (FLAC) was already making itself felt.

As Mary Robinson remembers it: 'I had been taught a course in Urban Legal Studies by Professor Garmolesky and that was exciting. It was new to me that law was an instrument of understanding and openness and potential for change and then I related that easily to an Irish environment in which so much needed to be changed. It was typical of me that I would write that – not that I necessarily wanted every law school to have a course in Urban Legal Studies, but I did want to say: "Open your eyes and see what law's about – it actually can change things." It probably is very indicative of my state of mind at that time.'

She concluded optimistically that the creation of courses in Urban Legal Studies in Irish universities 'would answer one of the basic demands of students, while fostering their latent idealism, that law becomes more relevant to them and to the environment in which they live. It would help meet the criticism that lawyers are an elite group who are unconcerned with social problems and disinterested in those unable to pay the costs of litigation. It would generate a new clinical approach to the study of law, encouraging research into housing and welfare problems in Irish cities and leading to inter-disciplinary courses with economists and sociologists which should be of benefit to all concerned.'

The 1969 general election offered her a first opportunity to put her principles into practice. It was a year in which Irish politics were in crisis. Decades of unresolved community tensions in Northern Ireland had led, first, to the emergence of a civil rights movement modelled in some respects on the American civil rights protests of the Johnson era, and then to widespread violence and arson, sectarian murders and a recrudescence of paramilitary conflict.

Irish society as a whole had become extraordinarily volatile in the preceding decade. In 1959, Eamon de Valera had retired at the age of seventy-seven to the presidency in the Phoenix Park after four decades in Irish politics. His successor as Taoiseach and leader of the Fianna Fáil party, Seán Lemass, had tapped into reservoirs of national optimism and creativity which many thought had run dry, launching a programme of economic development that staunched the flow of emigration and even encouraged many former emigrants to come home and take part in building a more vibrant country. The inauguration of Ireland's national television service on the last day of 1961 began to expand the national social agenda and introduced a long overdue bite and irreverence into the treatment of some national issues and controversies. The reforms of the second Vatican Council, which met in Rome from 1962 to 1965, gradually seeped into the consciousness of a sclerotic Irish Catholic Church whose younger members were becoming impatient at the immobilism of its hierarchy.

A new generation of younger politicians, especially on the left, encapsulated a hope that the sterile politics of the Irish civil war would at last be supplanted. In June 1969, Jack Lynch, Taoiseach and leader of the Fianna Fáil party, called a general election. Public and media attention focused on the Labour Party, which – although the smallest of the three main parties with just 22 seats out of 144 – had attracted a galaxy of new talent in the shape of television commentator David Thornley, former diplomat Conor Cruise O'Brien, and university professor Justin Keating. Earlier that year Labour had declared itself a socialist party and fielded ninety-nine candidates in the election; enough, theoretically, to provide it with an overall majority in the Dáil.

In the event, it was a false dawn. Although Thornley, O'Brien and Keating were all elected, the party was reduced to nineteen seats. Aided by a consummately crafted electoral gerrymander and by a campaign that appealed to a still conservative electorate by stressing Labour's 'alien ideology', Fianna Fáil now had a clear overall majority in the Dáil for the first time since 1944. There was comparatively little interest in the Senate election, held as usual some three months after the main contest, and such interest as there was became rapidly overshadowed by rising tension in the North.

The nature and composition of the Senate was not, in any case, calculated to kindle enthusiasm or ambition in any but the most doggedly devoted political breasts. As originally created in 1922, in the wake of the Treaty, it had been designed largely to provide disproportionate representation for southern unionists – that largely Protestant group of Irish men and women whose political sympathies lay with Britain but who had been cut adrift by the British government and left to fend for themselves in the new Irish Free State. In the Senate's early years W.B. Yeats and others used it sporadically as a sounding-board for minority opinion. Yeats once rose from his seat prophetically to warn an Irish government which was case-hardening the laws on divorce: 'If you show that this country, southern Ireland, is going to be governed by Catholic ideas and by Catholic ideas alone, you will never get the North. You will create an impassable barrier between south and north, and you will pass more and more Catholic laws, while the North will, gradually, assimilate its divorce and other laws to those of England. You will put a wedge into the midst of this nation.' The Senate's originally substantial powers were gradually whittled away by successive governments and it was even abolished briefly by Eamon de Valera in 1936. After its reconstitution in 1937 with limited powers – it could not initiate money bills and had limited powers to delay legislation coming from the Dáil – it had to some extent become a home for defeated or superannuated politicians.

The 1937 Constitution's version of the Senate was designed to be permanently controlled by the government of the day through the mechanism of having eleven of its sixty members directly appointed by the incoming Taoiseach. The electorate for another forty-three seats comprised approximately one thousand people who earned the right to vote by virtue of having been elected as members of various local authorities across the country. The huge majority of them were, of course, already members of one or other of the country's main political parties, which meant that independents – although they could readily secure nominations from voluntary associations – had for all practical purposes no hope at all of being elected.

The Taoiseach's eleven nominees and the forty-three members elected by county councillors left a balance of six, three of whom were elected by graduates of Dublin University, of which Trinity was a constituent college, and three by graduates of the National University of Ireland. This form of election to the Senate was an innovation of the 1937 Constitution, and one which solved an awkward problem for de Valera – up to then each of these two universities had been entitled to elect three members of Dáil Éireann. This was another device to ensure that the voice of Irish Protestants would be amplified in parliament, and was based on similar procedures in the British House of Commons which continued to give parliamentary representation to the universities of Oxford and Cambridge until well into the 1940s.

These university Senate seats, ironically, were the only ones which mirrored to any degree the supposedly vocational character of the upper house of the British parliament in that those who occupied them were generally politically independent and supported by strong vocational interests among their electorates – notably doctors and teachers. This was the staid and decorous environment which was unexpectedly enlivened by the appearance of a twenty-five year old woman who put herself forward in what appeared to be, at first sight, an utterly quixotic and hopelessly ambitious campaign.

Astonishingly, there were only four candidates, including Mary Bourke, for the three Dublin University Senate seats. This did not make it any easier to win a seat: the small size of the electorate – 6,625 – meant that there was a battle for every vote. The situation had to some extent been opened up by the announced retirement from politics of Senator W.B. Stanford, the venerable Trinity classicist. Conventional wisdom, however, suggested that this vacancy would be filled by former senator Owen Sheehy Skeffington, a liberal and a lecturer in French in the college who had unexpectedly lost his seat in 1965. The two incumbent senators were W.J.E. Jessop, who was over sixty, and John Ross, who was fifty, twice Mary Bourke's age. Jessop represented the powerful medical establishment, which tended to vote as a bloc. Ross, who had successfully contested the constituency in 1961 and 1965, represented conservative business interests. With Stanford's retirement, Skeffington was widely expected to win back a seat: his defeat in 1965 was probably the result of over-confidence on the part of his supporters, who would not make the same mistake twice. Few people would have rated the chances of Mary Bourke, a graduate of only two years standing, against either Ross or Jessop.

The Dublin University Senate constituency, like its National University counterpart, is in effect an amalgam of different constituencies – lawyers, doctors, business people, teachers, scientists and so on – geographically spread all over the globe and united only by their shared university experience. There was one significant difference, however, that marked off the Trinity constituency not only from the other Senate constituencies but even from that of the National University: its size. Partly because of the Catholic 'ban' on Trinity, the number of the College's graduates was small and had been so for years. As new graduates were added to the roll and older ones died, it grew but at a decorous pace. In 1969, the explosion of student numbers at third level as a result of free secondary education and increased economic prosperity had only just begun to appear on the horizon.

The ballot is a postal one and the constituency's three Senate seats are elected by proportional representation. Candidates therefore, however much they may have developed a power base in one or other of the occupational groups mentioned, have to appeal to as many constituencies as possible. It was an uphill task for anyone against one former senator and three incumbents, but it was not one that held much terror for the young part-time law lecturer and barrister. As Mary Robinson recalls: 'I've said – and it's true – that part of it was

Harvard arrogance. The sheer confidence of having been in that company for a year and seeing young people taking responsibility was an eye-opener. They were afraid of no-one and speaking for themselves. I was a bit younger than most of them. Most of them were married.

'Somehow, coming back to Ireland, I was asking all the questions. Very shortly after I came back I started at the Bar and began tutoring in UCD and an election was being called. I learned – but I suppose I knew it too from my days in College – that following that there would be the Senate election, and I began to take an interest in it and to ask: "Why should university senators be elderly male professors?"

'I remember that the more I asked the question, the more I knew the answer I wanted people to give me – I talked people into saying: "Why don't you go [for the senate]?" because I wanted to have a vehicle for change. In fact, I underestimated what I was asking, and the fact that it would be much more difficult than I imagined, but it kept getting that momentum.'

If, as has been suggested, the Senate had become to some extent a home for elderly politicians, why would the young Mary Bourke have seen it – rather than the Dáil – as her first objective? The answer is simple enough: wherever she would run, she would run as an independent; very few independents ever succeed in being elected to the Dáil and have little power if they do get there; and the university constituencies had a tradition of electing non-party candidates whose independence, even if it was somewhat lethargically exercised, was generally recognised. It was the obvious place to try.

Just as the campaign started, she won further recognition by being appointed Reid Professor of Criminal and Constitutional Law at Trinity. The Reid Professorship was a part-time position, established in 1888. It was part-time because then, as now, most newly-qualified barristers had to scratch around for a living in the courts of justice and the founders of the professorship thought that it would be an appropriate income supplement for bright young lawyers in their early years. In its original form, it had been designed to further the study of criminology; in practice, it was used by the Trinity law school to attract energetic young lawyers who might be expected to lecture, not just on criminology but on almost anything else as the occasion demanded. It was not so well-paid as to attract a flood of applicants: in 1969, when Mary Bourke was awarded it, it had been vacant for two years. When she vacated the position in 1975, it was turned into a full-time post, but for the time being it was one that suited her talents and her energy admirably and gave her a public platform.

In the summer of 1969, however, the Reid Professorship, for all the sonority of the title, did not make its holder a household name. Mary Bourke's campaign had to appeal, therefore, to all the variegated mini-constituencies or interest groups in the Trinity electorate and to do so virtually from a standing start.

One of her key helpers in this process was her younger brother, Adrian, who had been president of the Trinity Student Union in 1968-69. His own talents and contacts were now brought to bear on the task of getting his sister elected to the Senate. The Bourke brothers were something of a legend in their time in Trinity: passionately interested in rugby and in horse-racing, they had a way of making their presence felt and their views known. Trevor West, a young mathematician who was (and still is) actively involved in the college's many sporting activities, found himself 'volunteered' as Mary Bourke's election agent after he had been confronted by a posse of male Bourkes who would not take no for an answer. Later during the campaign she was to stay at his family home in Cork where she captivated his father, who in turn rallied the electoral troops in the southern capital. The house at 21 Westland Row became the nerve centre of activities: one of its rooms was turned into a war-room, with wall-mounted maps identifying key towns and individuals. At a certain stage each evening, the candidate would be sent to bed and the campaign team, fortified by bottles of stout and plates of bacon and eggs prepared by the stalwart Ann Coyne, planned the next day's strategy.

Envelopes were addressed to the electors, not least by Mary Bourke's schoolgirl successors at Mount Anville, and lists of friends and friends of friends were drawn up *ad infinitum*, to be targeted by teams of letter-writers. At one point a doctor in the south of England, himself a Trinity graduate who had written about 150 letters to friends and colleagues asking them to vote for Mary Bourke, contacted the election headquarters to tell them that he himself had received no fewer than eleven such 'targeted' letters from others, and that if he received any more he would be seriously tempted to vote for someone else. Ann Lane, a secretary who had worked part-time in the Trinity Student Union and had helped Adrian in his earlier campaigns for election to the Student Union, volunteered to help with the new venture and came in after work to type letters on a miracle of modern technology – an IBM golfball typewriter. Ann was to become Mary's full-time personal secretary in 1972 and, several generations of technology later, personal secretary to the newly-elected President of Ireland.

Mary Bourke was the first woman candidate in the Dublin University – indeed either university – constituency and the first Catholic. And her first election address was carefully crafted to avoid the pitfalls that she knew awaited her. She had to offer herself as a credible young candidate but one dissociated from wild-eyed radicalism; she had to appeal to a number of key occupational groups and she had to break new ground. Her appeal then was deliberately aimed at four key groups: she offered herself to the electorate 'as a young person, as a liberal, as a lawyer and as a woman'.

One of the primary characteristics of a university senatorship is, of course, that its holders, independent members of the Oireachtas, generally have no executive power. Their election addresses, therefore, tend to be short on specifics, to indicate attitudes rather than to make policy commitments and to gather support in as many quarters as possible without alienating it unnecessarily in others. The political language is coded and oblique. In many respects, Mary Bourke's address fitted this classic mode: what made it different from most of those of her predecessors and her competitors, however, was that, given the circumstances of thirty years ago, it took more risks.

The appeal to youth was problematic for two reasons. In the first place, young graduates are highly mobile, geographically speaking. In the late 1960s in Ireland, in particular, they were moving from job to job and from country to country. The electoral register maintained by the university authorities relied on information from the graduates themselves when they changed addresses and, as general elections took place every three or four years on average, huge numbers of ballot papers were routinely returned marked 'Gone Away'. Young voters would have been disproportionately highly represented in this group.

The second reason was that the older generation of voters – more settled in their ways, more likely to exercise the franchise – were likely to view the youth revolution of the late 1960s with an occasionally jaundiced eye. That revolution, launched in Paris, in Berlin and in the United States with unparalleled vigour, shook at least one national government – that of President Charles de Gaulle – and spawned a rash of analyses and predictions not calculated to reassure political and social establishments anywhere.

By the time this tide had reached the periphery of Europe it had lost some of its force, but nowhere was immune from its effects. Students in Dublin became more conscious of their rights; there were occasional sit-ins in university offices. Across the city, in University College, Dublin, several thousand students launched a peaceful occupation of the university's Great Hall in what came to be known as 'the gentle revolution': they were led by, among others, a bearded architectural student named Ruairí Quinn (known colloquially, and for obvious reasons, as 'Ho Chi Quinn'), who was to become a Labour Party politician, a colleague and supporter of Mary Robinson in the Parliamentary Labour Party (PLP) and Minister for Finance in the 1994-1997 government.

The Trinity protests were on the whole more decorous, although the college also harboured a small cell of students who were inspired by Mao's cultural revolution and achieved hitherto unattempted levels of disruption at university functions and public meetings. Mary Bourke's task was to harness the commitment of these young people and at the same time to avoid giving the impression that she was in thrall to their sometimes febrile enthusiasms. Her address approached the thorny question of student unrest with an even-handedness that indicated at the very least caution and possibly also the fact that her own political trajectory was only in its early stages. Student unrest, she observed, was a contributing factor to university reform because it was vital, socially committed and a challenge to the sometimes complacent members of the academic world. 'However', she added, 'I am not blind to the shortcomings of some of the methods employed by students in furthering their aims. Students are not exempt from the dictates of good manners.'

Her address also emphasised her own youth and her hope to 'contribute to the evolution of this state, looking to the future rather than to the past'. Young graduates themselves were not prominent among her major supporters but four key names were those of David Spearman, a young scientist; Brendan Kennelly, the young poet and lecturer in English; Howard Kinlay, a gifted student politician who was president of the Union of Students in Ireland in 1968, and was to die tragically young; and Trevor West.

This appeal to youth was balanced by other names designed to assure older voters that her head and her heart were not speaking different languages. A Church of Ireland bishop was among her nominators, and her list of supporters was well-freighted with names calculated to appeal to the older generation: one of them had graduated from Trinity fifty-five years earlier, in 1914; another, Thekla Beere, the first woman ever to be appointed secretary of a department of state, had graduated in 1923.

It was hardly taking a risk, in the Trinity constituency, for a candidate to appeal to the electorate as a 'liberal': Trinity graduates had long prided themselves on this adjective, however selective they might have been in their understanding of it. What was new was that whereas this stance was almost expected of the traditional run of male, Protestant candidates, it was astonishing territory for a Catholic and a woman to enter. And she struck a modestly specific note: the need for civil liberties in the Republic and the danger of a 'self-satisfied Ireland'. In the late 1960s, this could be readily decoded to mean principally one thing: the dominant attitudes of Irish Catholic society and its clerical leaders to the vexed questions of contraception and divorce. Pope Paul VI's encyclical forbidding artificial methods of birth control, *Humanae Vitae*, had been issued in 1968. Catholic Ireland, which had in large part expected the decision to go the other way, was in ferment; but all except the most courageous were keeping their heads well below the parapet. Divorce was another matter entirely. Seán Lemass, Taoiseach between 1959 and 1966, had put the matter on the agenda, not least because of its perceived significance to Northern Ireland, and had even set up an all-party Oireachtas Committee on the Constitution. However, it was to be almost three decades and two referenda later before the constitutional ban on divorce legislation was removed, and for a Catholic candidate in an election in 1969 – even in a predominantly Protestant constituency – to hint, however obliquely, at raising the matter in parliament was quite exceptional. As it turned out, this particular issue was low on Mary Bourke's agenda at the time.

The longest of her four sections, however, was that on the law. It burns with an unmistakable impatience to get at the business of law-making, to expose the political executive and the administrative bureaucracy to public scrutiny and accountability. And it exemplifies one of the Robinson core values: a passionate belief in law as an instrument of justice. It marked her off then, and does so to this day, from those of her contemporaries in the profession who see it primarily as a method for settling disputes and from politicians who see it as the articulation of the necessary compromises between conflicting interest groups in the society for which they have to legislate.

'In a way', she recalls, 'I think I have retained that sense – not that law is the answer to everything, but it's at the heart of structural and policy changes and you've got to get it right. You've got to be very faithful to the small print of it because there's no good in having good intentions with law and not having good drafting, or a good policy.'

The newest note of all in her address, however, was struck in the section on women. For all its caution, it broke distinctly new ground. The women who had been elected to the Oireachtas – apart from the firebrands like Countess Markievicz who had been elected in the heady days of the War of Independence – had almost universally been widows or children of former TDs who owed their seats to the conservatism of the Irish electorate and the dominance of the party system. There was a precedent in Northern Ireland where, in April 1969, Bernadette Devlin, a twenty-one year old civil rights worker, won a by-election to Westminster in the mid-Ulster constituency, becoming the youngest MP in that assembly, the youngest woman MP ever there and the youngest MP elected on universal suffrage. In Trinity's sister constituency, that of the National University, no woman was elected until nine years later when Gemma Hussey took a seat as an independent (she had been a member of the Fine Gael party since 1972 but did not accept the party whip in the Senate until 1980). Trinity itself had no teaching women fellows until June 1968 when, in a marked break with tradition, five were appointed.

'For too long', Mary Bourke told her voters, 'Irish women complained sporadically about discrimination, and yet on the whole were content to relax back into the sphere of influence to which they felt they belonged – the bosom of their family. Now, like women elsewhere in the world, they are beginning to play a significant part in the political, social and economic life of the country. This concrete achievement is a much more cogent argument than the slogans of an aggressive feminist. The more we are ready to branch out and fulfil ourselves in the life of the country, the more doors will open in the face of quiet ability and feminine qualities of efficiency and good humour.'

The same note, combining self-affirmation with an unwillingness to allow anyone else – even another woman – to write her political agenda, was evident in a shorter, personal letter to supporters: 'As a woman I would be proud to demonstrate that we can play a role in public life in Ireland without having to make an issue of it, or be an aggressive feminist.'

The election, when it took place on 12 August, saw Mary Bourke sweep into the Senate with an apparent ease that belied the frenzied efforts of the campaign. Only 4,630 graduates of the 6,625 electorate voted in the TCD Senate election of 1969. Owen Sheehy Skeffington re-took the seat he had lost in 1965, buoyed up by a wave of support from many graduates (including his cousin, Conor Cruise O'Brien), some of whom had wrongly assumed at the previous election that his seat was a safe one. W.J.E. Jessop retained the core medical vote and the Senate seat that went with it. Neither of these results could fairly be described as a surprise – but Mary Bourke's was. She out-polled Ross by 1,140 to 853 on the first count and was easily elected on the second count by a margin of 300 votes. Her reaction to the result was almost one of surprise: given that there were so few young graduates on the register, she said, it meant that 'the older generation are giving the younger a chance'. Serving notice of her future intentions, she added that there was scope for a real extension of civil rights in Ireland, instead of the 'mere verbal tolerance' which had been the rule up to now.

Nor was she the sole representative of the younger generation. That Senate contained, unusually, four members under thirty. Mary was not the youngest of them: two young Fine Gael politicians, John Boland and John Mannion, reached their twenty-fifth birthdays in October and November of the same year, a development which indicated that the role of the Senate as a rest home for former politicians was being supplemented by a new role as a forcing-house for political aspirants.

The election of 1969 was in some respects a watershed. The new Taoiseach, Jack Lynch of Fianna Fáil, was the first man to hold that position who had not taken part in the revolution of 1916 or the subsequent War of Independence against British rule. Even as the Senate election took place, however, there were potent signs that the past would not so readily be consigned to history: the political crisis engendered by developments arising from the contested civil rights movement in Northern Ireland was deepening. The count for the Senate election was held on 12 August 1969: on the evening of the following day, Lynch appeared on television to assure his countrymen that his government would 'not stand by' as a wave of violence threatened to engulf pockets of Irish nationalists north of the Border, especially in the embattled Catholic enclaves in Belfast. Fianna Fáil, which had been in government for twelve uninterrupted years, would in turn be riven by the political consequences of the Northern conflict.

CHAPTER 2

The Senate: The Young Dissenter

BY THE TIME THE SENATE met for the first time on 5 November 1969, Mary Bourke's youth and gender had already combined to make her something of a sensation. It is a measure of the standards expected of women at the time that she turned up dressed soberly in a suit and – to the delight of the photographers – a hat. The hat did not last for long, but was widely pictured, framing the Senator's alert young face in a manner that appears incongruous with the benefit of hindsight and looked so even then. Events were to show rapidly how unwise it was to judge this particular book by its cover: proper she might be, but not demure.

On her first day – uncharacteristically, as it was to turn out – Mary Bourke was speechless. The first business of the new Senate was the election of a Chairman and the majority Fianna Fáil party had, after an internal party caucus, decided to put Senator Michael Yeats forward for the position. Owen Sheehy Skeffington decided to oppose the nomination. The situation was replete with irony: not only was Michael Yeats a Protestant but he was a graduate of Trinity College and son of W.B. Yeats. But Michael Yeats was now also a member of Fianna Fáil, the party of Eamon de Valera and of Seán Lemass, and thoroughly wedded to mainstream Irish politics.

Under the Senate's procedural rules, more generally known as standing orders, any senator can call for a vote on any issue. If the Cathaoirleach or Chairman, however, believes that there is not widespread support in the House for a formal vote, he calls on any senators who wish to have a vote taken to stand. If there are fewer than six of them, no vote is taken, but their names are formally recorded as having 'dissented' from the decision not to have a formal roll-call vote.

Yeats's election was not opposed by either of the two Opposition parties, Fine Gael and Labour. In normal circumstances, therefore, there would not have been a vote, but when one was demanded from the Trinity seats, senators generally were invited to show their support for this call by standing up. Only two senators rose: Skeffington and Mary Bourke. One national newspaper managed to ignore her entirely, describing Skeffington as 'the only dissenter'. More perceptively, John Healy in the *Irish Times* described her as someone who 'promises to be the most charming dissenter in the House'.

The Yeats 'vote' showed at the same time both the best side of the Senate and the most corrosive side of Irish politics – the best in that all parties could agree on the appointment of a decent and honourable man as Chairman without bitter and petty party controversy. The latter side was shown in the ability of all the major parties to join forces to squeeze out or marginalise a potentially embarrassing independent voice, and to create, effectively, a kind of political cartel.

Mary Bourke erupted into this cartel with an energy and a willingness to take initiatives that surprised even some of those who eventually became her allies. As one might expect from a constitutional lawyer, she chose to play the game by the rules, but when she found that the rules worked against her, she explored the rule-book further until she found ways of exploiting procedures that had grown rusty from decades of under-use.

Initially, knowing that independent senators have effectively no chance of legislating for change, she confined her initiatives to putting down motions to draw the Senate's attention to issues she considered important. The problem about motions is that they are little more than flag-waving. They will never be discussed if the House (more precisely, the government majority in the House) decides not to allocate time for a debate. If motions were likely to embarrass the government, as Mary Robinson's motions generally were, the prospect of having time allocated for a debate was usually nil. There was no provision in 1969 for a regular allocation of time to Opposition senators – let alone the small group of independents – to debate matters of their own choice. As the Senate generally sat only on Wednesdays and even more rarely on Thursdays, the leader of the House (in 1969 the leader of the Fianna Fáil senators) could always claim, often enough tongue in cheek, that there was too much government business to be done.

Mary Bourke, or other senators faced with this procedural brick wall, could ask that time be allocated for their motions; they could jump up and down and protest; they could write letters to the newspapers; but in practice that was all they could do. The motions, accordingly, languished on the order paper for months and months. As her motions gathered dust, Mary Bourke went into action in other spheres. Rural medicine and health matters engaged her attention, and as the daughter of two doctors her comments were evidently well-informed. Increasingly, however, legal matters bulked large on her agenda. And the echoes of her American experience broke through sharply in a debate on a Censorship Bill in May 1970, brought in by the government to liberalise, to a limited extent, the severe laws which had been in existence since the 1920s.

Mary Bourke turned the traditional anti-censorship argument on its head, pointing out that while she was in favour of freedom of speech, the media could offend against public morality on political, religious, or social class grounds and not just in the highly visible area of sexual morality. Warming to her theme, she denounced John Wayne's Vietnam war film *The Green Berets*, for its 'clear bias' in favour of United States policy and its failure to represent a South East Asia point of view. Neville Keery, a Fianna Fáil senator (another Trinity graduate, and a Protestant to boot) was plainly nettled, and saw the opportunity to trap Mary Bourke into making an illiberal commitment. Would she censor the *The Green Berets*? he asked.

'Yes!'

It rapidly became evident to her that putting down motions which were never discussed would not advance the cause of civil rights or of anything else. In the circumstances, she accepted with alacrity an offer from the *Irish Times* to write an article on Northern Ireland in July 1970, and used this platform to launch a criticism of Article 3 of the Irish Constitution which proclaims 'the right of the Parliament and Government ... to establish jurisdiction over the whole of [the national] territory'. Article 2, defines the national territory as 'the whole island of Ireland, its islands and the territorial seas'. Both articles, taken together, have long been – and remain – a bone of contention for unionists: in the *Irish Times*, Mary Bourke described it bluntly as 'an unnecessary assertion of jurisdiction' and called on the political parties in the Republic to establish a consensus on a possible solution to the Northern problem. If her optimism on this score was unfounded, her article showed that her stance on the Northern problem, which was to embroil her in controversy fifteen years later, was of long standing. It is certainly significant that her electorate would have included, as it still does, a very large number of Protestant Trinity graduates from Northern Ireland who had come to Dublin for their university education and who had returned to live in the North. Trinity and the National University were in fact the only two parliamentary constituencies in which a substantial proportion of the electorate lived outside the State.

Newspaper articles and motions alone, however, were not enough. This made it inevitable that she would broach the possibility of legislation. A motion does not change anything: a law does. A Senate that refused to discuss laws was much more open to criticism than a Senate that refused to discuss motions, and draft legislation, because it is much more specific than a motion or resolution, attracts public attention far more readily.

Under the Constitution, any bill, except a money bill, can be initiated in the Senate. The problem about legislation is that it demands more support. Any individual senator can put down a motion in the Senate: to table legislation one needs three senators to sign a draft bill. A bill, also, needs to surmount the hurdles of full-scale parliamentary procedure. Not only does it need three sponsors but it cannot pass any stage of a five-stage process, through which all bills must travel before becoming law, without the formal approval of the House. The first stage is to get the permission of the House to print and circulate the bill. In principle there is no reason why any senator cannot photocopy the text of any bill and send it to every other senator in the post: but it is not an official legislative document and this does not get it an inch further in the parliamentary process. In addition, senators and governments who disapproved of the contents of any such bill would claim, however disingenuously, that any senator who circulated it privately was showing scant regard for the procedures of the House.

The first issue on which Mary Bourke decided to put down draft legislation was, in the late 1960s and early 1970s, undeniably controversial: contraception. But where was she to find her supporters for any controversial legislation? None of the political parties would support her and their nominees or representatives occupied fifty-four of the sixty Senate seats. Of her Trinity colleagues, Owen Sheehy Skeffington would have been a natural ally, but he died at the beginning of June 1970, before she had got into her legislative stride. The only other senator from Trinity was Professor W.J.E. Jessop, whose personal opinions on the issue may not have been unsympathetic but who was disinclined to support anything as public and as dramatic. In any case, she would have preferred someone younger.

For her second signatory, Mary Bourke therefore went to the National University of Ireland constituency. One of the three NUI senators was Professor P.M. Quinlan of University College, Cork, a doughty conservative who never hid his opposition to her views on this topic. The second was Professor Bryan Alton, who was repeatedly elected with the support of the medical fraternity and had been personal physician to both Eamon de Valera and Seán Lemass. He was an unlikely source of support, to put it mildly. The only new senator in the constituency was the author, John Horgan, a journalist four years older than Robinson, who had displaced a long-serving secondary school teacher and who drew his electoral support largely from among the middle-class Catholic readership of the *Irish Times*, for which he worked.

Horgan agreed to sign the bill but not without some misgivings about the possible effect on his political support, much of which was not only Catholic but clerical: in the event, his vote dropped sharply in the 1973 election, although probably not for this reason alone. But Mary Bourke now had two names. She did not get her third name until after the by-election to fill the seat left vacant by Skeffington's death, which took place in December 1970. The seat was taken, after a skilful campaign, by her former election agent Trevor West.

Coincidentally, this was also the month in which her long-standing relationship with Nicholas Robinson flowered into marriage. Nick was the boyfriend of her student days and a fellow law student, who had graduated and become a solicitor. He is also a witty cartoonist and although he practised as a solicitor into the 1980s his heart was plainly elsewhere and his interests in art, architecture and history have provided an increasing focus for his professional life. He is a member of an old Dublin family. His forebears were barrel-makers in the Liberties, one of Dublin's oldest working-class areas, but his father, Howard Robinson, is a chartered accountant whose small bank, the City of Dublin Bank, later amalgamated with a larger institution. The family is undeniably well-off.

Mary Bourke changed her name on marriage: a decade later, or even less, she might not have done so, but things were not so black and white then. In addition, complex family dynamics were evident. Even more significant than the change of name was the fact that the marriage was the cause of a major, though short-lived, family rift. Though religiously mixed marriages formed an integral part of the Bourke family history, the fact that Nicholas Robinson was a member of the Church of Ireland deeply upset her family, and her parents and brothers all stayed away from the small, almost private, ceremony held in the Dublin Airport church. The family differences were made up after a couple of months but they illustrate, as well as anything else, the steely determination not to accept facile compromises that was part of her inheritance.

In early 1971, Mary Robinson and her two allies went into action. Family planning, as it happened, was an issue that reflected all four of the major considerations she had specified in her election address: youth, liberalism, law and womanhood. She was not the first Irish political figure to raise these thorny issues in public but what made her unique was that she was the first to attempt to legislate for change. Other politicians in Labour and smaller left-wing parties shared her views to some extent but no party had formally aligned itself behind a proposal to change the law because all parties, no matter how progressive some of their individual members might be, still tended to be led from behind by the representatives of a conservative general electorate. The debate about family planning, such as it was, was carried on in occasional speeches from public platforms and letters to the papers – never in the national parliament, where no change in the law had been discussed since the 1930s.

The main ban on contraception in Ireland had been embodied in the 1935 Criminal Law Act. Strengthening the provisions of the legendary 1929 Censorship of Publications Act, the 1935 legislation had made the importation, distribution and sale of contraceptives a criminal offence. Publications that advertised contraceptives could be, and often were, officially banned or seized at Irish ports of entry by customs officials. The legislation was malign for a whole range of reasons. The major objective of the Act was to outlaw prostitution and the combination of contraception, prostitution and even abortion in its provisions was a powerful cultural allegation of guilt by association. A number of protesting voices – often tentative, generally Protestant – had been obliterated by the juggernaut of majority opinion.

The law was also to some extent operated in a socially discriminatory fashion. Mass-circulation British newspapers like *Reynold's News* which regularly carried small advertisements for contraceptives were banned; elite publications like the *Spectator* and *New Statesman*, which also did so, were not. People who could afford to travel and had the opportunity to do so could smuggle contraceptives into the country, especially across the land border with Northern Ireland. British firms manufacturing or retailing contraceptives developed new ways of circumventing the vigilantes who monitored the postal services. They were not always successful and the seizure of one particular contraceptive consignment by the postal authorities was later to prove the germ for one of the most significant legal cases ever won by the young barrister and senator from Trinity College.

Ireland had changed since the 1930s, however, and was continuing to change. The debate on contraception within the Catholic Church had reached fever pitch in the 1960s and when Pope Paul VI appointed a Commission in 1965 to review the Church's teaching on the matter, many thousands of Catholic women confidently expected a change. The decade also saw the rapid spread of the contraceptive pill, a phenomenon which had a number of effects, particularly in Ireland. Because its primary function was as a contraceptive, it ran the risk of being considered as illegal under the terms of the 1935 Act, which banned all contraceptives. It also, however, had a function, which was essentially a by-product of its primary function, as a form of medication which helped to regulate the menstrual cycle. The result was that doctors and women conspired to treat it as a 'cycle regulator', producing an incidence of 'cycle irregularities' in Irish women that shredded statistical norms.

A major benefit of this development was that the contraceptive pill, as medication, was provided free to many thousands of Irish women who qualified under the means test. The major disadvantage was that for many women, particularly those with a history of hypertension, it was dangerous and even life-threatening and therefore could not be prescribed by any conscientious medical practitioner. When Pope Paul VI rejected the advice of his Commission in 1968 and reiterated the Catholic Church's traditional stance on contraception, there was a subsequent surge in the Irish birthrate, but this did not mean that the problem had gone away or that the pressure for change would not continue to intensify.

On 26 February 1971 Mary Robinson notified the Senate that she had prepared a bill to change the 1935 Criminal Law Act: it was the inauguration of a process which was to take almost two decades to complete and which became symbolic, in a way, of the social and other changes that were taking place outside parliament and which parliament as yet reflected imperfectly and hesitantly. In its initial form, the bill did no more than repeal those section of the 1935 Act which totally banned contraception; in later forms, it would introduce some modest restrictions on the availability of contraceptives, not least to offset the anticipated criticism that removing all controls was simply going too far. After a few low-key exchanges designed to test the water, she and her co-sponsors finally went on the offensive in March 1971.

Thirty years later, it is difficult to convey the degree of moral courage necessary to stand up, as Mary Robinson did, on the afternoon of that day in March 1971 in the Senate chamber to request permission for her bill to be printed and distributed. The Senate chamber itself is not exactly designed for histrionics. Originally the ballroom of the townhouse of the dukes of Leinster – the building came into the ownership of the Irish Free State in the 1920s and has been used as the home of the Irish parliament ever since – the chamber is a graceful room with long Georgian windows and two massive fireplaces. The Senate Chairman sits on a raised dais in a bow-windowed alcove; the sixty dark blue leather-covered chairs in which the senators sit are ranged in front of him in a semi-circle. Microphones are not needed (although they were added in recent years for sound recording purposes) and there is only a handful of places for press and spectators.

Perhaps because it has little power, the Senate is a model of decorum, and sometimes prides itself on the absence of the bitter inter-party divisions that can feature in Dáil debates. The atmosphere on that day, however, owed less to the fact that Mary Robinson was part of a tiny minority in the chamber and more to the fact that behind the political majority that faced her, on both sides of the house, was the moral majority of the Catholic Church. This is what gave the occasion its David and Goliath texture.

David and Goliath were to meet many times before the contest was finally resolved. In the short term, Goliath sulked in his tent. Mary Robinson, although she had her three signatories for the bill, could not muster the six required to force a vote on her proposal that the first stage of the bill should be discussed (if passed, the House would give permission for the bill to be officially printed). The blushes of other senators, who might have agreed with her privately but who would have been bound by their parties to march into the lobbies to oppose her had a vote actually been taken, were spared.

At the same time, and unknown to those who read of her Senate activities in the newspapers, she rapidly became the target of a campaign – probably uncoordinated but none the less vicious for all that – by Irish men and women who felt that her stance on this issue threatened every value they held dear. In the decades since 1922, the sense of proud isolation and ethnic differences from England had engendered an attitude to contraception that bordered on fetishism. On one side of the argument, there were those – many of them Protestant, which of course only reinforced Catholic opposition – who argued that the never-ending flood of emigration and the deep poverty associated with large working-class families were evidence of the need for a more rational approach to the question of population control. On the other, there was a deep-rooted belief that the promoters of contraception were involved in a malign conspiracy to extinguish the Irish race. Some twenty-five years earlier, a pamphlet published by the Gaelic Athletic Association, Ireland's largest amateur sporting organisation with members in every parish in the country, described contraception as 'race suicide' and demanded: 'First offence warnings and petty fines for traffickers must be replaced, without mitigation, by penal servitude, expulsion of aliens and the lash.'[5]

The author of those words had died a few years before Mary Robinson entered the Senate, but she was to discover almost immediately that the passage of time had not softened this opposition. A deluge of hate mail, most of it anonymous, reached her office; used contraceptives were put through her mailbox; and she was left under no illusion that her modest proposal had touched an extremely sensitive nerve. She burned the hate mail, to the annoyance of later archivists, but as an altogether understandable reaction to a verbal assault which tested her psychological resilience to the utmost.

She had not only the government against her but virtually everyone else as well. Across the floor of the Senate she faced the Leader of the House, a battle-scarred (in every sense) Tomás Ó Maoláin, veteran of the War of Independence and of organisational struggles within his own party, now general secretary of Fianna Fáil. Owen Sheehy Skeffington had christened him 'Chairman O'Mao'. The leader of Fine Gael, the second largest party in the Senate, was Michael O'Higgins, a solicitor and a former TD, deeply conservative on family matters. The Labour Party was represented by a small number of trade unionists, who rarely spoke other than on industrial or labour relations questions. It was not promising territory.

Mary Robinson was quick to realise that she could turn all these procedural defeats to her advantage. Here she was, a duly elected member of the legislature, who was not even being allowed to print and distribute a bill she had drafted on a matter of keen public interest. The more she objected, the more the government, assisted either vocally or silently by members of other parties, dug in its heels. In March, she pushed for the second version of her bill to be printed and distributed: her initiative was rejected by Ó Maoláin, who, plainly nettled, said that she was behaving in a 'schoolgirlish, irresponsible manner'. Two months later, as she intensified her campaign, he remarked that she was 'new to this House [and] does not understand the difficulties which older hands would appreciate'. In later debates on the same issue, she and her supporters were to be described, less elegantly, as 'brazen-faced rubbernecks'.

Outside the Senate, however, events were acquiring an independent momentum which the 'older hands' would be hard put to resist. There was a growing consciousness among women of the need to set an independent political agenda. The year 1970 had seen the formal establishment of the Women's Political Association (originally the Women's Progressive Association – how delicately the issue of nominature was skirted around!) which was founded primarily to encourage greater participation by women in Irish public life: as well as Mary Robinson, early participants in its activities included two future Fine Gael government ministers, Gemma Hussey and Nuala Fennell. A loose confederation of other women's organisations had begun, in the late 1960s, to put pressure on the government to address their needs: the result was the creation in 1970 of the Commission for the Status of Women, which was to report formally in 1972. Public interest in Mary Robinson's apparently one-woman campaign to change the country's laws on contraception had been growing and there were rumours that Section 17 of the 1935 Criminal Law Act – the section that was targeted in her bill – might be challenged in the courts on constitutional grounds.

The Catholic bishops were alert to the danger, as they saw it, of change and issued a joint statement early in March warning that any change in the law on contraception would have grave social consequences. This attempt to mark the government's cards in a measured way was, however, seriously undermined by an individual broadside from the Archbishop of Dublin, Dr John Charles McQuaid, who stated bluntly, and in extraordinarily emotive language, that any change in the law 'would be, and would remain, a curse upon our country'. Some clerics were privately appalled at the intemperateness of his language, realising that it would polarise opinion dramatically on the issue, but there was nothing that they could do about it.

The days when Irish Catholics would accept such an ecclesiastical diktat were, however, fading fast. Two speeches in March 1971 highlighted the issue in ways which implied that the archbishop could not count on everyone's support. One was by Dr Paul McQuaid of the Mater Hospital's Child Guidance Clinic. The other was by Senator Neville Keery, who argued that the law was now being broken so frequently that it had become a 'mockery'. This was the setting for Mary Robinson's next attempt to move the bill, which was defeated without a vote on 31 March. By now, as it happened, she had realised that a simple measure to abolish Section 17 of the 1935 Act would not of itself be enough and had drafted a new version of her bill which would also have changed the censorship acts of 1929 and 1946: there was little point in allowing access to the means of contraception if people did not know where they could acquire them or read advice about the different methods involved.

The temperature continued to increase. On 12 May Mary Robinson again failed to get the Senate to discuss her proposal to publish the revised bill. Within days, the Irish Women's Liberation movement, in a protest which attracted an extraordinary amount of attention, went by train to Belfast in large numbers with the intention of buying contraceptives and declaring them defiantly to the customs officials in Connolly Station on their return. When they got off the Belfast train on 21 May, preceded by banners and brandishing packets of contraband substances (many of them, it turned out later, were packets of Aspros), the customs officials decided that it would be more politic to turn a blind eye to the protest, but the point had been made. Although Mary Robinson was not directly associated with protests like these, some of those involved – notably a number of journalists – were to play an important role in a focus group which assessed her chances for the presidency in 1990.

The hubbub outside the Dáil highlighted another problem with which the government was going to have to come to grips. If everybody in the country was talking about the issue except the senators and the TDs, what was the relevance of parliament itself? This was the context in which, at the beginning of July 1971, the government moved rapidly to answer the jibe that contraception could not be discussed in the Oireachtas and simultaneously to remove it from the agenda.

The speed with which they moved on the matter was a tactic in itself. Without notice, they announced that Mary Robinson could move the first stage of her bill in the Senate – and that they would be opposing it. They knew that defeating the proposal to publish the bill, although it would lead to bad publicity, meant that under standing orders she would be unable to bring the matter up again for at least six months. The other advantage was that, under procedural rules, only two speeches could be made on the issue – one by Mary Robinson, the other by a spokesman for the government.

The lack of notice meant Mary Robinson had not had time to prepare a detailed speech. She noted that since the government had not had the courtesy to inform her of their intentions, she would not be making a considered statement but a 'rather angry statement'. She contrasted sharply the government's declared intention to abolish partition with what she described as its maintenance of 'moral partition' and warned that she would continue to introduce legislation aimed at making Ireland a more pluralist and more tolerant society. The result of the vote was a foregone conclusion: the government forces defeated her proposal by 25 votes to 14. But Mary Robinson and her supporters also had the rare satisfaction of seeing Senator Michael O'Higgins, the leader of the Fine Gael group, joining the Fianna Fáil senators in the lobbies to vote down her measure. It was the first time for many years that the traditional civil war divisions in the Senate had been superseded, however briefly, by a division based on social and ideological differences.

Although the public at large may have been unaware of the finer tactical points being played out, a major political reputation was in the process of being forged. The extent of her leadership on the issue can be judged from the fact that when two Labour Party TDs, Dr Noel Browne and Dr John O'Connell, introduced a bill in the Dáil to reform the laws on contraception in February 1972, it was identical to Mary Robinson's. It was defeated in the Dáil, too, amid much huffing and puffing, and the strategic absence from the vote of some of Browne's and O'Connell's party colleagues provided evidence that not even in the Labour Party could unanimity on this issue be guaranteed.

The voting down of Mary Robinson's bill was to prove a Pyrrhic victory for the government, as later developments would show. At the same time, however, for all its lingering embarrassment at having a policy vacuum exposed by the young senator from Mayo, the government was also prepared to allow her considerably more room to manoeuvre in an area which suited its own purposes better – adoption. Adoption was not as controversial as contraception, except in one respect: like contraception, it was an area in which the influence of the Catholic Church was very strong. It was also an area in which, over the years, numerous anomalies had begun to emerge – among them the fact that the parents of a child born outside marriage could not, if they were of different religions, adopt their own child legally after they had married. The Catholic Church's interpretation of the needs of the child, which had been written into the original adoption laws with its approval, put religion at the core of the adoption process in a way that plainly interfered with the civil rights of others and this is why changing the law was such a sensitive manner.

There was also a suspicion that many young women who had children outside marriage – the term 'illegitimate children' was still in common, and legal, use – were being subjected to unfair pressure to surrender their babies for adoption. As the young women concerned had their babies, for the most part, in residential homes owned and run by Catholic religious orders, this was equally sensitive territory. As Mary Robinson pointed out, in Scandinavia over 80% of single young mothers kept their children whereas in Ireland 80% of young women in the same position gave their children up for adoption. Did Irish mothers love their children less or was there another explanation, and were Irish women being denied freedom of choice by religious, economic and social constraints?

The government knew that something had to be done, and agreed in the summer of 1971, without too much difficulty, to allow the Senate to discuss a bill which Mary Robinson had framed to change the adoption laws. They had no intention of accepting her draft legislation but, by allowing her to ventilate the issue, they could escape, or at least minimise, the level of clerical criticism or obstructionism that might have greeted them had they raised the issue directly themselves. It was also – unlike contraception – an area in which they were prepared to move forward and they knew that stressing the rights of the children involved gave them higher moral ground from which to operate than in the contentious area of family planning.

For all their criticism of Mary Robinson's impetuousness and supposed lack of realism, the government was now prepared to allow her to introduce and debate her bill on the understanding that she would not force it to a vote, but would withdraw it because the government would be bringing in its own legislation on the matter. In this way the government could allow discussion on this delicate matter to take place without having to show its own hand. Independent senators could be troublesome but they also had their uses.

Mary Robinson was, in many areas involving women, a unique bridge between the incestuous, male-dominated world of parliamentary politics, and the life lived by many women outside it. A classic example of this was her relationship with the 'Cherish' organisation for single parents, of which she was to be president from 1973 until her election as President of Ireland in 1990.

Cherish was itself one of the offspring of the Women's Liberation movement. The Dalkey 'branch' of the movement (it is difficult to find an appropriate terminology, not least because it nourished a healthy suspicion of many of the classic forms of organisation) decided to organise a project around the social reality of the 'unmarried mother'. This was many years before this inherently pejorative phrase had been banished from the lexicon; at the time, even to mention it in public marked something of a breakthrough, and the reality of single parenthood was masked by social disapproval, and the voluntary or involuntary surrender of children for adoption.

Maura O'Dea was a single woman who had had a child in 1970. She had a good job and was able to fend for herself, even in those unpromising times. She was asked to give a talk on the problems facing women in her situation to the Dalkey group and, after the evening had ended, was asked whether she would help another, less fortunate young woman in similar circumstances. Over the next couple of years, the network mushroomed. An advertisement in the *Evening Press* in 1972 produced scores of replies, and the imminence of the general election focused the group's attention, not only on the prospect of legislative reform, but on the politician who seemed most likely to be sympathetic, and to help them achieve it.

There was really only one candidate. In the autumn of 1972 Mary Robinson was invited to give a talk for the group on the adoption laws and the need for reform. Maura O'Dea (now Richards) remembers that when Mary Robinson came out she was pregnant with her second child, William, and was 'awfully tired', but that she stayed as long as the group wanted to talk to her. It was not long before they asked her to be president of the organisation, but initially she demurred. She had two reasons: the first was that she wanted the organisation to have a proper structure – in effect, to be incorporated. The second was that she was, as she said, 'too young to be president of anything' and, in Maura Richards's words, 'didn't quite understand what we wanted, or how to help'.

Once the incorporation problem had been resolved, Mary Robinson became Cherish's president. The organisation itself mirrored the tensions in the women's movement of the day – tensions between members who regarded the group's social and mutual support functions as primary, and members who regarded its political activism as central. The tensions, however, never got out of hand, and over the decades which followed, Cherish became a powerful advocate of the rights of single parents, seeing many of its objectives enshrined in law.

In all of this, Mary Robinson was a central figure. She came to Cherish's first Christmas party in 1973 with her own children, and frequently asked Maura O'Dea into her offices in Merrion Square for consultations on legislation she was drafting or on the issues which most affected single parents. In public, she used Cherish's annual general meetings each year to focus attention on issues of particular concern: in 1980, for example, on the crippling rents which single mothers were having to pay, and, in 1982, in the middle of the controversial abortion amendment campaign, she argued that the 'real pro-life issue' was the 4% of Irish children who suffered from a legal disability because they were stigmatised as illegitimate.

Mary Robinson was now in it for the long haul. She was also learning that, when you met an immovable object, a detour was sometimes better than a confrontation. The following year, not long after the first Report of the Commission on the Status of Woman had been published, the Labour senator Evelyn Owens button-holed the Fianna Fáil Senate leader in a Leinster House corridor and began to twist his arm persuasively about the need for a debate on the Report on the basis of a non-controversial motion. Mary Robinson, who was passing down the corridor at the same time, remarked wryly that perhaps this was sometimes a better way of doing things.

The adoption debate itself was notable for one sharp exchange between Robinson and Ó Maoláin, in which Robinson underlined the role of the Catholic hierarchy in the drafting of the original legislation, quoting impeccable academic sources for her statement. The veteran Fianna Fáil politician, nettled, retorted that his government had never had to go to any bishops for permission to legislate. There was, in the exchange, an echo of the old days when Catholic bishops were loud in their denunciations of the political forebears of Ó Maoláin's party, especially during the Civil War, when they condemned those Republicans (including Ó Maoláin himself) who had taken up arms against the legally constituted government of the state.

The Catholic hierarchy, of course, had played a major part in the creation of one other key document – the Irish Constitution of 1937. While they had not been involved in the drafting on any formal basis, they had been closely consulted. Dr John Charles McQuaid, then in charge of his religious order's boy's school at Blackrock, Co. Dublin, and a personal friend of de Valera, had with other clergy been closely consulted on the section dealing with marriage and the family; the Archbishop of Armagh and Catholic Primate of All Ireland, Cardinal McRory, had been consulted – as had Vatican officials – on the section which ultimately bestowed the recognition of a 'special position' on the Catholic Church.

One section of the Constitution which bore the marks of this process particularly clearly was the section which prevented any Irish government from legislating to introduce divorce. Seán Lemass, who had been Taoiseach between 1959 and 1966, had raised the matter privately through intermediaries with Archbishop McQuaid in 1965 but had dropped the subject rapidly in the face of the trenchant opposition he encountered on that occasion. It had remained on the agenda, however, not least because of its perceived significance in relation to Northern Ireland, and was discussed, extremely tentatively, by the informal all-party Oireachtas Committee on the Constitution, which Lemass set up before he left office in 1966 and which finally reported on 23 December 1967.

The committee's handling of the problem was crab-like in the extreme and begged a number of extremely important questions. Unaware or heedless of the fact that it was venturing into hotly disputed theological territory, it recommended that the Constitution be changed to allow divorce for Irish citizens whose religion did not forbid it. For this reason, among others, its recommendation on divorce died a sudden death. It was to be almost three decades and two referenda later before the constitutional ban on divorce legislation was removed.

This was the context of a proposal at a meeting of the Irish Theological Association in December 1971, to set up a working party to carry out its own review of the Constitution. This Association was an independent organisation of theologians, for the most part Catholic ones, and its independent status meant that it was tolerated rather than approved of by the bishops. The working party was set up in January 1972 to examine ways in which the Constitution might be said to be divisive on religious grounds. It was a time when paramilitary violence in the North was reaching unprecedented heights, and when Northern unionists, pressed to defend their political position, frequently cited the Republic's Constitution as a major obstacle to community harmony.

The working party's terms of reference were largely drafted by the man who was to become its chairman (and later chaplain to President Mary Robinson), Dr Enda McDonagh. Professor McDonagh was professor of moral theology in St Patrick's College, Maynooth, who had done his doctoral study on the Second Vatican Council's declaration on religious freedom, and was, like Mary Robinson, from Co. Mayo. This was not their first meeting. Knowing of his interest in the Constitution, the young barrister had once telephoned him to ask him to speak at a meeting, introducing herself with the sort of flourish that indicated it was an invitation he ought to have difficulty in refusing: 'This is Mary Bourke from Ballina.'[6]

It was Mary Robinson's interest in constitutional reform and her ability in this sphere, rather than her geographical origins, which secured her an invitation to take part in the working party: it was the first time any woman had been invited to serve on such a committee. Other members included the high-profile barrister Seán MacBride; Louis MacRedmond, a former editor of the *Irish Independent* who had reported with distinction for that paper on the second Vatican Council; and two prominent Protestants, Dr G.B.G. McConnell, a Presbyterian, and Mr Justice T.C. Kingsmill Moore, an Anglican.

Mary Robinson, according to one of the group, was 'very clear-headed, thoroughly democratic, and respectful of religion'. The Working Party's report on 16 May 1972 [7] went far beyond the cautious and circumscribed comments of politicians. It not only recommended the deletion of the 'special position' of the Catholic Church (this was eventually achieved in a non-controversial referendum in 1972), but devised a much longer shopping list to accompany this modest proposal. Drawing on the United Nations International Covenant of Civil and Political Rights, the US Constitution and the French Constitution, it specifically recommended changes to the Preamble to the Constitution, because it reflected 'the predominant religious strand in the Irish tradition'; removal of the constitutional ban on divorce so that 'the social implications of change can be examined on their merits'; the amendment of the law on contraception (although strictly speaking this had nothing to do with the Constitution – here Mary Robinson's influence can be clearly seen); the amendment of the laws on adoption (again not, strictly speaking, a constitutional matter); and the Catholic Church's regulations on mixed marriages, which manifestly had nothing to do either with the Constitution or with public legislation. It also expressed some lightly coded objections to other sections of the Constitution, 'particularly in its limited recognition of the rights of women'.

For the remainder of her first term in the Senate, Mary Robinson concentrated on doing exactly what she promised her electorate she would do: probing draft legislation with a legally trained brain that helped her to sniff out threats to civil liberties, sometimes in the most unlikely areas, and to pinpoint existing inequities.

She was also involved with others in the campaign to widen the basis for what were considered 'women's issues' beyond the important but narrow confines of family and sexual life. The Council for the Status of Women, which had been set up by the previous government, had issued an interim report on equal pay. Mary Robinson insisted that the CSW report be added to the order paper although it was not to get a debate until after the 1973 election. Outside the Senate, she drew attention to its implications for women generally, at a meeting of the Women's Political Association, in a speech which was almost a blueprint for her own future political and legal activity.

What was needed, she argued, was a new appraisal of tactics. Because the agitation and lobbying by women's organisations had not been effective, there was a need for more effective lobbying and legal action on specific, pragmatic issues which illustrated the pattern of discrimination and injustice.

'Instead of a general complaint about discrimination against married women in public employment, there ought to be five or six actions lodged by women who have had their contracts of employment terminated on marriage. Instead of complaints about lack of equal pay, there ought to be picketing or other collective activity to press home legitimate claims for parity on wages and salaries.' This in fact was the technique ultimately adopted, some two decades later, by a group of women who successfully sued the government in Europe – with Mary Robinson as their lawyer – because they had been discriminated against under the social welfare code.

There was one area, however, on which Mary Robinson – like most other senators – was almost silent, at least within the confines of Leinster House. This was the question of Northern Ireland. During the entire 1969-73 period, the Senate debates were almost innocent of references to the North while, outside, the politics of partition festered within the political parties. Divisions of opinion within the ruling Fianna Fáil party on the issue were to lead to Jack Lynch's unprecedented decision to sack two of his senior ministers – both of whom were later cleared in the courts of charges of illegally importing arms for use by Northern nationalists – and to a political crisis which nearly brought down his government. In the North, the same tensions and the violence they engendered saw the heady days of optimism for civil rights give way to brutal paramilitary campaigns, to the suspension by Britain of the Northern Ireland parliament in 1972 and eventually to direct rule from London in 1974.

In the Senate, it was almost as if these heady events were being totally ignored. They were not so much ignored, however, as avoided. The tensions within the government on the Northern issue, and the vacillation about a policy response to a situation over which that government had no effective control, made public discussion of the issue a high-risk prospect. Passions ran so high on the issue that, in both Dáil and Senate, politicians shunned set-piece debates. They were, quite simply, afraid that what might be said in the heat of the moment might make matters even worse or provoke retaliation by loyalists against beleaguered pockets of nationalists, particularly in Belfast. When the Senate came to discuss the Northern Ireland problem in August 1971, therefore, it was with a hesitation that amounted almost to diffidence. The circumstances demanded that something be said: internment had been introduced in Northern Ireland two days earlier and hundreds of Catholics, many of them with no links to the new generation of paramilitaries, had been rounded up and imprisoned. But what could be said in or by a legislative assembly which had no power to intervene? The motion was deliberately non-contentious; speeches were carefully phrased; everyone was walking on egg-shells.

Mary Robinson's contribution to the debate did not differ from others in its brevity and its low-key approach. Like the others, she had no ready-made solution for the North's problems, beyond suggesting that the re-introduction of proportional representation there or the establishment of a committee-based system of government might help matters (both were later carried out by the British government, although without notable success). She raised one significant warning flag, however: nothing that happened in the North, she argued, would ever make internment acceptable in the Republic. It was a position she stuck to even when it cost her dearly in terms of political support. Three years later, it was to involve her in a major controversy with Conor Cruise O'Brien, who had been one of her warmest admirers, and who launched a sharply focused attack on her when he was a Cabinet minister in the 1973-77 coalition government.

All this, however, was in the future. One of the few occasions on which the question of the North again obtruded into the placid surroundings of the Senate was in December 1972 when, in the wake of the loyalist bombings in Dublin, the government introduced stringent new security laws. In the Senate, Mary Robinson argued unavailingly that, because this was effectively a response to a national emergency, it should be treated as emergency legislation and should automatically expire, or have to be renewed, after ninety days. The national mood was against her and against the few who supported her stand. On this and on other matters, progress was to be continually uphill: it was a direction in which Mary Robinson became increasingly used to travelling.

CHAPTER 3

A Liberal Voice

THE SENATE, OF COURSE, was not a full-time occupation. For all that, Mary Robinson put as much work into it as if it had been, and considerably more than her fellow-senators from Trinity, as she did not blush to point out in her 1973 election literature. At one point, some six months after her election, she thought briefly of mounting a one-woman picket on the august assembly, marching up and down outside under a banner proclaiming: 'I am under-employed.' A decade later she was still accusing the Senate of being 'an under-used body which fails to give value for money', because of the attitude of successive governments, neglect by the media and the 'tame acquiescence of senators themselves'.

She was lending her time and her energies to an ever-increasing number of organisations, including Cherish and the Women's Political Association. She was simultaneously lecturing in Trinity on a wide range of legal subjects as Reid Professor and travelling to the Western Circuit to appear in civil and criminal cases the length and breadth of Connacht. There, considerably to her surprise but not, one imagines, to her discomfiture, a jury foreman once winked at her. In the higher courts in Dublin, where she was also beginning to appear in a small but significant number of cases with constitutional implications, the stakes were higher and the proceedings more solemn.

What marked her out early on, however, and in a way which displeased many of her barrister colleagues, was her potent combination of a lack of solemnity with her ability to carry an argument. It was not that she was unserious – she could be deadly serious when the occasion demanded – but that she did not mind the publicity attendant on some of her more high-profile cases and even, in the eyes of some of her more jaundiced contemporaries, seemed to court it. The legal profession is not bereft of star performers or even of barristers who have cultivated high-profile careers in politics while continuing to practise at the Bar. If Mary Robinson wanted to look for an exemplar, she would not have had to look very far: Paddy Lindsay, one of the most technicolour characters to grace either politics or the Bar, was also from Mayo, and migrated between Dáil and Senate throughout the 1950s and 1960s, at one stage serving as Minister for the Gaeltacht.

But the Bar in the seventies had become an altogether more drab place. The idea that cases might hit the headlines other than in the greyish columns of the *Irish Times* devoted to court reports was anathema, and barristers who figured in them were regarded as in some sense letting the side down.

What also struck her contemporaries about Mary Robinson, but more positively, was how modern she was and modern in a way most barristers at the time were not. Her research was always impeccable and solicitors who met her to discuss a case would find themselves furnished with a long memorandum and told that they could now concentrate on the core of the case.

Given her track record, it was hardly surprising when she was engaged as junior counsel in the case brought by Mrs Mary McGee in the High Court in Dublin on 8 June 1972. Mrs McGee challenged the constitutionality of the 1935 Criminal Law Act after a package of contraceptive jelly, which had been sent to her by a firm in Britain, was intercepted by customs officials and impounded. It was probably something that happened on many occasions to others. However, Mrs McGee's medical history made it imperative that she should use a barrier method of contraception rather than the contraceptive pill, which was widely available in Ireland on prescription although technically not for purposes of contraception.

The McGees were also fighters and with the help of Mary Robinson and their other counsel they constructed a case which argued that the action by the customs officials effectively violated their constitutional right to marital and personal privacy. The Constitution, as it happened, did not contain any such explicit right of privacy and it was partly on these grounds that the High Court rejected Mary Robinson's arguments and Mrs McGee's case on 31 July. An appeal was promptly lodged to the Supreme Court where, eighteen months later, the constitutional arguments would finally triumph.

The McGee case judgement, delivered by Mr Justice Brian Walsh in December 1973, accepted that Article 41.1 of the Constitution, which recognised the Family (it uses the capital letter) as 'the natural primary and fundamental unit group of society, and as a moral unit possessing inalienable and imprescriptible rights, antecedent and superior to all positive law', also embodied this implied right to privacy. On the basis of this right, the court held that the authorities had acted unconstitutionally in depriving the McGees of the necessary means to plan their family.

This was not only a bench-mark in Mary Robinson's legal career; it also served notice on the political establishment that Walsh and his colleagues on the Supreme Court bench were taking seriously the suggestion, made privately to both Walsh and Cearbhall Ó Dálaigh by Seán Lemass when he appointed them in 1961, that the Irish Supreme Court should be more like the US Supreme Court. The subsequent development of constitutional jurisprudence about individual rights, which flourished under Walsh in particular, proved fertile ground for Mary Robinson and other lawyers to explore in the 1970s.

In the meantime, Mary Robinson published her Family Planning Bill privately in December 1972, effectively thumbing her nose at the political establishment. This had no practical purpose in legislative terms, but it served a political purpose – keeping the issue alive, and ensuring that her record in relation to it was highlighted to her constituents as the country moved towards its next general election.

As 1973 dawned, Jack Lynch's government moved onto an election footing. The Dáil was dissolved at the beginning of February and a general election called for 28 February. The date was significant. Legislation had recently been passed to give all citizens over eighteen the right to vote (up to then the franchise had been restricted to those aged twenty-one or over). To vote, however, you needed to be on the electoral register and the new electoral registers, bearing the names of some 140,000 new voters aged between eighteen and twenty-one, would not come into force until the beginning of April. Mary Robinson, acting on behalf of a student named Reynolds, appeared in court to challenge the government's decision effectively to disenfranchise all these young people. She lost her case, but the publicity was almost as good as an election campaign in itself.

The Labour Party had abandoned its long-maintained no-coalition stance and had made an electoral pact with Fine Gael. This might not have been enough on its own but for the fact that, after sixteen years of uninterrupted Fianna Fáil rule, the electorate was also hankering for a change. The two opposition parties came back with an overall majority and the aura of expectation was palpable. The new Taoiseach, Fine Gael leader Liam Cosgrave, was regarded – accurately enough – as an honest but old-fashioned and conservative politician. His heir apparent, Garret FitzGerald, however, epitomised the political stance of many middle-class liberals and Declan Costello, the new Attorney-General, had been a principal author of the 'Just Society' policy document which had endeavoured, with only limited success, to harness Fine Gael to a progressive social and economic agenda.

Labour ministers included Conor Cruise O'Brien, who signed Mary Robinson's 1973 election address as a supporter and whose genius for political and intellectual polemics would see him constantly in hot water, and Justin Keating, a university professor and former member of the Irish Communist Party. The government was, in some respects, an ill-assorted bunch but its members worked well together and were, at the end of the government's term of office, firmly cemented by adversity. Its urban, middle-class, university and legal components would have known Mary Robinson well and some of them would have met her socially: in August 1973 the Robinsons were holidaying in the south of France in company with, among others, the new Foreign Minister, Garret FitzGerald, the new Labour Minister for Industry and Commerce, Justin Keating, and the head of the EEC office in Dublin, Denis Corboy. One feature of the holiday was a working lunch of all four at which prospects for the forthcoming Irish EEC presidency were explored.[8]

These politicians would have shared some but by no means all of Mary Robinson's views on the need for social and institutional reform. In any case, she was still an independent, an outsider, looking through a glass darkly at the cockpit of party and cabinet politics where the real decisions were taken. She took her independence seriously. When Neil Blaney, a former Fianna Fáil minister who had been sacked along with Charles Haughey by Jack Lynch just before the arms trial in 1970, asked her to nominate another ex-Fianna Fáil TD, Paudge Brennan, as a Senate candidate (nominations in certain cases had to be signed by a minimum of four Oireachtas members), she did not reject it out of hand but eventually declined to do so for political rather than personal reasons.

The 1973 Senate election campaign, although better organised than its predecessor in 1969, was carried on at a frenetic pace as her legal practice expanded and the needs of her family made themselves felt. Shortly after her marriage to Nick, they had bought No 17 Wellington Place, Dublin 4, from Nick's brother Peter. It was a graceful two-storey over-basement Georgian house, small enough to be manageable and big enough to absorb the mountain of files associated with her legal and political work. Her first child, Tessa, had been born on 2 October 1972 and juggling family, law and politics became the order of the day. In the mid-1970s the household was put on a more even keel when Ann Coyle, the Mayo woman who had been the major-domo in the Westland Row house, returned from a sojourn in England to take up housekeeping duties. Ann, generally known as 'Nan', remained with the Robinson household until her death in 1982, a culinary legend and a loving presence for Mary's children as she had been for Mary and her siblings years earlier.

In March 1973, just as her campaign got off the ground, Mary Robinson's mother died while on a visit to Dublin. The loss of this strong, independently-minded and professionally active parent would have been a major blow at any time: coming when it did, it forced Mary Robinson to draw on all her personal resources and resilience at once.

Her election address was notable for its emphasis on Trinity and the needs of the college; but it also stressed the need for promoting the functional and economic links between North and South in mutual cooperation within the European framework (Ireland had, on 1 January 1973, become a member of the EEC) and underlined her role as first president of the Women's Political Association. 'There is still a long way to go,' she noted, 'and indeed it is disappointing not to see women more visibly involved in Irish life. But the impetus is there.'

She warned her supporters not to succumb to the 'Skeffington syndrome' – the belief that she was so assured of victory that they could lend, as it were, their first preference votes to other worthy candidates. The tactic worked but without disadvantaging Trevor West, who was also standing again. She received almost 1,500 votes on the first count in her constituency, 50% more than the charismatic figure of Dr Noel Browne, the former Labour deputy (he had exiled himself from the centres of power because of his opposition to coalition) and radical left-winger, who was also a Trinity graduate. Browne was also elected, together with Trevor West who came from behind to overhaul W.J.E. Jessop and thus leave the Trinity medical tradition without a voice in the Senate for the first time in many years.

In many respects it was a changing of the guard. There was even a change in the Phoenix Park where Eamon de Valera, now aged ninety, had been President for fourteen years, the maximum allowed by the Constitution. Virtually blind and increasingly inactive, he moved into private retirement and his place was taken after a keenly contested election between Erskine Childers, a former Fianna Fáil minister and, like Douglas Hyde, Ireland's first president, a Protestant, and the Fine Gael politician Tom O'Higgins. The Fianna Fáil election machine rebounded from its defeat in the general election to secure the Park for its candidate. Childers set about his presidency with a sense of urgency which, for all that it was also characterised by an unmistakable sense of self-importance, was in marked contrast to the invisibility of his predecessor.

The new government presented Mary Robinson with a different sort of challenge than the increasingly out-of-touch Fianna Fáil administration which had preceded it. It was packed with energetic ministers anxious to make their marks after a long period in the political wilderness. Many of them sympathised with, even if they did not fully share, Mary Robinson's personal agenda. Membership of the EEC, in addition, had brought with it not only economic benefits but social imperatives. Not least because of the requirements posed by Europe, some of the targets identified by Mary Robinson were achieved: women in the public service received equal pay in June 1973; in July the marriage bar was abolished. But as some problems receded, others came to the fore.

In Leinster House, the new government had decided that it had to grasp the nettle of the McGee case. Effectively, there had been no legal controls over the importation and sale of contraceptives since the Supreme Court had declared Section 17 of the 1935 Criminal Law Act unconstitutional in December 1973. This meant that a conservative case could be made for legislation, i.e. something had to be done to control the situation created by the Supreme Court as a result of which the Irish public, young and old, had, technically at least, unlimited access to all forms of contraception.

In March 1974 Mary Robinson introduced in the Senate yet another family planning bill to regularise the situation. This was the third bill she had introduced on the issue and it was notably more conservative than either of its predecessors, although it did not shrink from the basic job that needed to be done. It was certainly too conservative for some contemporary family planning activists at the time: Dr David Nowlan, a member of the Irish Family Planning Association and a senior journalist on the *Irish Times*, commented: 'Senator Robinson herself has come to seem like some sort of revolutionary heroine, leading the battle for human rights through a reactionary Irish parliament. But her bill, if passed, would give Ireland the most conservative and restrictive legislation on contraception in Europe, with the possible exception of Malta and possibly Portugal.'[9]

The new Minister for Justice, Paddy Cooney, intervened in the debate to announce that the government would be bringing in its own bill. Such support as there was for Mary Robinson's proposal rapidly evaporated and it was defeated by 32 votes to 10. What happened next was a pantomime of political ineptitude that left everyone, including Mary Robinson, gasping with disbelief. The opposition by religious groups to the government's extremely modest proposal was so intense, and the sense of apprehension among politicians so pronounced, that the government announced there would be a free vote on the issue. It was, however, described as a 'government measure' and on that basis large numbers of visibly reluctant government back-benchers were herded into the lobbies to support it.

To everyone's astonishment, the Taoiseach, Liam Cosgrave, then voted with the main opposition party against the 'government bill'. He had kept his intentions private until the end despite being questioned by colleagues in the Cabinet room. His vote, and those of some of his colleagues who had seen just in time which way he was planning to vote and hastily switched sides to join him, ensured the defeat of the proposal.

The confusion had a simple explanation. Everyone assumed that a 'free vote' meant that, while members of the two parties in government could abstain or vote against the measure if they perceived it as an issue of conscience, the Cabinet at least was four-square behind it. This assumption helped to persuade many government TDs to take the risk: if their own Cabinet ministers were being brave, they could troop into the lobbies behind them without risking too much political fall-out. In the event, the Taoiseach's action in voting against the measure left them out on a limb, exposed to the wrath of their more conservative electors.

Mary Robinson's response was withering in its intensity and merciless in its mockery. The government, she suggested, could do with some intensive marriage counselling and 'we need government planning even more than family planning'. Behind this broadside came the lawyer: public discussion of what had happened was confusing two issues – the free vote and collective Cabinet responsibility. It had been quite inaccurate to describe the bill as a 'government measure'. If members of the Cabinet understood they had a right to vote against it – and if it had been introduced in the context of a genuinely free vote – it might well have been a better bill.

The Dáil defeat meant that the whole issue was kicked off the public agenda for the remainder of the lifetime of the government – not without audible sighs of relief. Mary Robinson made one last attempt, in December 1974, to re-introduce the issue in the Senate but it had run out of steam. Not even after she joined the Labour Party almost two years later did she – for reasons that are discussed below – get more than a token acknowledgement of her efforts.

Her relations with the Labour Party were in fact going through a sticky patch at this point. The issue was Northern Ireland. The introduction of internment in the North had heightened previously latent republican feelings in the South and by late 1974 they were, in some quarters, at fever pitch. On 16 October John Mulcahy, the editor of *Hibernia*, organised a public meeting in the Mansion House in Dublin to protest against internment in the North and invited Mary Robinson onto a platform which included Tom Hadden, the Belfast lawyer and later co-founder of *Fortnight* magazine, Fr Denis Faul, the Dungannon priest who had highlighted discrimination against the Northern minority, and the actress Siobhán McKenna.

Everybody on the platform, as might have been expected and was certainly intended, condemned internment. What set the meeting alight, however, was Fr Faul's decision to condemn not only internment but what he described as 'murder gangs'. Asked from the floor whether the IRA were murder gangs, Fr Faul replied, without qualification, that they were. The meeting erupted in a symphony of booing and catcalls and the chairman, John Mulcahy, briefly lost control of the proceedings. Order of a sort was restored after a veteran Derry republican in the audience, Seán Keenan, came onto the platform and appealed for calm, adding his own view that there should be 'pickets on every British establishment in Dublin, the greatest of which was Leinster House'.

These sentiments were applauded by the protesters and also by the chairman but otherwise went for the most part unremarked. A little over a week later, however, a slow fuse which had been lit in Leinster House by these events burnt through to its explosive charge and Conor Cruise O'Brien, Minister for Posts and Telegraphs, went thunderously on the offensive. Up to this point, O'Brien's personal relationships with Mary Robinson had been extremely warm – after his cousin Owen Sheehy Skeffington's death, he had backed her unreservedly for the Senate in the 1973 campaign and his support counted for a lot in the Trinity electorate, of which he himself was one. Now, in a carefully scripted speech to a Dublin audience, he attacked Mary Robinson's role in the meeting on the two grounds best calculated to damage her: it was a betrayal of the liberal cause and it was, if only by inference, a slur on the parliament in which she herself sat.

His reference to the liberal agenda was a telling one. In the 1950s the *Irish Times* had published a lengthy controversy in its correspondence columns about 'the liberal ethic', a debate in which (then Senator) Owen Sheehy Skeffington had been prominent. Among large sections of Dublin Protestant opinion and a growing number of Catholic middle-class intellectuals, the word 'liberal' had become almost a badge of honour, signifying opposition to repressive legislation, to domination by the Catholic Church of social legislation and institutions, and support for civil rights generally.

In his Dublin speech O'Brien put his own liberal credentials firmly on the table: although he had argued against repressive legislation such as the Forcible Entry Act and the Offences Against the State (Amendment) Act while in opposition, liberals had to recognise threats to democracy when they were real and unmistakable. For these very reasons he had supported – also in opposition – legislation to transfer dangerous prisoners to military custody and the establishment of the Special Criminal Court. What was critical now, he argued, was the need to defend parliament because, if parliament 'fails to provide an adequate response to armed conspiracy and thereby succumbs to that conspiracy, then it will be succeeded by a dictatorship'. He went on: 'A member of our parliament sat on that platform while Mr Seán Keenan was applauded for describing that parliament as a British establishment. She appears to have made no public protest at this proceeding although she continues to hold her seat in the institution thus held up to contumely.

'I think this was a great pity. Senator Mary Robinson (for it was she) is a lady of considerable ability and style who has fought with courage and effect in the Senate for at least one important and genuinely liberal cause. The Mansion House proceedings were so profoundly illiberal as actually to cast scorn not on any given political party, not on the government, but on the central institution of democracy, parliament itself.

'Nor is that all. The Senator, who is also a professor of law, ably attacked the practice of internment without trial and made the case for reliance on the ordinary courts. But she is not recorded, in any reports I have seen, as referring at all to the difficulties which can be experienced in certain circumstances by the courts in dealing with armed conspiracies. She is not reported as referring to the murder of two judges in Belfast last month by that same armed conspiracy whose admirers were so vocal in that room that they were only quelled by the denunciation of the democracy in which we live. The only comment she is reported as having made on judges in Northern Ireland was an aspersion on their integrity.'[10]

It is not for nothing that O'Brien was known colloquially as 'The Cruiser'. Being attacked in these terms by such a heavyweight controversialist would have been a bruising experience for campaigners even more seasoned than Mary Robinson. Nonetheless, she defended her position the next day in a radio interview which, despite the shortcomings of the medium, adequately conveyed her determination to stick to her guns. She defended, in particular, her liberal voice against any attempt to 'squeeze it out, stifle it, contain it or stereotype it' and she warned of the danger of leaving the condemnations of internment solely to those engaged in active republicanism. O'Brien, she added, was using the weight of his office in an attempt to smear liberals by implying that they were in deliberate – or, worse still, confused – alliance with republican activists. On the lethal accusation that she had impugned the integrity of Northern judges, she hit back fairly and squarely: 'He said I had attacked the integrity of judges. In fact, I condemned the collective silence of the legal profession, including the judiciary, at the operation of internment. They operate side by side with a system which undermines the legal process and is a fatal flaw in building up society, creating confidence and building, in an alienated minority, trust and faith in the system.'

If O'Brien had been, in effect, accusing her of inconsistency in failing as a liberal, to defend liberal democracy, Robinson was responding by arguing that her own definition of liberalism was broader and more inclusive than his. In the process, she was identifying issues and commitments that would mark her own career consistently into the 1990s: a concern for the politically alienated minority in the North which was in no way inconsistent with her concern for a psychologically embattled majority there; and a concern for the rule of law, in the classic sense, which translated into her later critique of the Republic's special criminal court system, a critique which was even more detailed and probably more telling than her opposition to internment. Her debate with O'Brien remains, in some sense, at the core of the argument about what constitutes liberalism in Ireland today.

Back in the Four Courts, she was meeting with considerably more success than in the political arena. The government's continuing inaction on adoption was challenged by a couple who succeeded in May 1974, with Mary Robinson acting for them, in having one section of the 1952 Adoption Act declared unconstitutional. This finally forced the government to draft amending legislation which was passed in July 1976. If this was a highly technical issue which affected only small numbers of people, however, another which involved Mary Robinson was not. This concerned the question of whether or not women had a right to serve on juries.

Mairín de Burca, an able, left-wing political activist, had been among those who had noticed that women were virtually absent from the juries empanelled to deal with civil and criminal cases. The selection of juries was governed by the 1927 Juries Act which confined jury service to ratepayers. This had the effect of excluding everyone living in rented accommodation, whether public or private, effectively many working-class people. It also excluded women because, although some women were ratepayers, they were dealt with by the Act in a different way from their male counterparts. De Burca decided to challenge the constitutionality of this practice in the courts up to the level of the Supreme Court; and Mary Robinson was an almost inevitable choice for the legal team.

The difference between male and female ratepayers, as Mary Robinson later pointed out, was that males were not only eligible for jury service but could be compelled to attend and punished by the law if they refused. Female ratepayers, on the other hand, were eligible for jury service but could not be compelled to attend, and indeed actually had to apply to have their names put on the jury list. With the concern for research that characterised many of her major legal and political initiatives, Mary Robinson pointed out that in the ten years between 1963 and 1973 only nine women in the entire country had applied to serve on juries, four of them in Dublin. Of these nine women only five had actually been called for jury service. Two had been challenged when the juries were being empanelled and only three had actually served on juries in the entire decade, two on a criminal jury and the third in a civil case.

The Supreme Court allowed Mairín de Burca's appeal against the High Court decision (which had gone against her) in December 1975. By March 1976 the government, acting with a despatch that had been noticeably absent on the contraception issue, legislated in the Juries Act to democratise jury service for the first time in almost half a century. The Act also created certain exceptions from jury service, including lawyers and – prophetically – the President.

The same theme – the belief that law should serve ordinary people and should not be merely the preserve of an elite – underpinned yet another initiative with which Mary Robinson was closely associated during this period: the establishment of the Free Legal Aid Centres (FLAC). The name speaks for itself: it was the brain-child of a group of socially committed young lawyers, who recognised that access to the courts was illusory for many working-class people and who wanted to open up avenues through which good and cheap or free legal advice could be available, even in civil cases, to those who needed it most. Mary Robinson was, from the beginning, not only an ally but an advocate for the scheme which opened its first centre in Coolock in Dublin in April 1975.

It was at around this time, early in 1976, that Mary Robinson began to consider the possibility of actually joining a political party. She had already turned down 'ardent' proposals from both Fianna Fáil and Fine Gael.[11] The author, John Horgan, co-sponsor with her of many Senate initiatives, had joined the Labour Party in the summer of 1975 and was already actively involved in seeking a Dáil nomination for the party in the Dublin South constituency. Was it, she might have wondered, a time for all good women, as well as men, to come to the aid of the party? And which party?

In fact, 1976 was possibly the worst time for an independent to think of joining any political party with the possible exception of Fianna Fáil, then in opposition. The 1973 coalition government, which had come into office with high hopes of permanently breaking the cycle of Irish politics, had run almost immediately into the brick wall of the oil price rises which rocked economies everywhere in the world. As the Arab leaders doubled the price of their oil and then raised it again, energy-dependent economies reeled under the effect and prices of energy-related products like plastics rocketed.

In Ireland inflation galloped out of control, reaching an annual rate of 26% at one stage, and mortgage rates rose with it, eating into the income of home-owners and provoking round after round of wage claims. Borrowing enthusiastically in an attempt to keep the wolf from the door, the government succeeded only in temporarily blunting the edge of public discontent. Although Labour was the minority partner in the coalition, it had succeeded in persuading the government to adopt a wealth tax (death duties were abolished in a compensatory move, leaving Ireland with one of the lowest rates of taxation on capital of any developed country). To an electorate of which farmers, large and small, still formed a significant part, such a measure was portrayed by its opponents as incipient communism. The terrier-like Minister for Finance, Richard Ryan, was satirised as 'Red Richie', or 'Richie Ruin'. The latter years of the government's term of office therefore saw the development across the community generally of a mood of sullen disillusion and an unspoken determination to vote them out of office at the first opportunity, come what may.

The government knew that they faced major problems but consistently under-estimated them. They took one significant step to offset the unpopularity which they recognised was out there in the constituencies waiting to bite them – but it was a move that fatally back-fired. This was the decision to re-draw the constituency boundaries to maximise the effect of the core vote for the two government parties and consign Fianna Fáil to the electoral wilderness for the second time running. This feat had never been achieved by any non-Fianna Fáil government.

The problem about the gerrymander – or Tullymander as it became popularly known after the Labour Minister for Local Government, James Tully, who supervised the scheme – was that it had a built-in self-destruct mechanism. It was framed on the assumption that the government could retain its majority even if there was a modest swing against it. Once the swing reached certain critical proportions, however, the advantage conferred by the proportional representation system would be transferred to Fianna Fáil, with an electoral bonus in seats disproportionate to its share of the overall vote.

Although none of this was known at the time, the situation was still bad enough in 1976 to suggest that anyone who jumped aboard the coalition ship was an idealist at best, foolhardy at the very least and arguably someone with an extreme taste for political masochism. In these circumstances, for someone seen as a middle-class liberal to join Labour rather than Fine Gael was even more incomprehensible.

The difference, in a sense, was that Labour still lacked the self-confidence to canvass new recruits actively, especially given the horrendous criticism and internal party problems that had been generated by the accession of people like O'Brien, Keating and Thornley. Fianna Fáil and Fine Gael were both broad-spectrum parties: though Fine Gael was more evidently liberal on social issues, it did not monopolise this territory, and Fianna Fáil could claim more social radicalism than the other large parties. Less self-consciously, Fianna Fáil and Fine Gael were given to canvassing actively for members and potential Dáil candidates, especially among the younger members of the professions; and they would have had more confidence in their ability to manage even as potentially contrary a spirit as Mary Robinson. In a bigger party, she would be less visible, less de-stabilising.

Mary Robinson joined the Labour Party with a well thought-out agenda, as she later made clear. She had become ever more conscious of the limitations of the legal process as a way of bringing about profound social change, even though she had also come to accept that the political path was strewn with obstacles and that politicians as legislators often tended to give a belated expression to public opinion rather than to lead and shape it. On the other hand, she regarded judge-made law as 'sometimes a weakness. You do get break-throughs in the courts, and sometimes they're helpful, but the best way forward is by making policy consciously through the legislature – that can sometimes be slow.'

Her own sentiments left her with no real option in party terms. In addition the Labour Party, for all its vacillation on some issues, was the only major party which had given serious consideration to any of the measures she had proposed in the preceding seven years and its members in the Senate had frequently supported them. Labour senator Evelyn Owens, in what was a complete departure from normal party practice, had even been given permission by her party to co-sponsor Mary Robinson's adoption bill.

'I was increasingly aware', she recalls, 'that the real way to make change was through the structure that effected change, which is a political party. Effectively the only political party that I could join in that sense was the Labour Party and I joined with great motivation.'

She first made an approach to Labour's general secretary, Brendan Halligan, through Evelyn Owens. A meeting was set up but had to be cancelled when an IRA bomb killed the newly-appointed British ambassador to Dublin, Christopher Ewart Biggs, on 20 July 1976 and threw the entire political system into a tail-spin. She eventually joined the party formally at the end of the month. She was taking a major risk but was not to know at the time how much of a risk it actually was. The next nine years were to see her accused of opportunism, careerism and worse. The aura of political frustration and failure would be hung around her neck like an albatross; her good faith and her political principles would be jeered at and discounted; and none but a small and apparently dwindling band of personal supporters would continue to see in her something of the bright hopes that had marked her early career.

It was an intellectual commitment rather than one based on any personal relationships. The leader of the Labour Party at the time was Brendan Corish, a slow-spoken, silver-haired member of a political dynasty from Wexford. His father, Richard Corish, had been a TD from 1920 to 1945. Brendan, who won the seat at the by-election after his father's death, had been elected leader of the party in 1960 and, at the time that Mary Robinson joined the party, was Minister for Health. Although Mary Robinson respected him they were in some sense on opposite sides of the fence. 'I remember not being close to Brendan Corish, particularly because he was very concerned at the fact that I was very much involved in family planning legislation. I remember acknowledging that he and I would have a lot of differences on many issues. But he was very honest and very committed and I had a lot to learn from people like him.'

All this, however, was in the future. Her immediate task was to justify to her electorate her decision to abandon her independent status and immerse herself in the grubby world of political compromise, deal-making and patronage with which party politics was inevitably associated. 'Gradually I have become convinced', she wrote at the time, 'that the problems which torment this society – problems of inequity and the attitudes which foster it and all the ills which grow from inequity – cannot be solved piecemeal. I now believe that only within the framework of a socialism which evolves around those ills and advances a coherent view of their possible remedies can we truly progress ...

Independence without commitment becomes a tyranny. I have tried to balance both.' Interestingly, there was little negative feedback – very little feedback of any sort, in fact. It was hardly an endorsement, more a suspension of judgement.

Joining the Labour Party, however, does not carry automatic membership of the Parliamentary Labour Party (PLP) even if the applicant is already – as Mary Robinson was – a member of the Oireachtas. The PLP is comprised of people who signed a pledge to obey its rules before the election: anyone who joins after the election must apply and be accepted. The PLP, it turned out, had mixed feelings about its potential new recruit. Her application to join the PLP lay on the agenda for some time as members side-stepped gingerly around it. Finally Michael D. Higgins, then a senator, moved that it be accepted and the deed was done. There was some muttering at the back of the room, and the words 'you'll regret this' were heard from one participant, although identifying the Doubting Thomas was impossible.

CHAPTER 4

The Labour Party:
Battles Lost and Won

THE PARLIAMENTARY LABOUR PARTY as a whole responded to its new recruits with modified rapture. John Horgan was a journalist and his arrival raised unmistakable apprehensions about the possibility of leaks to the media from the conclave of the parliamentary party meeting. Mary Robinson was a woman, which in a sense was even worse. The parliamentary party culture was overwhelmingly male. It had only two female members: Evelyn Owens, an exceptionally able and sensitive trade union official who was never afraid to speak her mind to her male Labour colleagues; and Eileen Desmond, TD, from Cork, the widow of a former Labour TD, who had become a formidable politician in her own right (and was later briefly to become Minister for Health). What both had in common was that they were imbued with Labour Party culture and could be trusted implicitly not to rock the boat. Mary Robinson came into the Labour Party with a record of rocking boats all over the harbour and some of the crew of this particular vessel gave the impression that they were anxiously checking whether the life-jacket was still under their seat.

There were some notable exceptions, particularly Owens, Ruairí Quinn, Michael D. Higgins and Justin Keating, but by and large the welcome she received was tempered by reserve. It was also tempered by the attitude, exemplified in the hard-nosed stance of ministers like James Tully, that policies and attitudes mattered less in the long run than votes and that the true worth of any politician could best be measured by his or her willingness and ability to rack up the votes that would win a seat in the Dáil. This was hard political currency and the only one with a real exchange value for the professionals.

Mary Robinson attended her first meeting of the parliamentary party on 28 October 1976 and, after the normal courtesies had been extended, was immediately enmeshed in controversy. Party discipline was the issue. In late

1976 Labour, with the coalition issue still an irritant, had been in power for over three years. The external shocks to which the economy had been subjected were creating widespread difficulties for TDs in vulnerable seats, who were looking anxiously over their shoulders and becoming more jittery by the day. The Labour ministers, on the other hand, had been welded by adversity into an increasingly coherent group with their Fine Gael counterparts, a process accentuated by the very serious security situation in which ministers and their families had to live, with constant armed guards, threatening telephone calls and other forms of pressure created by the Northern Ireland situation. There was a feeling among some Labour rank and file members that the ministers had lost touch with the party grass-roots and this, combined with the general edginess, was encouraging some members to kick over the traces.

The most serious disciplinary problem had occurred just before Mary Robinson joined the party when David Thornley, the Trinity College politics lecturer who had swept into the Dáil on the Labour ticket in 1969 (he had stood ineffectually in the Trinity Senate constituency as an independent in 1965, ending up second from the bottom with 308 votes) had the party whip removed from him by a vote of PLP members. This meant that he was expelled from the PLP, was no longer subject to its discipline and could no longer claim its privileges. The real sanction was the likelihood that the party's central administration would refuse to ratify his selection as a candidate at any subsequent general election unless he mended his ways. Thornley's offence had been to appear at a banned Sinn Féin commemorative rally outside the GPO at a time when public opinion in the South was turning dramatically against the paramilitary activities of the IRA in the North.

The discipline problem had two aspects. One was that the PLP had to vote formally to expel a member; this gave rise to all sorts of tensions. The second was that voting against the party was the crime that generally gave rise to expulsion; in the Senate some members, not least Michael D. Higgins and the author, finessed this issue by abstaining on a number of controversial issues without imperilling the government majority. So Mary Robinson's first PLP meeting had before it a motion put forward by two of the most conservative members of the PLP, Michael Pat Murphy from Cork and Stevie Coughlan from Limerick, proposing that anyone who voted against the party or abstained would automatically lose the whip: no need for divisive votes and angry speeches. Motions at PLP meetings are generally discussed and voted on in short order, especially when they involve party discipline: leaving them on the order paper would simply encourage the wounds to fester. And the PLP, like all political party groupings in the Dáil and Senate, is master of its own destiny and procedures: there is no higher authority to which anyone can appeal.

Mary Robinson was immediately in the thick of the argument, trying to persuade her new-found colleagues that there should be a distinction between voting against a party decision, which was a deliberate act, and mere abstention. Automatic exclusion from the PLP for the latter offence, she thought, was going too far, although the party should have a strict code of discipline and should not be afraid of implementing it. Her suggestions fell on deaf ears. Coughlan wanted automatic loss of the whip extended to TDs who made injudicious utterances even outside the Oireachtas, and the Coughlan/Murphy motion was passed by 25 votes to 3. Life was not going to be easy for Mary Robinson.

She used what opportunities she had to insert the items which had been on her personal agenda since 1969 into the Labour Party's action plan, but it was a difficult task for at least three reasons. The first was her insistence on debating issues at the PLP regardless of the fact that she was almost bound to lose any votes. The second was the combination of pre-election nerves and leadership tension which affected the party. For some time in the run-up to an election, no political party wants to take avoidable risks. In addition, a number of her potential allies at the PLP were not always available. Like her, they were all also actively cultivating constituencies – particularly if, like Ruairí Quinn and Michael D. Higgins, they were still only senators. The author, who had been her ally in the Senate, also fell into this category and was, paradoxically, less available than when they were both independent members of the Senate. In addition, Labour had its fair share of political backwoods men, long-serving holders of seats outside the main urban areas (in 1965-69 there was only one Labour TD in Dublin) who thought, probably accurately, that supporting contraception would be, for them, a messy form of political suicide.

The third factor was the leadership issue. In 1976 Brendan Corish had been leader of the party for sixteen years. Although not particularly old (he was fifty-eight) his health had been giving him some problems since 1973 and it was an open secret that he would be retiring after the election. Two candidates were shaping up for the succession stakes: Frank Cluskey and Michael O'Leary. Each of them knew that the support of non-Dublin TDs, especially those from the Munster area, would be vital in the contest. In these circumstances, Mary Robinson's chances of swinging the whole party behind her were slim.

Top of her agenda was the family planning issue, on which the party was eventually to muddle through to a classic compromise. It was evident to Corish, then Minister for Health and therefore the Cabinet member who might well have to carry the poisoned chalice of family planning legislation, that a vote in the Dáil on the issue would expose deep divisions in his own party. The fact that it would probably also expose divisions in other parties was, in the circumstances, scant consolation. Mary Robinson discussed the latest version of her bill privately with Corish in early December 1976 and the first compromise (suggested by Ruairí Quinn at a later meeting) was that she should be permitted to move the bill in the Senate, that the Minister (Corish) would sit in on the debate but without making a speech and that the debate should be adjourned to some unspecified date in the new year.

This proposal failed to elicit much support and in February 1977 when Quinn repeated his proposal, Corish made it clear that, in his view, there was not the slightest prospect of a unanimous party position on the matter, and suggested that any legislation on the issue should be the subject of a free vote. It was not until the following month that Mary Robinson, with the valuable support of Conor Cruise O'Brien (despite their earlier clash on internment), secured the party's agreement on a compromise: the measure could be debated and voted on in the Senate and if it was carried a date would be set for the next stage, on the strict understanding that it would actually not be discussed again in the lifetime of the present Senate, i.e. on this side of the anticipated general election. The matter would not be settled until 1979 when Minister for Health Charles Haughey would secure passage of a Family Planning Act.

Conor Cruise O'Brien was not always to be found on Mary Robinson's side of an argument. Indeed there were times when O'Brien himself was raising eyebrows right across the Labour Party spectrum. He had already criticised her severely in 1974 on the issue of Northern Ireland. Now, he had become even more critical of the Constitution than had Mary Robinson, believing that it was too fundamentally influenced by a malign Fianna Fáil nationalism and arguing that the whole document should be dispensed with and a new one written. Mary Robinson and other would-be reformers hesitated to adopt such a line, more conscious than O'Brien, perhaps, of the possible identities and proclivities of those who would be composing its replacement.

This issue had surfaced notably at a meeting in the Gresham Hotel in January 1977, when Robinson, Dr Enda McDonagh and O'Brien were all on the platform. O'Brien, as a government minister, was the focus of attention and not necessarily to the delight of his Cabinet colleagues. Only days earlier the government had introduced what was to be its last Budget, a modest and ultimately unsuccessful attempt to turn back the tide of public opinion that was now flowing heavily against them. In the course of his speech, O'Brien hinted broadly that people like Mary Robinson who were prepared to settle for piecemeal if substantial constitutional revision were naive. The resultant storm of controversy was to obliterate the paltry good economic news in the budget.

There was no risk that Mary Robinson would be seen as a single-issue politician. In the same brief period before the general election, she pushed the party hard on two different issues: adoption and penal reform. In the case of adoption, she believed that the situation was so inflexible that a constitutional amendment would be needed to reinforce the rights of children. The PLP established a group of eight people to meet the Attorney-General, Declan Costello, to discuss the issue, but almost as soon as this proposal had been agreed Costello became a judge and his successor, John Kelly, did not have any time to take the matter further. On the question of penal reform, the party decided to set up a sub-committee whose deliberations, such as they were, were rapidly overshadowed by the imminent election, and which never produced a report.

Mary Robinson had already decided that there was no sense in accepting the obligations of party membership without also accepting the implicit imperative to create another Labour seat in Dáil Éireann and in the process to move closer to ministerial power, to that magic circle within which politicians can actually decide what they want to do and do it, instead of merely talking about what they would like to do if they had the chance.

The problem was that, by the latter part of 1976, there were relatively few constituencies available for latecomers. Candidates were already in place in most constituencies which were even vaguely winnable and there was little point in a quality candidate like Mary Robinson heading off for the wilds of Leitrim, or even her native Mayo, to mount a quixotic campaign against hopeless odds. For one thing, she was now effectively a Dubliner by adoption, and the intense localism of Irish politics might have told against her, even in Mayo. As well as that, Labour was to all intents and purposes invisible in Mayo and it might have taken even more than her legendary family connections in the constituency to win a seat for the party there at this time. Discussions with the general secretary of the party, Brendan Halligan, rapidly identified one possible option, the Dublin constituency of Rathmines West, and by August she had already signified to a number of local Labour Party activists that she proposed seeking a nomination there for the forthcoming general election.

The constituency had a number of advantages. As the four-seater constituency of Dublin South Central in 1969, it had elected Dr John O'Donovan to the Dáil in the Labour interest, but O'Donovan had subsequently performed poorly and lost his seat in 1973. It had since been reduced from four seats to three, of which Fianna Fáil and Fine Gael were virtually guaranteed one each. The head of the Fine Gael ticket was Minister of Finance Richie Ryan, a solicitor who had been a Dáil deputy since 1959 and in normal circumstances could have expected to be elected with a healthy vote surplus but not enough to elect a second Fine Gael candidate.

Labour strategists hoped that Ryan's spare votes would help Labour take the third seat, with the middle one going to Fianna Fáil. The constituency had a mixture of settled working-class and middle-class housing and a strong sense of local identity. Artisans and civil servants rubbed shoulders with shopkeepers and the lower gentry. It was a comfortable, easy-going sort of place with well-rooted traditions. Mary Robinson's house was almost on the edge of the

ABOVE: The Bourke family home: Victoria House, Victoria Terrace (otherwise Emmett Terrace), Ballina. The house was bought by Mary Bourke's father, Aubrey, and is impressively situated, facing across the River Moy to St Muiredach's Cathedral.
(*Reproduced courtesy of Michael O'Sullivan*)

BELOW: Mary Bourke, *centre*, with her brothers, *from left to right*, Oliver, Aubrey, Henry and Adrian at Miss Claire Ruddy's private preparatory school. Miss Ruddy's school – one of a number of such schools patronised by middle-class parents in the larger provincial towns – existed until 1969. Its proprietress was an independent-minded woman with a fondness for the Irish language and the classics. (*Sunday Tribune*)

Mary Bourke as a student in the sixties speaking in the *Irish Times*-sponsored student debating competition. Her co-debater was the future Attorney-General, Harry Whelehan. (*Irish Times*)

LEFT: Sartorial standards in the Senate were restrained in 1969, and newly-fledged women senators were expected to appear in hats. This was Mary Bourke's first day as a Senator. Her – much later – appearance in a trouser suit was a break with tradition that was more in character. (*Irish Times*)

BELOW: Mary Robinson's second election to the Senate, May 1973. By this time she had already established a considerable reputation, and her place as one of the three Trinity senators was virtually assured. (*Independent Newspapers*)

ABOVE: Mary Bourke with fellow TCD academics Kadar Asmal, *left*, and the Rev Terence McCaughey, *right*, in the mid-1970s. Asmal was a fellow-lecturer in the Law faculty while McCaughey still lectures in Irish. All three were prominent in the Anti-Apartheid Movement and a number of other civil liberties organisations. Asmal, who was also a member of the African National Congress, was appointed a minister in Nelson Mandela's first government. (*Irish Times*)

BELOW: With Nobel and Lenin Peace Prize winner, Seán MacBride SC. MacBride, son of Maud Gonne, was a mercurial character who had been Ireland's Foreign Minister in 1948-51, and specialised in high-profile constitutional cases at the Bar. Mary Robinson, in her early legal career, worked with him on a number of cases. He died in 1988. *(Irish Times)*

ABOVE: The Wood Quay protest attracted widespread support in Dublin, and was the focus of a number of marches and court cases involving Mary Robinson. *Above*, the scene outside Leinster House at a major protest in 1978. (*Irish Times*)

Mary Robinson participating in a 24-hour vigil outside the Department of Justice in Dublin in October 1978 to protest against the decision to open Loughan House, a purpose-built secure centre for juvenile offenders. It was the focus of considerable opposition by civil rights and child welfare groups and was eventually closed down. (*Reproduced courtesy of Derek Speirs/Report*)

ABOVE: Mary Robinson as Joan of Arc by Littleman (cartoonist Billy Drake) in *Hibernia* in 1978. The unflatteringly-drawn background figure is her husband Nick, a friend of Littleman's and a fellow cartoonist. (*Reproduced courtesy of Littleman*)

BELOW: Mary Robinson, *back to camera*, addressing a public protest meeting in 1979 on the need for a proper system of free legal aid. She was involved with this movement from its inception and, as President, donated a £4,000 prize that she had been awarded to the network of Free Legal Aid Centres which were eventually established. (*Reproduced courtesy of Derek Speirs/Report*)

ABOVE: With husband Nicholas shortly after the birth of their youngest child, Aubrey, at Holles Street Hospital, Dublin, in May 1981. Aubrey's introduction to politics was not long delayed: he was being breast fed and so became a constant feature of the election campaign in Dublin West in the same year. (*Irish Times*)

LEFT: As a Labour senator after 1976, Mary Robinson was much in demand by different sections of the party organisation. Here, she speaks at a party seminar on housing in February 1980. (*Reproduced courtesy of Derek Speirs/Report*)

Every inch the Senator – Mary Robinson thanks her supporters at the conclusion of the January 1983 Senate election campaign. (*Independent Newspapers*)

LEFT: In 1982, pressure groups forced the government to introduce an amendment to the Constitution in an attempt to give constitutional backing to the criminal law already in place on abortion. Mary Robinson, seen here speaking at a meeting in February 1983, was active in the anti-amendment campaign. However, she was not – as was alleged during her election campaign for the presidency – an office-holder in the anti-amendment movement.
(*Reproduced courtesy of Derek Speirs/Report*)

BELOW: At home in Sandford Road, Ranelagh, the Georgian terraced house where Mary Robinson lived with her family until the move to Áras an Uachtaráin in the Phoenix Park in 1990. (*Irish Times*)

Mary Robinson with Dick Spring, leader of the Labour Party, at Leinster House on 4 April 1990, immediately following the decision by Labour's Administrative Council and Parliamentary Labour Party to nominate her as a candidate for the presidential election, although she declined to rejoin the party. (*Irish Times*)

ABOVE: Presidential election headquarters, Merrion Square, Dublin: *from left*, Ruairí Quinn TD, chairman of the joint election committee; Bride Rosney, strategist and future presidential special adviser; Brenda O'Hanlon, press relations specialist, and Fergus Finlay, adviser to Dick Spring. These four were key players in Mary Robinson's successful campaign. (*Irish Times*)

LEFT: A campaign meeting in Mary Robinson's home town, Ballina, Co. Mayo, on 22 October 1990. (*Irish Times*)

Candidate going down, votes going up: on the escalator in the major shopping centre at The Square, Tallaght, Dublin, 5 November 1990. Directly behind Mary Robinson is Pat Rabbitte, the Workers' Party TD for the Dublin South West constituency and Minister of State 1994-97. Behind and to the right of Nick Robinson is Mervyn Taylor, Labour TD for the same constituency and later Minister for Equality and Law Reform 1992-97. (*Irish Times*)

LEFT: Brian Lenihan TD, the Fianna Fáil candidate, Mary Robinson, and Austin Currie TD, the Fine Gael candidate, outside Radio Telefís Éireann just before the radio debate between the contestants, 22 September 1990. (*Reproduced courtesy of Derek Speirs/Report*)

BELOW: Photograph used in the poster campaign for the presidential election: the occasion was a canvass in St Stephen's Green, Dublin, where Mary Robinson met these four voters. As the result of an oversight, their names were not recorded at the time, and election workers had to scour the Green for days afterwards to identify them and get their permission for the photograph to be used.
(*Reproduced courtesy of Conor Horgan*)

Nicholas Robinson at home in Ranelagh during the election campaign. More often, he was on the road with the candidate, offering invaluable moral support and good advice. (*Irish Times*)

At the end of the long campaign, Mary Robinson and her father, Dr Aubrey Bourke, face the future cheerfully. (*Irish Times*)

constituency, a factor which is important in politics dominated by localism. She had a national reputation and she was prepared to pitch in and do the work.

Mary Robinson, however, was not the only person who had her eye on Rathmines. Brendan Halligan had been fleetingly interested in the nomination but had gone elsewhere when it became clear that the local Labour standard-bearer, councillor Michael Collins, would not make way for him. Labour party activists loyal to Noel Browne, had scouted the area and there had already been something of a tussle between Collins and a dentist, David Neligan, who also fancied his electoral chances. Collins worked in a dairy company and was a stalwart of the Workers' Union of Ireland. Neligan was more left-wing and pro-active. By the time Mary Robinson arrived on the scene, they had agreed a compromise of sorts as a result of which effective control of the constituency organisation was shared between branches loyal to each of them. Suddenly there was a new element in the equation, although Collins had been approached by party headquarters and had agreed to Mary Robinson's entry into the lists.

When Mary Robinson told David Neligan in August 1977 that she would be looking for a nomination in the constituency, he had not at that stage declared his own candidacy. Within the constituency, two new branches were formed, largely composed of female party members who supported Mary Robinson, creating a situation in which each of the potential candidates (David Neligan declared in September) controlled two branches and the voting delegates from these branches. In theory, and provided the constituency opted for a three-candidate strategy, this guaranteed Mary Robinson a nomination.

The anticipated early date of the election, however, created another problem. In the process of putting its administrative house in order and, in particular, in order to restrict the phenomenon of 'paper branches', the party had decreed that branches had to be in existence for a minimum of six months before their delegates could vote at a selection convention. Under the old rules, paper branches could be formed with a very small number of members and comparatively undemanding financial obligations to the party's head office. TDs or those who aspired to election nominations could bankroll such branches relatively cheaply: all they needed were two people who could be relied on to turn up to a selection convention and vote for the approved candidate. And such branches could be created and registered almost up to the eve of the convention itself.

The minimum period rule was designed to make all this more difficult. It did not, of course, make it impossible. And it had the side-effect of creating a problem for the party in constituencies which were winnable but which did not have a candidate of the right calibre. In such constituencies, there was generally an additional problem in that unelectable candidates held the local party organisation (and hence the election nomination) in an iron grip and often refused ratification to branches being organised by rival aspirants. In an attempt to balance both ends against the middle, the party's executive, the administrative council, acted against 'paper' branches by creating the six-month rule, while simultaneously extending its own powers by giving itself the right to add candidates to those chosen by the local organisation if necessary. The downside of this was that added or 'imposed' candidates ran the very serious risk of alienating local party supporters and ensuring only that the party contested the election with an admirable candidate but with a truncated or alienated party organisation at grass-roots level.

In Rathmines West (and in Cabra, another Dublin constituency where veteran trade unionist's son Michael Mullen was looking for a nomination for the seat previously held by his father), the imminence of the election meant that branches which had been formed for the express purpose of securing nominations for Mary Robinson and Michael Mullen Jr were just outside the six-month time limit. Brendan Halligan then came up with an ingenious solution, which was endorsed by the administrative council, in the hope that it would avoid the necessity to 'impose' either of them as a candidate on an unwilling local party. The six months were to be interpreted not as calendar months but as lunar months. On this basis, Mary Robinson's and Michael Mullen's branches just squeezed under the wire.

Anybody who knows the Irish Labour Party could have predicted that this 'solution' might not meet with universal acceptance. In fact Griff Cashman, a disadvantaged potential candidate in Cabra, took an action in the High Court to declare the result of the selection convention there invalid and the case dragged on for weeks, tainting Mary Robinson's selection process as it did so. In the case of Rathmines, however, the party leadership had grounds for believing that the constituency organisation would in any case agree to run three candidates – Collins, Neligan and Robinson. In the 1990s this would be regarded as foolhardy in the extreme in a three-seater constituency but the conventional wisdom of the day was that this was the best way of avoiding damaging party splits and indeed offered the possibility of maximising the party vote.

On the basis of this understanding, the constituency chairman and director of elections, Dublin solicitor Niall Connolly, decided that constituency harmony would be improved if Mary Robinson's two controversial branches did not vote at the selection convention. He had already had intimations that she would be added to the ticket by the administrative council, if necessary. To his surprise, however, the branches controlled by Collins at the selection convention voted for a two- rather than a three-candidate ticket, Collins having apparently decided that while he would abide by party policy, he did not see why he should facilitate it.

Collins and Neligan were therefore nominated alone and, in an atmosphere of some confusion and not a little recrimination, Mary Robinson was soon after added to the list by the administrative council. David Neligan promptly withdrew his nomination in protest and vanished across the Liffey to help Noel Browne's election campaign in Artane, leaving the field to Collins and Robinson. It was an inauspicious beginning, to put it mildly. The media, always ready to pounce on evidence of a Labour 'split', focused gleefully on the banana-skin element which had already marked the campaign and Mary Robinson started running, but from behind. As Niall Connolly put it in his report to party headquarters afterwards: 'The late entry of Mary Robinson added to difficulties already apparent in the form of lack of preparation for the election. In addition the constituency appeared unwilling to take any steps until the selection problem had been resolved. In the event, the constituency had neither unity of purpose nor intent for action.'

For all the ominous rumblings, the campaign was equable enough and Mary Robinson's chances were not discounted. 'Her controversial entry to the campaign in Rathmines West could work against her,' one commentator suggested, 'but her "public image" will do her no harm and she will appeal to non-aligned voters whose first preferences will swell her percentage of the Labour turnout.'[12] Although subsequent events proved this prediction over-optimistic, it was in some respects far-sighted, as can be seen from the vantage point of the 1990s. In the short term, however, Mary Robinson had an uphill task and it was not made any easier by the evident unwillingness of the party leadership to commit the same sort of energy and resources to her election as had been done in the case of earlier and equally high-profile acquisitions by the party.

The constituency was divided into two areas and each candidate had an individual director of elections: Mary Robinson's director was her husband, Nick. The party secured a campaign headquarters at the top of Rathgar Road which was ideal in every respect but one: nobody had checked the roof which leaked copiously. After one downpour, Connolly entered the headquarters to find Nick Robinson sitting in solitary splendour doing election work at a table in the only part of the office that had not been inundated. Not that Nick always got his way: he made a valiant but unsuccessful attempt to have 'Here's to You, Mrs Robinson' adopted as the party's campaign theme for the constituency. His suggested amendment of the words to 'Here's to you, Collins-Robinson' failed, unsurprisingly, to elicit a positive response in the Collins camp. At the end of the campaign, Collins loyalists told the director of elections that in their view he had been '90% fair'. In the context of the Labour Party in 1977, this was praise indeed.

The defeat, when it came, was bruising. Labour, like everyone else, had underestimated the extent of the swing against the government. Its share of the national vote declined by more than two points, from 13.7% to 11.6%, and it lost four seats. Its net loss, however, was only two as Ruairí Quinn and John Horgan both won seats against the swing. In Rathmines, victory had actually been tantalisingly close. Mary Robinson polled 2,854 votes, some 500 ahead of Michael Collins, and when he was eliminated she received a large share of his transfers but failed to win the last seat by a margin of some 400 votes. Ben Briscoe, the Fianna Fáil candidate who was elected to the third seat just ahead of Mary Robinson, had in fact polled a hundred votes less than the combined Labour total of 5,231 but squeezed past Mary Robinson with the help of votes from an unsuccessful third Fianna Fáil candidate.

Some of the recrimination was misplaced. The Labour vote in Rathmines West had actually gone up from 16% to 19.5%; taking into account that the constituency boundaries had been substantially re-drawn prior to the election, this meant in reality that the party's vote had held steady or even increased slightly in the face of the national swing against it. Again, some people made an issue of the fact that many of Michael Collins's votes had not transferred to Mary Robinson on his elimination, hinting at the possible effect of bad blood between the candidates. Many of Collins's votes at this stage, however, would have been votes which he had received on transfer from lower-placed, non-Labour candidates, who could not have been expected to transfer onwards to Robinson in large numbers in any case. In the event, the transfer rate from Collins to Robinson was some 75%, which was entirely respectable in the circumstances.

Moral victories, however, count for little in politics and Mary Robinson was, in the wake of this result, neatly slotted by journalists and others into her little box. She was the gallant loser, the intellectual who couldn't make the grade. She had gone out into the yard where the big boys play and had come running back in with a tear-streaked face. Time to turn our attention to more important things.

Needless to say, this was not Mary Robinson's view of what had happened. But she was now faced with two urgent problems. What was she to do in relation to her Dáil aspirations? Should she run again for the Senate – and, if so, in which Senate constituency? As a high-profile defeated Labour candidate, she could normally have expected a Senate nomination from the party on one of the 'vocational' panels on which, in certain circumstances, election could be all but guaranteed. Her other options were to retire from politics, or to contest the Trinity seat again, unsure of the effect on her electorate of her abandonment of independence and her recent defeat at the polls.

The problem of finding a Dáil constituency was to resolve itself over the next few years as the old Rathmines West constituency was eventually dismembered, parts of it being hived off into Dublin South East and other parts of it helping to create the new constituency of Dublin South Central. Mary Robinson could hardly move into South East, which was Ruairí Quinn's stamping ground, and South Central was heavily over-populated with Labour candidates. They included Frank Cluskey, the gruff, witty, ex-butcher TD, carved in one piece from the Dublin proletariat, who became leader of Labour after Brendan Corish's resignation in 1977. (Cluskey would have been closer to Mary Robinson's positions than Corish on many issues but his concern for party unity led him to blunt the edge of some of her more controversial initiatives.) In the short term, therefore, she bided her time, probably expecting that another constituency would turn up, as in due course it did.

This left the Senate problem. Biting the bullet, she wrote to her Trinity constituents to explain how she had worked out her position, making it clear in the process that she had seriously thought of not running again. She also indicated – and it would have surprised her Labour colleagues had they been fully aware of it – that had Labour gone back into government she would have declined to join the party group in the Senate. Their puzzlement would have arisen from their inability to understand how someone who was prepared to accept the Labour whip in the Dáil if the party was in government felt she could not accept it in similar circumstances in the Senate. She realised the necessity of explaining the rationale for her position and wrote in a post-election letter to electors:

> The experience of eight years of public life has left its mark. I no longer feel that it is an adequate personal contribution to assess each proposal on its merits and act independently of the political parties. My political commitment has deepened and I am convinced that I can make a more substantial contribution within an overall political framework and as part of a team. In July 1976 I became a member of the Labour Party and earlier this month very narrowly failed to win a Dáil seat in the constituency of Dublin Rathmines West. Had the Coalition been returned to office, I feel it would have been inappropriate for me to have continued as a Trinity senator to take the government whip. However, Fianna Fáil are now in government with the largest majority in the history of the State and I believe I have a constructive role to play in continuing, as I have done for the past eight years, to scrutinise legislation carefully, to speak out doggedly on minority issues, to advocate reform where there is need for reform and to point out injustices and discriminations where these exist.

She elaborated in an interview with the author: 'I would have been very aware that there was much more scope when you were in Opposition and I was very much committed to and aware of the fact that, if I wanted to achieve the rounded change I now wanted to achieve, it had to be grounded in a political framework. Law makes specific *ad hoc* changes, whether it's legislation or the courts, but in politics you work with colleagues. It's harder and it's messier but that's the way you do it if you want to achieve. But if I were in government then the room to manoeuvre and the possibility for doing things would have been less, and I would have felt, I think, that I was not being true to what the Senate seat was about. It's fairly pragmatic, but it bore out that there is a huge difference between being a government backbencher in the Senate and being among colleagues in Opposition.'

Behind this rationale was another one, which is necessary to explain her evident willingness to accept the role of a government back-bencher (as she might have become) in the Dáil but her unwillingness to accept the same role in the Senate had Labour been returned to office. This secondary rationale related to the nature of the constituency in each case. If she had been elected to the Dáil, it would have been on the basis of a universal adult franchise: this mandate would have carried corresponding obligations and indeed she had signed the party pledge before the election. The Trinity electorate, on the other hand, was a restricted, elite one which did not carry a mandate at the same level of significance and, moreover, preferred its senators to be as independent as possible. A back-bench Labour senator, had Labour been in government, had more responsibility and less power than would have been palatable.

Perhaps in anticipation of Mary Robinson's election to the Dáil, the number of candidates in the Trinity constituency had grown again and there were now a dozen contesting the three seats. This time Dr Noel Browne was not among them. He had been re-elected to the Dáil, having been expelled from the PLP for standing as an independent candidate against an official Labour candidate in the 1977 general election.

Many of the other candidates were examples of the triumph of hope over experience but the competition at the top was tough. Replacing Browne in the battle for the left-of-centre vote was Conor Cruise O'Brien, who had not only lost ministerial office with the defeat of the coalition but also his Dáil seat. Then as now, for a sitting minister to lose his Dáil seat was highly unusual, but O'Brien's public profile had been consistently controversial and he had become a favourite target for Fianna Fáil politicians in particular. The Trinity constituency was a natural safety net for him and one which he landed in gratefully. One problem remained: he was still, technically, Labour Party spokesman on Northern Ireland, although it was increasingly obvious that his outspokenness on this issue was causing major waves within the party. After a private passage of arms with the party's leader, Frank Cluskey, who insisted that O'Brien submit all statements on Northern Ireland to him before publishing them, he resigned from the PLP on 19 September 1977. He now shared a constituency with Mary Robinson, whom only seven months earlier he had implied was naive: as things turned out, she was to prove the longer survivor.

Mary Robinson's Senate election campaign was not helped by the fact that she had to travel to Strasbourg in the middle of it to fight a case that was particularly important to her. This was the case of Josey Airey, a Dublin woman who was attempting to bring a case in the High Court for a full judicial separation from her husband. Such actions were rare, in spite of the fact that they were virtually the only legal remedy for broken marriages. A more common one, known colloquially as the 'Irish divorce', was for one of the partners in a failed marriage, usually, but not exclusively, the husband, to emigrate to England and establish a domicile there in order to take out British divorce papers. The reason why so few actions for judicial separation were taken out in the Irish courts was basically financial. In the six years to 1978, only 255 people initiated court proceedings for judicial separation and fewer than ten decrees were granted in any one of those years.

Josey Airey, in deciding to take on the legal establishment and the legal system virtually on her own, was flouting conventional wisdom. Initially, she represented herself in court because she could not afford lawyers and there was no State scheme under which she could be provided with free legal aid, as this was a civil rather than a criminal case. After fighting her case unsuccessfully through several levels of the Irish judicial system, she eventually reached the European Court of Human Rights. This court accepted that the Irish government had a case to answer after she charged that it had violated articles 6 and 8 of the 1950 Convention of Human Rights – to which Ireland was a signatory – guaranteeing citizens the right to legal aid in civil cases. It was a fascinating case but Mary Robinson can hardly have welcomed the fact that it came right in the middle of her re-election campaign. The Airey case was to continue its process through the customarily slow judicial system for another two years before the Commission eventually ruled in her favour. In July 1977 not many people would have put money on her chances but for Mary Robinson the case was something not far short of a crusade. With Strasbourg out of the way, at least for the time being, the election campaign was wrapped up. The result – her vote total dropped considerably, although she was never in serious danger of losing her seat – made it clear that she had been re-elected despite her conversion to Labour, rather than because of it. She and Nick celebrated her re-election to the Senate on 17 August by departing for a holiday in Spain: the Airey case apart, it had been a bad year.

She rebounded from the Dáil defeat and the stress of the narrow Senate victory with initiatives both inside and outside parliament. Within the PLP, she effectively served notice that the questions she wanted to raise would not be allowed to vanish from the agenda. In short order, she was to raise the question of penal reform; to circulate a draft bill on Freedom of Information (finally legislated for in 1997, two decades later); produce a statement on nuclear energy; and secure the PLP's agreement for the tabling of a private members' bill on children's rights. Few of these initiatives, as it turned out, came to fruition, and some were buried in sub-committees from which they never re-emerged. They indicated, however, that the pace she set at the beginning was to be maintained.

Outside the Oireachtas, an issue was emerging which increasingly engaged her attention and which provided yet another significant component of the coalition which was to help ensure her victory in 1990. This was the growing protest about Wood Quay, a large, four-acre site sloping down from the eleventh century Christ Church Cathedral to the river Liffey. It had been acquired over the years by Dublin Corporation as a site for its new civic offices, which would re-house officials scattered in unsuitable accommodation over the city. It was also, however, the focus of a growing sense of excitement among archaeologists because it overlapped to a considerable extent the area in which, more than a thousand years earlier, the Vikings had established the city that later became Dublin.

There had been a somewhat desultory archaeological excavation of this and adjoining sites since the early 1960s: Wood Quay itself was first dug in 1974 and, although the Corporation's initial plan was to allow the National Museum to organise a short excavation in 1975 before building commenced, a number of individuals, alerted to the possible richness of the site, began to organise themselves into a protest movement. In April 1975 Mary Robinson and others were raising the matter in the Senate during a debate on the National Museum: there was a growing sense of concern that the museum authorities were not taking the Wood Quay finds sufficiently seriously. Specifically, she called for an overall body which would supervise the Wood Quay excavation and report future digs.

A year later, on 8 April 1976, an organisation called the Friends of Mediaeval Dublin was launched. Although not primarily a 'Save Wood Quay' grouping, it became, under Fr F.X. Martin OSA, almost synonymous with the movement that emerged rapidly and found itself in confrontation with Dublin Corporation, the corporation workers' trade union and the government.

Initial anxiety about what the Corporation was doing gave way to outright alarm and, in November 1977, Fr Martin went to court in the first of many battles to protect the site. Mary Robinson was his junior counsel; the senior was Donal Barrington, who was appointed to the Supreme Court in 1996 after a distinguished legal career in Ireland and as a judge in the European Court of Justice. Her fellow-junior was T.C. Smyth, appointed a High Court judge in 1997.

The issue, however, presented certain problems for the Labour Party. Although Labour councillors, TDs and senators were, by and large, sympathetic to the Wood Quay protest, they were also sensitive to the position of the major trade union involved, the Local Government and Public Services Union, five hundred of whose members actually marched publicly in support of the Corporation's plan in September 1978. Labour issued a policy statement on 2 October 1978 suggesting a compromise under which the offices would be re-designed and re-located on a part of the Wood Quay site which had already been bull-dozed. At a PLP meeting a few days later Ruairí Quinn, also a councillor on the Corporation and an architect, reminded members that Labour now had a policy on Wood Quay and urged colleagues to consult him before making statements on the issue.

This was in all probability a shot across Mary Robinson's bows and to that extent may have been partially successful. On 6-7 December, a two-day debate was held in the Senate on the whole issue at the instigation of National University of Ireland senator, Gus Martin. His motion was to preserve the whole of the Wood Quay site but it would have had no executive effect if passed. The Labour Party position, which Mary Robinson now advanced, was that a smaller set of civic offices could be built on that part of the site which had already been excavated down to bedrock and where no archaeological remains existed any longer. The remainder of the site should be properly excavated and used as the basis for a purpose-built museum. This proposal, defensible enough in itself, was seen by some of the more radical Wood Quay activists as a betrayal. In the event, Gus Martin's motion was defeated by the narrowest of margins, 21 votes to 20. Quite unexpectedly, two government-appointed senators, T.K. Whitaker and Gordon Lambert, voted against the government. To even more general surprise another NUI senator, the historian John A. Murphy, voted with the government. Unaccountably, Mary Robinson was absent when the vote was taken. Had she been present and voted against, the vote would still have been lost, on the casting vote of the chairman.

On 11 December the Labour compromise was put to the Corporation and defeated by one vote, 19-20. Again, it is not clear that its passage would have had any executive effect but it would at the very least have given added momentum to the campaign for the Quay.

Significantly, the height of the campaign coincided with the 1979 local government and European elections. Michael O'Leary, deputy leader of the Labour Party and a candidate for the European Parliament, was among those who successfully seized on the Wood Quay issue to heighten his profile. More modestly, Mary Robinson set her sights on Dublin Corporation, as did a number of other Wood Quay supporters. The Corporation, after all, was in charge of the site and the prospect of carrying the battle right into the enemy camp was irresistible. On 30 March Mary Robinson was officially selected as a candidate for the No. 9 area in the election to Dublin Corporation; at the election in June, she won a seat easily, along with a number of other pro-Wood Quay activists in other political parties. The surprise of the election was the defeat of Dublin's Lord Mayor, Councillor Paddy Belton, who had defended the Corporation's Wood Quay strategy, by a twenty-six year old pro-Wood Quay schoolteacher from Glasnevin, Mary Flaherty, who had never held public office before. She is still, at the time of writing, in national politics as a Fine Gael TD.

The pro-Wood Quay group, including Mary Robinson, now had an effective majority of twenty-four members of the forty-five seat Corporation. That they were unable to stave off the ultimate destruction of the site in 1984 was due, essentially, to the fact that members of the Corporation have little executive power: most of it has been legally confined to officials. And the officials were more conscious than the councillors of the immense legal bills and bills for damage that would materialise if the building contractors, who had a binding contract with the Corporation, were to sue. The long battle, however, had cemented a number of key friendships and alliances.

Mary Robinson became closely identified in the public mind throughout this period with the Wood Quay protest. Later, when the site was occupied by protesters, she was a frequent visitor; her husband, Nick, acted as solicitor for Fr Martin and for some of the occupiers. The legal battles she and the other members of the team planned succeeded initially in having the site declared a national monument by Mr Justice Liam Hamilton (now the Chief Justice). The result was to stave off the bull-dozers, sometimes at the eleventh hour, for the best part of seven years, by which time priceless archaeological information had been acquired, along with a huge range of artefacts. The Robinsons' legal expertise and friendship, the Friends of Mediaeval Dublin declared later, had been 'a continual source of comfort and strength'.[13] The final compromise in 1984 satisfied nobody and was in effect a defeat for the protesters; but the experience of protest welded those involved in it into a community of interest which was to re-emerge later as a powerful influence on her election campaign for the presidency. Almost unnoticed among them at the time was Bride Rosney, a Kerry-born post-primary teacher and an activist in the Teachers' Union of Ireland, whose already evident skills as a strategist gave her a role as one of the *ad hoc* executive committee formed by the occupiers. In 1981, by which time she was a close personal friend, she was godmother to Mary's youngest child, Aubrey, and was later to play a major role in her campaign in the Dublin West constituency.

Like many others, she found Mary Robinson cold and distant at first until the reserve gave way to an intimate friendship which has been the good fortune of a small and heterogeneous group of people around her. The same traits were noted by an American academic, Thomas Farel Heffernan, whose book about the Wood Quay controversy is a model of its kind. 'She holds a law degree from Trinity and has another law degree from Harvard. She has great presence before audiences. Her public voice, in fact, is often so grave and magisterial that it seems to be coming from someone other than the pretty young woman in the front of the room. Her private conversation is warm and enjoyably seasoned with irony.'[14]

Her public profile was to prove useful in highlighting other concerns. One of the features that distinguished Mary Robinson from many middle-class women who became active in what was loosely known as the 'women's liberation movement' in that period was her commitment to workplace equality. It was not that other women did not fight the same corner; but few of them had her public profile, and consequently they had to carry on the fight across tables with employers, at meetings of trade unionists (where they as often as not had to fight their case against their male trade unionist colleagues), and out of the public gaze.

Mary Robinson was a member of first one, and then two trade unions. As a Trinity lecturer, she was a member of the Irish Federation of University Teachers (IFUT). After she joined the Labour Party in 1976, she added to her credentials by joining the Irish Transport and General Workers' Union (ITGWU). She was, it must be said, following a trail staked out by others, including David Thornley and John Horgan: at the time, it was almost *de rigeur* for an aspirant Labour TD to join one of the big general unions (if they did not already belong to one). It was partly a question of proving one's *bona fides*. It was certainly not for financial gain: the contribution by a union like the ITGWU to a member's Dáil election campaign fund in the 1970s would typically have been of the order of £300.

Her commitment to women in the world of work and to the trade union movement has been – and continues to be – central to her beliefs. 'I really felt that it was a deepening of my own commitment, that it needed to be rooted in a desire for a broader political change which took on board economic and social rights – particularly trade union rights. At an early stage, becoming a member of what was at that stage the ITGWU – as well as being a member of IFUT – was a commitment to a kind of sense of belonging there that actually I've never lost. I will never change those spots.'

As well as marking a high point in the Wood Quay saga, 1979 marked an extraordinary burst of activity outside parliament by Mary Robinson that reflected her commitment to equality. From the mid-1970s to the mid-1980s, in particular, her political agenda had included an emphasis on women and work that was not often noted by mainstream, and male-dominated, media more conscious of the marketability of sexual politics. She was under no illusions that 'it was not the guarantee of equality under our Constitution, but rather the obligations on Ireland of membership of the EEC, which led to the enactment of equality legislation in the mid-1970s'.[15] In 1977 she told the Council for the

Status of Women, in what proved to be something of an understatement, that the statutory commitment to equality of pay and opportunity posed 'the greatest single challenge of the 1970s', and the following year was remarking wryly that 'there will never be a time when it will be "convenient" to bring about equality of treatment and social justice'.

Not entirely coincidentally, she was fighting at this time a landmark case through the Labour Court to establish pension rights for her husband: under the antediluvian pension scheme for politicians, the widows of politicians were entitled to pensions under certain circumstances, but widowers were not. The case was finally resolved in her (or, more properly, Nick's) favour on 12 May 1979. In 1980 she was pointing out to a European Youth Forum in Brussels that only forty-seven of 19,000 trade apprentices in Ireland were girls, and arguing that the special factors which contributed to female unemployment and low wages should be tackled as a matter of priority. By April 1981 she was matching practice to precedent in a particularly dramatic way, by having herself expelled from the Senate after provoking a major row about the transfer of a women Senate usher to other duties. She thus became the first university senator to be expelled for disorderly behaviour, a development foreseen by at least one hostile journalist, who had described her not long before in *Hibernia* as being 'as hard-headed and as hard-necked a politician as any Fianna Fáil grass-roots operator'.

At the beginning of July 1979, she appeared in court for the Murphys, a married couple who alleged that the tax system was discriminatory because the tax allowances given to a couple were less than double the tax allowances given to single taxpayers. The court decision, when it was given in October, went against the government which promptly appealed to the Supreme Court, where it lost again on 24 April 1980. Within a week of the initial Murphy decision, the Josey Airey case was decided in Strasbourg, also in the plaintiff's favour: damages would be awarded on 5 February 1981.

For any lawyer to be on the winning side in two such actions within such a short space of time would have been exceptional. And one of her losing cases in Europe was also interesting, although for an entirely different reason and one which highlighted the extraordinarily small world in which Irish lawyers and politicians moved. This was the so-called Lee case.

The plaintiff, a Sligo farmer, had taken an action against the Minister for Agriculture, first of all in the Circuit Court, claiming that he had been unfairly deprived of an EEC grant because the work he had carried out fell outside the scope of the particular EEC directive under which certain types of grant were administered. He at first carried on the litigation himself, urged on by a local county councillor who convinced him that he was right to do so. He eventually found a solicitor, Adrian Bourke, Mary Robinson's brother, who employed Mary as the barrister in the case and pursued it all the way up to the European Court of Justice. Lee lost his case there but his journey was not entirely fruitless as this was apparently the first case in which the Court granted legal aid to a plaintiff. Nor was this the only noteworthy feature of the proceedings: in the lengthy interval between the institution of the case and the decision of the Court of Justice, the pertinacious county councillor had gone on to higher things – so high, in fact, that he had become Minister for Agriculture and was now defending the decision which as a local public representative he had attacked like a terrier. His name was Ray McSharry. And counsel for the State in the Strasbourg hearing was none other than Harry Whelehan, future Attorney-General, who was shortly to take silk on the same day as Mary Robinson herself.

Mary Robinson's legal workload was combined with a high level of Senate activity. On 9 July 1979 the Fianna Fáil Minister for Health, Charles Haughey (to become Taoiseach on 6 December) finally secured the passage of a Family Planning Act, which he described unhappily as 'an Irish solution to an Irish problem'. Extraordinarily restrictive, it required married couples who needed barrier family planning methods to get a prescription from their doctor before being allowed to purchase them at pharmacies. The fact that Mary Robinson had already secured the Labour Party's support for her own bill gave that party a legitimate excuse for voting against all aspects of Haughey's bill; otherwise they might have had difficulty in explaining their opposition to its few commonsensical proposals.

The easiest thing for an opposition politician to do is to seek targets on the government benches and in 1979 there was no shortage of them in that quarter. Mary Robinson, however, was continually serving notice that a certain independence of spirit had not been quenched by her institutional affiliation. The Labour Party itself, she commented pointedly, had 'put people off socialism'.[16] The more conservative members of that party, who might not have been unduly dismayed at this critique, would have been far more exercised about two more salvoes from her in the autumn. One of them, on the eve of the visit to Ireland by Pope John Paul II in September, warned tersely of the 'grave risk of Catholic triumphalism' in relation to Northern Ireland. To stand aside from the crowd on this occasion required more than a touch of moral courage. The country virtually came to a halt during certain sections of the papal progress around the country and, by warning of the dangers of over-reaction to the visit, Mary Robinson risked having herself bracketed with the very small number of people who objected somewhat shrilly to the very fact of the visit itself. Undeterred, she returned to the same territory within a week when she pointedly criticised what she saw as 'discriminatory' provisions in a draft deed of trust being prepared by the Department of Education for community schools.

This document, which was to be the foundation for a major re-organisation of second-level education, explicitly conferred rights on the Catholic school authorities which she and a number of others felt were wrong and possibly even unconstitutional.

By the end of this period, it was evident that her relationship with the Labour Party was never going to be entirely comfortable and might even become mutually disadvantageous. There had been no honeymoon. She had a greater freedom to criticise her own party when it was in opposition and she exercised that freedom heedless of the scowls from those for whom party loyalty outweighed all other considerations. This is not to say that she cherry-picked issues or chose Labour merely as a flag of convenience. She was an active member of four Labour committees: the economic policy committee, the environment committee, the European Affairs Committee and the Labour Lawyers Group. Any two of these, given the Labour Party's propensity for lengthy committee meetings and reams of documentation, would have amounted to a recipe for serious overwork. Four of them smacked of political masochism. But she took it all on cheerfully, fought and lost her battles and hoped for better times ahead.

CHAPTER 5

Divorce and Abortion:
The Litmus Tests

WITH FAMILY PLANNING out of the way, at least for the time being, the next political issue involving conservative opinion in general, and the Catholic Church in particular, rapidly emerged: this was the question of divorce. Article 41.3.2 of the Constitution stated bluntly: 'No law shall be enacted providing for the grant of a dissolution of marriage'. In fact, divorce had been possible in the Irish Free State for a brief period after 1922, but couples who wanted to get one had to secure the passage of a private bill through the Dáil and Senate. When applications were made for a number of these politically and socially embarrassing pieces of legislation, the Free State government promptly legislated the loophole out of existence. Eamon de Valera's 1937 Constitution was designed to ensure that it could never be re-opened.

The Airey case provided the pro-divorce movement, as yet unstructured, with the critical momentum it needed. The foundation of the Divorce Action Group (DAG) on 14 April 1980 marked the beginning of a major campaign on this issue which was to experience bitter defeat in a referendum in the summer of 1986 and eventual victory in quite a different referendum a decade later. At the outset, however, the DAG was confident of victory. Opinion polls increasingly showed a small majority in favour of a change in the Constitution or at the worst indicated an evenly divided electorate. Mary Robinson, although not formally associated with the work of the DAG, was an enthusiastic supporter from the beginning. In fact, within days of its launch, she was presenting to the PLP a draft bill to amend section 41.3.2. of the Constitution.

Under the Constitution itself, all proposals for amendment have to first take the form of a bill which has to pass through Dáil and Senate before being submitted to the people in a referendum. The form of amendment would be to delete the sub-section of the Constitution. As Mary Robinson and others realised, however, the Irish electorate might be slow to accept this proposal if it meant giving politicians in general and the government in particular the right to decide the principles which should govern whatever form of divorce law might eventually be introduced. Radical voters, depressed by the limited scope of the Family Planning Act, would be concerned about the restrictions that would be introduced. Conservatives, appalled that any form of divorce should have been legalised, would have been even more apprehensive about what weak-kneed politicians might now do to further rend the fabric of Irish society.

The Robinson draft, therefore, attempted to steer a course between these two polarities. The amendment was phrased in such a way as to support the institution of marriage itself, while catering for the circumstances of marital breakdown. It would also place a priority on seeking reconciliation wherever possible, and ensuring the physical and economic protection of vulnerable family members. On the other hand – and this, seen in retrospect, was the most explosive element of the package – it placed a positive duty on the State to afford a means for the dissolution of marriages. Mary Robinson did not want to see the passage of an amendment which would leave the position neutral or unclear and, she reasoned, a government which had been put under a legal obligation to act in a certain way by the Constitution itself would be better protected against opposition and threats from vocal minorities. As events would show, she seriously under-estimated the potential downside of this mandatory provision.

For the time being, the discussion was carried on in private. The problem about divorce was that, although it was supported by a majority within the Labour Party and by minorities of varying sizes within the other parties, and despite the fact that the final decision would fall to be made by the electorate and not by any party or government, nobody wanted to be first into the breach – not even the Labour Party. Even an apparently innocuous step, such as typing out the text of Mary Robinson's draft bill and sending it to the media as a press release, would have almost certainly caused an immediate rift in the PLP.

Frank Cluskey was hyper-conscious of the need for party unity as he had been elected on a narrowly split vote (initially 8-8 and then, in a second ballot, 9-7) and frequently had to engage in some rapid footwork to keep both ends of the party in touch with the middle. His own views were also relevant. He came from a solid Dublin working-class background and, although he could be as irreverent and cynical about ecclesiastical power-plays as any Irish socialist, he was slow to take dramatic initiatives in such sensitive territory. His wife, to whom he was devoted, had died tragically in September 1978 and he was still in a state of emotional shock. On a personal level, however, he had a high respect for Mary Robinson and, although he disagreed from time to time with her tactics (or felt that she failed to appreciate the political constraints which affected his own decisions) the relationship between them was warm and respectful.

The rank and file of Labour, as Mary Robinson knew well, would have been much more substantially in favour of the measure than their parliamentary representatives. Among her allies were the Labour Women's National Council, to whom she circulated the draft bill. When the PLP met in May to discuss the issue again, she was told sharply that this was a breach of the understanding about confidentiality, and the party set about sorting out the details of its approach. Cluskey noted that while he had had doubts about divorce in the past, he was now in favour of the issue but warned against a confrontational approach. What was on the table was an approach from the Taoiseach, Charles Haughey, which in effect opened the possibility that there might be all-party agreement on referring the matter to the Law Reform Commission (LRC). This would provide political insurance for everyone if it could be arranged. The LRC, headed by a senior judge, advises the government on contentious area of legal change, although its recommendations do not have to be accepted.

Cluskey proposed writing to Haughey to take him up on his offer of an all-party approach and Mary Robinson found herself outflanked. Virtually everyone agreed with Cluskey's proposal except for Michael Pat Murphy, a Labour TD from Cork South West, who argued trenchantly that the party should not support any law opposed by the Catholic Church. Mary Robinson tried to harden the proposal by suggesting that a copy of the text of her bill go with the letter to Haughey but this was not agreed, although there was no formal vote on the matter.

It became increasingly obvious, however, that while the Law Reform Commission was being asked to deal with problems arising from marital breakdown, the question of divorce was conspicuously absent from its agenda. The situation was complicated by the fact that Noel Browne, now an independent TD, had tabled a draft bill of his own and could move it in the Dáil at any time, putting Labour in an embarrassing position, because not all of its members would vote for it on a free vote and some might even vote against it, free vote or not.

It took almost a month for Haughey to clarify the matter, and when Cluskey came back to the PLP to report that, as he suspected, divorce was not going to be discussed by the Commission, the party was finally forced to a decision. Mary Robinson insisted that for the party to support her bill would be the best possible option: it had already supported her on a draft bill on illegitimacy and the precedent had been well established. Cluskey, on the other hand, had worked out another strategy, which would have the benefit of maintaining party unity while not involving any betrayal of principle: the party would put down a motion in the Dáil, urging the creation of an all-party committee to examine this most controversial of questions. If the other parties refused, they would have to accept the burden of responsibility for refusal to change and the party could decide not to support Browne's bill on the grounds that the all-party approach was one with a better chance of success. This proposal was supported by the author, who now found himself on the other side of the fence from Robinson for the first time in more than a decade because, while prepared to accede to this tactic, she felt that now there was nothing to be lost in simultaneously publishing the text of her bill and pushed it to a vote. The only two people to support her in a poorly attended meeting were Justin Keating, who seconded her amendment, and Ruairí Quinn: she lost 10-3.

The summer intervened and the air leaked slowly out of the balloon. In November, Mary Robinson returned to the fray, suggesting that the party was dragging its feet on the issue. It was incontrovertible but the delay was in some sense explicable if not excusable. The political system was again going on election alert and the contest, when it came in June 1981, was to inaugurate a period of profound political instability and change.

Mary Robinson had now moved constituencies and had been adopted as one of the three Labour candidates in the sprawling Dublin West constituency, an area of middle-class housing, socially deprived working-class estates, open fields and the remnants of a few small rural villages. Insofar as it was becoming an overspill area for central Dublin, however, and populated to some extent by young married couples in starter homes, it appeared to offer Mary Robinson a measurably better chance than had Rathmines. There was also a welcome for her from local party activists which was an encouraging change. The candidate situation, however, was initially complex. Three candidates had been chosen: Michael Gannon, a trade union official, John O'Connell Jr, a son of the Labour TD in the neighbouring constituency, Dr John O'Connell, and Mary Robinson. Then Gannon withdrew for personal reasons, followed closely by O'Connell who bowed out for political reasons (his father had severed his connections with the party and was standing as an independent). This left only Mary Robinson. The candidate list was again brought up to three with the addition of Ann McStay, a woman from the settled working-class estate of Ballyfermot at the eastern end of the constituency, and Eamonn Tuffy, a teacher, at the western end. Tuffy, coincidentally, was of an age with, and had grown up in Ballina at the same time as, Mary Robinson but they had not shared the same social level: Tuffy's father had once rented land from Mary's grandfather.

The campaign was a good-natured one although there were times when the other two candidates felt slightly irked by the media spotlight which was still focused firmly on their Senate colleague. 'Here's to you, Mrs Robinson', now at last made its debut as a campaign song (it was to feature strongly in the presidential campaign as well) despite the presence of two other candidates on the ticket who were not similarly orchestrated. Mary was breast-feeding her baby son Aubrey throughout the campaign – the name sounded strange to at least some of her potential constituents who helpfully baptised the infant 'Strawberry'. And the BBC even came and did a documentary about her, featuring one splendid shot of Mary Robinson walking down a street canvassing votes, with her two fellow-candidates, Tuffy and McStay, bringing up the rear, each holding one of the straps of the carrycot within which young Aubrey was peacefully asleep.

It was, nonetheless, a difficult election for a number of reasons. The constituency was heavily marked by social dislocation, exclusion and poverty in contrast to the more closely-knit, traditional working-class society of Rathmines. Mary Robinson – who still lacked the touch she found during the presidential campaign nine years later – appeared ill at ease in the face of the welter of often irremediable constituency problems which faced her on her walkabouts. The constituency also had one of Dublin's most thorny social problems: encampments of travelling people, who were regarded with scant respect and often downright hatred by the settled community. Mary Robinson's instinctive sympathy with them as underdogs was to flower later in the mid-eighties when she appeared in a number of landmark cases against local authorities, forcing them to provide alternative camping sites for travellers facing eviction from roadside sites. But in 1981 such an issue had only negative implications for aspiring politicians unless they were prepared to engage in covert anti-traveller propaganda.

The utterly unpredictable factor in the political equation in Dublin West in 1981, however, was the hunger strike, then in progress by IRA prisoners in Belfast's Maze Prison. Ten hunger strikers were to die during a long and highly-charged campaign: it coincided with the general election in the Republic, where four hunger-strikers were actually successful candidates (although they were never able to take their seats). Another hunger-striker, Tony O'Hara, was a candidate in Dublin West, where he drew a substantial number of votes away from the established parties – especially the votes of disaffected younger voters. Mary Robinson came ninth out of fifteen candidates on the first count in this five-seater constituency, two places and seven hundred votes behind O'Hara. She was eventually to overhaul O'Hara and finish in seventh place but she was never close to winning a seat. The writing was on the wall for her Dáil aspirations and indeed she contemplated, in the immediate aftermath of defeat, not even running again for the Senate. She eventually changed her mind but made her position clear in her Senate election address to the Trinity voters: 'If a genuine issue of principle were to arise on which I had to choose between obeying the party whip and following my own conscience I would not hesitate to follow my own conscience and pay the price of so doing.'

In the same address could be discerned the lineaments of the political position on Northern Ireland which was to lead her ineluctably out of the Labour Party five years later. 'Time is not on our side in seeking a political framework within which to make progress', she said. 'I do not believe that framework should be founded on secret negotiations between the Dublin and London governments which exclude knowledge and participation by the representatives of the communities in Northern Ireland. It is essential ... to involve Northern representatives directly in any such discussions, because a political vacuum at present would lend encouragement to the advocates of violence in pursuit of their goals.'

She was in second place on the first count in the TCD constituency, indicating that her electorate were feeling more sympathetic to her than they had been after her conversion to Labour and her Dáil defeat in 1977. It was just as well. In the following seventeen months there were three general elections: Mary Robinson's election total for the period, of course, was four, as the 1981 general election defeat was followed by two more in 1982 as well as her successful bid to retain her Senate seat. In the meantime, as minority governments scrabbled to stay in power, hopes of progress on the divorce and other contentious questions faded rapidly, and a new and even more highly-charged issue was forced onto the public agenda: abortion.

Paradoxically, Mary Robinson and those who shared her views within the PLP had more success on the abortion issue than on the divorce issue, in that the party divisions were forced out into the open and the majority of the party opted publicly to oppose the conservative position. It was also a case, however, of winning battles but losing the war. Whereas the pro-divorce campaign was ultimately successful, although it took a decade longer than most campaigners, including Mary Robinson herself, expected, the outcome of the two referenda on the abortion question went resoundingly the other way.

Abortion was first raised in the run-up to the June 1981 election campaign by some fourteen pressure groups gathered under the general title of the Pro-Life (i.e. anti-abortion) Amendment Campaign, founded in January of the same year.[17] The campaign, although it was influenced by abortion controversies in Britain and the United States, in fact travelled in a diametrically opposite direction to the trends in those countries. In Britain and America, the pressure groups concerned succeeded in widening already existing abortion legislation; in Ireland, the campaign, influenced by fears that the Irish Constitution would be used to prise open the door to legal abortion, was aimed at the insertion of what was thought to be a cast-iron anti-abortion amendment in the fabric of the Constitution itself. This additional safeguard was thought necessary because the principal law against abortion – the unambiguous 1861 Offences Against the Person Act – could, even if only in theory, be changed by the legislature at any time.

A PLAC delegation met both the Taoiseach, Charles Haughey, and the leader of the opposition, Garret FitzGerald, at the end of April 1981 to seek a pre-election commitment that if they assumed office they would introduce an amendment 'to guarantee the right to life of the unborn child'. They met Frank Cluskey some two weeks later to seek a similar commitment. The first such pledge was given rapidly by FitzGerald and subsequently formed part of his party's election manifesto. Haughey, although agreeing in principle to the request, was slower to signal positive acceptance of it. Once FitzGerald had committed Fine Gael, however, Haughey's options were closed off and he gave a similar assurance within two weeks. Although Labour stated firmly its opposition to abortion, it reserved its position on the question of amendment and was alone among the major parties in not including its commitment to an amendment in its election manifesto.

FitzGerald assumed office as the leader of a minority government after the June 1981 election. Labour was on-side but only just and Mary Robinson herself argued unavailingly that there was 'no place for a coalition deal with Fine Gael in the process of recovery and strengthening of the Labour Party'. She was now a back-bench Labour senator while her party was sharing in government – precisely the position she had told her electors in 1977 that she was unwilling to assume. This necessary adjustment was also and evidently painful: increasingly, if she were to be true to her own views, she would have to be publicly critical of the government of which her own party was a member.

The Labour Party had a new leader: Cluskey had lost his seat in the election, and had been succeeded by Michael O'Leary, a witty and politically agile trade unionist from Cork who had been defeated by Cluskey for the leadership in 1977. Garret FitzGerald's determination to re-assume power led him to offer O'Leary a coalition agreement which, in the circumstances, was more generous than Labour might have expected and it was accepted by the party at a special conference in Dublin. The problem was that the package was to prove undeliverable.

FitzGerald's government was bedevilled by controversy and misjudgement. One of his decisions was to raise the minimum age for entry to primary school from four years to four and a half – a move which was designed to reduce the need for employing additional teachers and which induced near-apoplexy in the Irish National Teachers' Organisation (and in many harassed parents, especially mothers). Mary Robinson threatened publicly to vote against the measure but as it did not involve new legislation the opportunity did not arise. She had in any case already publicly announced in

September 1981 her decision not to run again for the Dáil. It was, effectively, the first stage in a withdrawal from representative politics although it did not appear as such at the time. In January 1982 she resigned from her position on the Corporation, a move which was greeted by the once-supportive *Irish Times* with the observation that 'in the past eighteen months she was rarely seen'.

She recalled her feelings at this particular set of experiences in an interview with the author: 'I was very frustrated. During that period I would have compared Dublin City Council with the Senate and thought: "I'm damned if I'm going to be a government back-bencher, doing nothing in the one arena in which I feel I have some hope. I can do nothing in this other arena." I was constantly angry, and angry that people weren't angry, at how little city councillors could do. The experience has served me in this [presidency], because I have respected greatly all elected representatives and worried at the lack of a proper balance. It should be bottom up and it's not. It's a very inappropriate system, to say the least.'

FitzGerald's government fell on 27 January 1982 on an absurd budgetary provision which would have extended Value Added Tax to children's shoes (on the grounds, an earnest FitzGerald informed the Dáil, that some adult women had feet so small that they could buy and wear them tax-free). The demise of his government was welcomed by the more conservative forces in Irish society for, in addition to his budgetary flat-footedness, he had not actually done anything to introduce the promised constitutional amendment on abortion. Worse again, he had actually gone on record, in a radio interview, to state his intention of embarking on a 'constitutional crusade', evidently with the intention of liberalising that by now forty-four year old document.

Charles Haughey was returned as the head of another minority government and repeated his commitment to a constitutional amendment on abortion along the lines urged by the conservative lobby groups. Now, for the first time, opposition began to emerge. The Labour Party chairman, Michael D. Higgins, was one of a small band of politicians who made their views known early on. Another was Mary Robinson, who described it bluntly as a 'rubbishy academic exercise'.[18] She was among a number of prominent campaigners – including journalist Mary Holland, Catherine McGuinness (another lawyer and fellow-senator of Mary Robinson's in the Trinity constituency) and Anne O'Donnell of the Rape Crisis Centre – who met in a Dublin hotel in April 1982 to formalise a national campaign. The Anti-Amendment Campaign, as it became known, had fourteen different groups affiliated to it by June 1982; fifteen months later that number had grown to sixty.

The AAC was, inevitably, a very broad coalition, including individuals and organisations who were strongly opposed to abortion but who felt that the proposed amendment was divisive and unnecessary, as well as individuals and organisations who were prepared to argue for the introduction of legal abortion in certain limited circumstances. From time to time the tensions within the organisation showed, and were always there to be exploited by the PLAC, but by and large the coalition held. The Robinson perspective, according to the most detailed study of these events, was to play a crucially important part. 'She adopted what might be referred to as a causalist approach to the problem of abortion in Ireland. Such an approach identified the factors alleged to cause abortion, attacked the amendment as an inadequate response to the problem and specified other measures considered more effective. The reform of the illegitimacy laws, provision for sex education within Ireland's schools, and more widely available contraception services ... were commonly cited.'[19]

Within the Labour Party itself, the temperature was rising rapidly as segments of the organisation, notably the Labour Women's National Council, increased the pressure on the PLP. That group discussed the question in June, but without coming to any firm conclusions. The pressure on Michael O'Leary increased, forcing him to issue a somewhat nuancé statement at the end of July. It was necessary to read the text of what he said closely to see that he was not opposing the idea of an amendment as such, but the prospect of an amendment which would 'have the consequences of re-introducing clauses of a denominational character'.[20] The party was in fact deeply divided on the issue. Seven of the fifteen TDs elected in February 1982 had signed the 'pro-life' pledge sent to all candidates before the election. Even though three of them – including Dick Spring – later changed their minds, this left a hard core of four who were prepared to support a constitutional amendment. On the other side of the argument, Conor Cruise O'Brien's constituency council submitted a motion to the party's annual conference calling for 'free and safe abortion in Ireland'.

The arguments were focused nationally by the publication of the government's wording on 2 November 1982. Mary Robinson was one of the first to attack its alleged ambiguity which, she said prophetically to the PLP, would throw the whole matter back into the lap of the courts, and might even call into question the constitutionality of the 1861 Act. By then Labour had again changed its leader: Michael O'Leary had abandoned ship after the party's annual conference had rejected his proposals on electoral strategy and he had been succeeded by Dick Spring. Spring, for all that he had originally signed the pro-amendment pledge before the 1981 election, now proceeded with considerable courage to lead the party in the opposite direction. It was accepted, however, that the tensions within the party were at some level irreducible: the compromise was to allow members a free vote on whatever was put to the Dáil.

The whole business was now thrown back into the melting-pot when

Charles Haughey's government lost power and was succeeded, at yet another election on 25 November 1982, by a new coalition led by Garret FitzGerald, with Dick Spring as Tánaiste. What followed was a bizarre sequence of events. FitzGerald's government produced a wording for the amendment which attempted to deal fairly with the complex legal issues involved, but was not specific enough for the anti-abortion campaigners. Fianna Fáil, seeing the government was seriously embarrassed, opposed the FitzGerald wording and proposed its own which was supported by the bishops. This was too much for some conservative Fine Gael and Labour back-benchers who sided with the Opposition, ensuring the defeat of the government's wording and its replacement by the Fianna Fáil formula. That formula was to prove deeply defective and would reinforce, even within Fianna Fáil, a feeling that the Constitution was not the most appropriate place for matters as complex as this.

Mary Robinson thought that certain judicial data in Ireland precluded the possibility that the Irish Supreme Court would react in the same way as the US Supreme Court had done. However, she had also warned – again prophetically – at a Labour Party meeting in January 1983 that if the proposed amendment were passed an injunction could be issued to prevent a woman going abroad for an abortion. It could in fact, she added, even open the way to abortion. Later the same month, she made it clear that her immediate priority on being re-elected to the Senate would be to make an urgent plea to the government and in particular to the Taoiseach, Garret FitzGerald, not to proceed with the amendment bill in the Dáil.

'It has', she said on that occasion, 'become a litmus test for the kind of society we are going to have in Ireland during the eighties. If the referendum goes ahead it will confirm the worst fears about those who are concerned about the influence of the majority Church on legal and social developments in the state. If it is dropped, it will signal that we have taken a significant step in the direction of a pluralist and tolerant society.'

By March 1983, the matter was moving towards a conclusion and Mary Robinson was among those who launched a specifically Labour Committee Against the Amendment, whose other members included Barry Desmond and Ruairí Quinn. Paradoxically, the success of this mini-campaign was to reinforce the views of some Labour deputies that they should vote against any and all amendments, and ensure that the Haughey text rather than the FitzGerald one eventually passed through the legislature. On 4 May, Mary Robinson had her last word in this particular debate when she spoke to the Senate for two and a half hours, reading documents into the record from opponents of the amendment, including some prominent Protestant churchmen, 'so that it can't be said that we did it in ignorance but in the teeth of their opposition'. It was, the *Irish Times* concluded, 'a remarkable performance'.

She was to appear once more on stage in a last-ditch attempt to torpedo the amendment legally, arguing unsuccessfully in the High Court on behalf of a married couple: the wife, who was pregnant, claimed that her pregnancy was prone to complications and there was a fear for her life in the event of the amendment being enacted. The referendum, when it was finally held on 7 September 1983, was passed by 67% to 33% on a low turn-out of 54.6%.

In the circumstances, it might have appeared foolhardy of the government to offer itself up for another drubbing by going back to the electorate with a proposal to change the Constitution to allow for divorce. But the two parties were committed to it by their joint programme and there was a strong hope among the defeated forces in the Anti-Amendment Campaign and its subsidiaries that this much at least could be salvaged from the wreckage. This campaign and the rapidly heightened profile of the Northern Ireland issue on the agenda of both Irish and British politicians were to be the major elements of Mary Robinson's own political involvement for the next few years.

The divorce debate had in fact been re-started when Garret FitzGerald's government took office in 1981. Fine Gael's agreement with the Labour Party on that issue at the time, embodied in a document which was approved by a special Labour Party conference in the Gaiety Theatre, was for an Oireachtas Joint Committee to examine marriage laws in a broad context, including the prohibition on divorce.

This was an obvious attempt to tie all parties into a joint approach and thus take out political insurance against the possibility that one party (in effect, Fianna Fáil) would take the moral high ground and appeal to a conservative electorate as the only party prepared to vote against the measure. Initially Fianna Fáil reacted exactly as Labour had feared, by refusing to participate and setting up their own internal committee to look at the matter.

Mary Robinson was furious. Even the Gaiety agreement, she argued, represented a compromise on the party's original, unvarnished commitment to introduce divorce legislation. Marriage law was in crisis, laws and remedies were totally antiquated, 'ordinary people are oppressed, suffering and discriminated against in their human relationships and yet we witness a classic example of the political football'.

'Above all', she added, 'the Labour Party must oppose any attempt to hive off this issue to the all-male and apolitical advisory committee set up to advise the Attorney-General. This is a fundamental issue of social policy which must be kept firmly in the political arena, and on which the Labour Party must secure progress. In mid-1977 nullity was deferred to the Law Reform Commission, and four years later we await action! Let us not repeat that mistake ...' Seething with frustration, she published the text of her own draft bill, which was embodied in two crisp paragraphs:

> The State pledges itself to guard with special care the institution of marriage and to protect it against attack. The State shall take measures to ensure adequate preparation for marriage and to promote the stability of marriage.

> It shall be the duty of the State, in making provision in cases of marital breakdown, to seek reconciliation between the parties to the marriage, to provide for the physical and economic protection of vulnerable family members and to afford a means for the dissolution of marriages which have broken down irretrievably.

Agreement was not finally reached between the parties on the establishment of a joint committee until two elections later, in June 1983, but Mary Robinson and one or two other Labour TDs were still suspicious. In September she pointed out that the committee's terms of reference did not mention divorce but merely 'the problems which follow the breakdown of marriage'.

As a member of the committee herself she was to play a major part in its deliberations but her tactics on legal matters did not always meet with the approval of some of her PLP colleagues. On an unrelated controversy, the PLP at one stage secured the attendance at one of its meetings in November 1983 of the Fine Gael Minister for Justice, Michael Noonan, to explain the detailed implications of the proposed Criminal Justice Bill. It was unusual, but not unprecedented, for a Fine Gael minister to attend a PLP meeting. Mary Robinson was well prepared: toting a number of law books into the meeting to buttress her case, she proffered three full pages of amendments to the bill and argued in particular that one controversial section was totally unacceptable. Some of her PLP colleagues were unimpressed; others, silently outraged at what they perceived to be a waste of valuable ministerial time, almost levitated with suppressed indignation.

A measure of the problems involved in reaching consensus on divorce was that the deliberations took more than two years to complete. By February 1985 it was clear that a majority of those on the joint committee favoured the removal of the constitutional prohibition on divorce, and by early November arrangements for the projected legislation which would have to be passed to facilitate the referendum were at an advanced stage. In the PLP, all was sweetness and light and there were general congratulations to Mary Robinson in early November 1985 for the work she had put into what was described as a magnificent bill. It was a far cry from the footdragging and nervous tactics of five years earlier, but the battle was far from over.

Coming up to the referendum on 25 June 1986, Mary Robinson spoke with increasing frequency at Divorce Action Group and other meetings, often on successive nights. Like many others, she was working herself to the bone in order to ensure passage of the amendment. Almost up to the end, the pro-divorce position held a narrow lead in the opinion polls but, some ten days before the vote, the lead started to slip dangerously and then evaporated in the face of a highly sophisticated and successful campaign aimed at convincing women in particular that the passage of the amendment would leave them dangerously insecure financially. The referendum proposal was defeated by 63% to 36%: on a less threatening issue than abortion, the liberal component of the electorate had added only 3% to its total. It was to be another decade before any government would have the courage to tackle the issue again.

CHAPTER 6

The Labour Party: Political Dog Days

BY THE TIME THE DIVORCE REFERENDUM was held, however, Mary Robinson was no longer a member of the Labour Party. The parting of the ways came in 1985 on the issue of Northern Ireland, but it was at the end of a long process which had begun several years earlier. That process had seen the development of her belief that the Labour Party had not proved the effective political vehicle that she had hoped it would and that the compromises which membership necessarily involved were becoming increasingly frustrating and non-productive.

As noted in previous chapters, Mary Robinson had failed in 1981, her second attempt, to be elected to the Dáil. In 1982 she had resigned from Dublin Corporation, concealing to some extent the depth of her dissatisfaction with the powerlessness of that body. In the same year she had a lengthy discussion about the party's development and presentation of policies affecting women with a senior party colleague, and confided in him that she had begun to wonder whether, in fact, she couldn't do more on the outside than on the inside. In the circumstances, he found it hard to argue against her. It was during the period when the religious right was politically ascendant; Labour itself was deeply and publicly split on the issue of the so-called 'abortion' amendment; and it seemed increasingly unlikely that she would ever find herself translated from the Senate to the Dáil.

The problem about that was that Cabinet positions, for which her track record and her now substantial experience amply qualified her, are effectively confined to members of the Dáil. Eamon de Valera once appointed a defeated minister to the Senate and then re-appointed him to the Cabinet, but the minister concerned died shortly afterwards. The precedent (which is provided for in the Constitution) was not repeated until the short-lived government of 1981-82, when Garret FitzGerald appointed one of his party's senators, Professor Jim Dooge, to be briefly Minister for Foreign Affairs. If Mary

Robinson was to look for a Cabinet position from the rarefied atmosphere of the Senate, she would – unlike Jim Dooge – be competing with Labour members of the Dáil whose seniority and longevity gave them powerful leverage.

In the shorter term, however, the prospect of making a substantial contribution to national debate on Northern Ireland suddenly manifested itself. Her appointment as an alternate member to the New Ireland Forum when it was established at the end of 1983 was both a recognition by the Labour leadership that she had a major contribution to make and an opportunity for her to perform on a wider stage.

To understand what led to the creation of the Forum, it is necessary to go back to the beginning of the 1982-87 coalition government led by Garret FitzGerald and to the initiatives taken by that government in relation to the Northern Ireland issue. The politics of Northern Ireland had effectively been in crisis since 1969. The old Nationalist Party, for years the political vehicle for nationalist opinion in the North, had been superseded, in the wake of the civil rights movement, by the Social Democratic and Labour Party (SDLP). The Northern Ireland parliament at Stormont had been prorogued and eventually abolished in 1972. A brief experiment with a power-sharing executive collapsed in 1974 in the face of a political strike by loyalist workers which successfully intimidated the British government. In the nine years between then and 1984, Britain had ruled Northern Ireland directly and within the North itself there was a political vacuum. The danger of this situation, from the point of view of both the SDLP and the Irish government, was that Sinn Féin, the political wing of the IRA, would increasingly colonise Northern nationalist opinion and wean Catholic voters away from the SDLP towards more extreme solutions.

These were the circumstances in which FitzGerald's government proposed the establishment of a new body, to be known as the New Ireland Forum. The Forum was open to all political parties on the island which abjured the use of violence for political ends and would – Dublin politicians generally hoped – fill the North's political vacuum. It might also, with luck, articulate a new strategy, or suggest initiatives, to move the situation forward. The risk was that underlying differences between the Republic's political parties on the Northern issue would surface to fracture any semblance of an agreed approach to this difficult area.

The Forum was formally established under the chairmanship of a distinguished academic, Dr Colm Ó hEocha, president of University College, Galway. Sinn Féin had effectively ruled itself out of membership, as the paramilitary campaign in the North was at full strength. The unionist parties were invited but – as might have been expected – did not come, although some unionists did attend on a number of occasions as individuals. The Alliance Party, which represents both Catholics and Protestants in Northern Ireland and which strives to distance itself from mainstream nationalism and unionism, agreed to attend; so did the SDLP, the main vehicle for nationalist political opinion.

The format of the Forum did not give all members the right to intervene on all issues: each party allocated its members and alternate members to particular aspects of the Forum's work. Mary Robinson was involved in the close questioning of a number of key witnesses, notably members of the Catholic hierarchy. Her own agenda was clearly signalled early on in two days of discussions on women's topics, when she questioned Sylvia Meehan, head of the Republic's Employment Equality Agency, about the significance of disunity for women on the island, North and South. Sylvia Meehan emphasised, in her written submission to the Forum, that the situation of women had to be seen as a crucial factor and called for economic and social planning that would have built-in provisions for child care and the reorganisation of working time. Questioned by Mary Robinson about divorce, she pointedly agreed that this was a change which ought to be made immediately and not just in the long-term context of a united Ireland.

The political, as contrasted with the social, dimensions of the problem were teased out by Mary Robinson in her questioning of Chris McGimpsey, an independent unionist, who warned that 'if we continue to meet with a virtual unionist forum at Stormont and the SDLP continue only to work for peace and reconciliation through a forum in Dublin, the void will eventually get so big there will be no future and when there is no future for politics and reasoned thinking all that is left is the gun'.

It was on the religious issue, however, that Mary Robinson really got into her stride, focusing in particular on a theme which she had made peculiarly her own for at least a decade: 'the importance of removing from our Constitution and laws those elements which are seen to be divisive on religious grounds'.

'This', she commented, 'is a forum for a new Ireland including the whole of the island of Ireland, not just Northern Ireland. Perhaps I could make the question clearer by referring to a very significant passage in the opening this morning by Bishop Daly.[21] It was a passage that was applauded by members of this Forum. He declared with emphasis that the bishops would raise their voices to resist any constitutional proposals which might infringe or endanger the civil and religious rights and liberties cherished by Northern Ireland Protestants. The question is why are you not raising your voices now in relation to the Protestants and others who are not of the Catholic faith in this part of the country? Surely they too are entitled to full civil and religious liberties and if we are to reach out to a new Ireland must we not create the basis of confidence that is the framework that we would have?'

She followed this up with an inquisition on the Church's attitude to divorce, to mixed marriages, and even to the question of the constitutional amendment on abortion, which had one of her episcopal witnesses suggesting that she might do equally well as a canon lawyer. By the end of the day, she had not elicited much by way of concessions, except for a number of declarations by churchmen that they regarded law as a matter for legislators rather than for ecclesiastics, and a veiled hint that in the somewhat unpredictable circumstances in which a 'new Ireland' might take shape, different legislation might be inevitable.

In the private sessions of the Forum, Mary Robinson was active on issues other than those of church, state, and women on which she had shone in public. One of the key points at issue was what form of future constitutional arrangements the Forum would recommend. There were effectively three options: a unitary state, a federal state, and a confederal state. Fianna Fáil, the largest party, was firmly committed to the unitary state model – in sharp contrast to the position consistently adopted for almost half a century by Eamon de Valera and Seán Lemass, that party's first two leaders, who always accepted that there would be a Northern Ireland legislature. The tension between the parties on this issue was most evident in the weighting that would be given to the other two options. Both Labour and Fine Gael were resisting moves by Fianna Fáil to categorise them merely as 'suggestions'. Mary Robinson was the toughest of those Fine Gael and Labour members opposing the attempt to commit the Forum to the unitary state model, and neither she nor Frank Cluskey was prepared to yield on the issue.

The Report of the New Ireland Forum, when it was finally published, was the occasion for a minor crisis. Its carefully phrased conclusions were to some extent hijacked by the Fianna Fáil leader Charles Haughey, who again stitched his commitment to the prior claims of the 'unitary state' solution into the record. This was of less significance in the end, however, than the impromptu response it evoked from the British prime minister, Margaret Thatcher, which set nationalist Ireland by the ears. Each of the constitutional solutions advanced to the island's political problems, Mrs Thatcher stated firmly, was 'Out'. Given more time, she might have framed her rejection more diplomatically, but the message would undoubtedly have been the same. A flurry of diplomatic activity ensued between Dublin and London in an attempt to rescue the situation, which now risked giving greater credibility to Sinn Féin and to paramilitary forces in the North and making the last situation even worse than the first.

The Report of the Forum sank without trace, but what went down with the ship was not only the fragile and probably unrealistic consensus on the constitutional issue but a substantial body of research material on economic and social issues which broke new ground in many areas but which was now lost to sight. Mary Robinson was one of the few people publicly to decry this loss when, in August 1985, she commented in withering tones on the fact that all references to equality for women had been deleted from the Forum's report. Nuala Fennell, the recently appointed Minister of State for Women's Affairs, had, she said, been given 'a job without power'. And, 'for reasons that stem from our political culture, women should not look to parliament as a primary source of innovation and change. This limited and mainly reactive role for parliament poses serious problems for our democracy.'[22]

The North retreated from the public agenda rapidly, although frustration at the lack of progress led to the inauguration of highly confidential Anglo-Irish negotiations which, as will be seen, were to produce the Anglo-Irish Agreement in November 1985. Meanwhile, a rare opportunity presented itself for Mary Robinson to move from the Senate back benches to a position of real political power and influence. This was in 1984 when the Fine Gael-appointed Attorney-General, Peter Sutherland, was appointed by the government to the position of Ireland's member of the EEC Commission.

Dick Spring, the Labour Party leader, at first argued for a Labour appointment to Europe but effectively used the claim as a bargaining counter. Once the Sutherland decision had been agreed, he was in a stronger position to press for the right to appoint Sutherland's replacement. FitzGerald agreed without too much difficulty, partly because he knew – or thought he knew – that Mary Robinson would be the appointee.

This underlines the quite different perception of Mary Robinson's talents in the two parties. FitzGerald admired her intellect and enjoyed her company. But Spring had quite a different agenda and proposed instead his friend John Rogers, with whom he had studied law at Trinity and who was also a trusted adviser. Spring's colleagues were almost as astonished as FitzGerald – not because they disagreed with Spring about Robinson, whom they regarded as 'too committed to causes to provide the cold, clinical advice that a government needs',[23] but because Rogers was a junior barrister with comparatively little experience.

More than a dozen years later, the episode is still fresh in Mary Robinson's memory. 'Yes, I was very disappointed. I believe that I was, to say the least of it, shortlisted, and indeed met Dick Spring on the matter. He gave me no indication of what he would do, but he knew my interest and I knew he was considering me. I didn't know who else he was considering.

'The way I saw it at the time was that I felt uniquely motivated, qualified and skilled. I didn't know John Rogers very well. To be quite honest, I felt that he made a very good job of it – but I didn't rank him *ex aequo* with me at the time, and I thought that Dick Spring had chosen a pal as opposed to someone who – if he but knew it ... It was another part of a dawning on me that I wasn't having much influence of the kind I wanted to have where I was. The deeper commitment I felt in the Labour Party was simply not translating into being able to use my skills effectively – not, I really believe, in an egotistical sense, but in a pragmatic sense.'

Since 1985, when she resigned from the Labour Party, some commentators have found it fashionable to explain her decision solely in terms of personal pique at the failure to appoint her to the attorney-generalship at this time. It was undoubtedly a major disappointment and added to the doubts she was experiencing at that time. On the other hand, a year is a long time to bear a grudge of that kind before acting on it, and those who know Mary Robinson well would give little credence to the idea that she would behave in this way. Her approach to politics, furthermore, has been entirely functional: what needs to be done, and when and where is the best place to do it? On this score, she has been as severe a critic of herself as anyone else. Reflecting on her complete failure to capture a seat in the Dáil, or to make the necessary impression on the hard core of the Labour Party that would have given her a better chance, she mused: 'In retrospect, I failed to see, and to reconcile, differences within the party. It was partly my own inexperience and clumsiness and there wasn't time to prepare.'[24]

The fact that she did not resign immediately after Rogers's appointment shows, not vacillation but a simple assessment that there was still more benefit in staying in than in moving out. The process of evaluation, however, was ongoing. In May 1984 she was musing publicly that 'I have paid a high price for my involvement in the Labour Party in giving up my independence, and I could go back to [independence].'

What brought matters to a head was the conclusion of the Anglo-Irish Agreement in November 1985. This provided, among other things, for the creation of a joint Anglo-Irish secretariat in Belfast and the setting-up of a structure of inter-governmental meetings which would review progress towards a political solution and act as a kind of early warning system to head off possible misunderstandings between the two governments. To counter-balance this development, which it was recognised would cause considerable problems for Northern unionists, the Irish government, for its part, formally recognised that there would be no change in the constitutional status of Northern Ireland without the consent of the majority there and accepted that its role in the government of Northern Ireland, although embodied in the structure of the proposed Anglo-Irish Conference, was effectively only advisory.

The problem about the Agreement, as Chris McGimpsey had to all intents and purposes predicted a year earlier at the Forum, was that it had been arrived at as the result of a process from which political majority opinion in Northern Ireland – the unionists – had been effectively excluded. Because the process was inter-governmental, only the Irish and British governments were involved;

but the SDLP had a privileged access to the Irish government and therefore an input into the content of the final agreement, whereas Northern unionists had no such input through the British government. Almost regardless of its outcome, therefore, the process was bound to produce intense unionist suspicion; the proposal for an Anglo-Irish conference turned suspicion into outright opposition. All Unionist MPs at Westminster resigned in protest and fought the resulting by-elections on a straightforward anti-Agreement platform. All but one were returned.

Within the Labour Party, Mary Robinson was becoming increasingly uneasy, particularly about the intense secrecy in which the discussions were – necessarily, from the point of view of those most directly involved – taking place. As it happened, the closing stages of the negotiations also coincided almost exactly with the plans to move the bill in the Dáil on the constitutional referendum on divorce, with which she had also been closely associated. The date for moving the bill was tentatively scheduled for 19 November.

On 13 November, two days before the Agreement was signed, the PLP met in a special session, not to discuss the Agreement itself, because it had not by that stage been finalised, but the procedure by which the party would be associated with it. The Tánaiste and party leader, Dick Spring, told the meeting that he would consult with members after the document had been finalised. Mary Robinson immediately objected, on the grounds that this meant that party members were being prevented from making any contribution before the text had been agreed. The procedural motion was agreed, nonetheless, by a substantial majority. Mary Robinson went to Spring privately before the finalising of the Agreement and explained her concerns in some detail. She was, she said, worried about any proposal which was based on inter-governmental structures alone and which was being negotiated without the involvement in any way of the majority community in the North. She expressed the belief that such a proposal would have all the weaknesses of the Sunningdale arrangement (the agreement between the Irish and British governments in 1973 which formed the basis for the unsuccessful power-sharing Assembly to govern Northern Ireland), and that it would be unacceptable to all sections of unionist opinion, and not just to extremists.

The morning after the Agreement was signed, it was discussed at a joint meeting of the Fine Gael and Labour parliamentary parties in Dublin, where it met with general and warm approval – except from Mary Robinson who warned about the dangers of pressing ahead if it emerged that no section of unionist opinion would support it.

'When I read the text of the Agreement', she declared publicly two days later, 'it confirmed my worst fears in that regard. I asked whether any fallback position had been prepared to avoid the grim prospect of civil disruption in the

North over the coming months. To my surprise and dismay, the media were informed after that meeting that there had been unanimous support for, and endorsement of, the Anglo-Irish Agreement. Regrettably, I cannot give that support and endorsement because I do not believe it can achieve its objective of securing peace and stability in Northern Ireland or on this island as a whole. I hope I am wrong.'

Announcing her resignation from the Labour Party on the issue, she noted: 'This has been one of the most difficult and painful decisions that I have had to make in over sixteen years as a senator. I particularly regret having to take such a negative view of an international agreement forged by persons of the calibre and integrity of Garret FitzGerald, Dick Spring and Peter Barry, with the active support of John Hume and his colleagues in the SDLP. In the circumstances, I feel it is the only honourable course for me to take.'

Her resignation was greeted with genuine shock: Dick Spring accepted it with 'considerable sadness' and in a letter to her intimated that while there were risks inherent in the government's approach there were also risks in doing nothing. Everyone was surprised that in her private discussions with Spring she had not intimated that this was a resigning matter. But, she explained, 'I cannot oppose something which is fundamental to the government and still remain within the Labour Party. My political future is absolutely secondary to all of this.'

The following day, the *Irish Times* commented editorially that 'Mary Robinson had a point in her resignation from the Labour Party. There is no long-term good for anyone in Ireland if the unionist people, the Protestant people of the North, do not have a reasonable say in their own fate. We are at a stage when this may be beginning to be worked out.'

This somewhat hesitant verdict betrayed a lingering sense of apprehension which was quickly obliterated by the general endorsement of the Agreement in the Republic and by public fascination at the frantic – and, it appeared, doomed – attempts by unionist politicians to torpedo it. More than a decade later, fundamental unionist consent to the operation of the Agreement seems as unattainable as ever: Mary Robinson was to say, in the week in 1989 in which she announced her retirement from representative politics, that she derived little satisfaction from having been proved right.

In 1997, a dozen years later, she was unrepentant. 'It was a very difficult decision and it was a very difficult time. And I did *not* vote against the Anglo-Irish Agreement, because nobody wanted an Anglo-Irish Agreement more than I did. It's not that I was wise. It was just that I was in touch with Northern Ireland, I think, more than a lot of people, and I mean really in all kinds of ways – constituency ways, university ways, theatre ways, friendship ways. I had an awful lot of weird, out-of-politics friends but they were telling me what the situation was. Most of the friends I had in Northern Ireland had nothing to do with politics.

'When we had that first meeting of the Fine Gael and Labour parliamentary parties after the Agreement, I raised my voice, Frank Cluskey raised his and so did Paddy Harte. I think we were probably the only three who did so openly. And I think I was the most overt, because I was saying publicly what I had been saying privately at some length. Then I came home and I turned on my television and I heard the chairmen of the parliamentary parties say that there had been "unanimous agreement", and I snapped. I talked to Nick and I said: "I'm better going back to the independent benches. I must be able to say publicly what I've been trying to say privately – but nobody's been paying a blind bit of attention."'

Within days of her resignation, she was hinting that party affiliation had not been a totally negative experience: the idea of joining any other party had been 'totally alien' to her, and she had sought, 'and to some extent received' within Labour the possibility of a different approach to society's problems on both economic and social grounds. But there was no going back, as anyone who knew Mary Robinson could easily have predicted. The parting was not without trauma on her side, so much so that she suggested that she might not even stand again for the Senate. As it turned out, she was to fight one more Senate election in 1987, now again as an independent.

The fact that her decision was taken after a discussion with Nick is a pointer to the centrality of her relationship with her husband and to his unseen but often critically important presence. Her own marriage is one based on total equality.[25] Nick, as an artist and writer, has his own sphere of operations: he would be more likely to choose the loose covers and the curtains for the house but, in his own words, 'Mary has the knack of putting her children first and knowing when there is something to be sorted out with one of them.'[26] Even as a young woman, her father recalled, she could be found with 'ten kids in the back of the car', taking them off for a picnic. And the informality of the private quarters in the Áras, as of the family home on Massbrook, Co. Mayo, is a guessed-at and closely-guarded family secret.

There are hints, here and there, that like many other working women she had to pay a price for the juggling of domestic and professional responsibilities. In the Law Library in her early years as a barrister, she was not regarded as 'clubby'. Insofar as clubbiness resides in a willingness and ability to retire to the other bar for a leisurely gin and tonic after work, this was an option which was simply not available to her. When she first qualified, she was one of a very small number of women barristers: for a time after she was called to the Inner Bar in 1980, she was the only female 'silk'.

Her increasing political involvement, especially after 1975, on top of her legal work and her responsibilities to her family, left little time around the edges. Invited to a meeting on neutrality by the Labour Party Lawyers' Group in November 1984, she replied apologetically that she would try to attend for the early part of the evening although it was an extremely awkward time for domestic reasons. By the beginning of the summer holidays, according to one associate, she would be 'picking herself up off the ground' after months of legal work, politics, and inevitable domesticities. What enabled her to bounce back, time after time, was another largely unsung female characteristic: sheer physical resilience. The workload she was to assume as President was, in itself, a standing reproach to many of her predecessors and male contemporaries.

As her direct political involvement began to assume a lower place in her scale of priorities, her focus was increasingly turning back towards her first love, the law. Ironically, on the very day that her resignation from Labour was published in the daily papers, the Supreme Court handed down a decision in her favour. Even more ironically, it was a case – possibly the only one of its kind – in which Mary Robinson appeared for the State, defending it against a constitutional challenge to the Gaming and Lotteries Act 1956. This case, Cafolla v. Attorney-General, was part of the campaign by the gaming industry in the 1980s to have the maximum prizes under the Act increased. Mary Robinson helped to defeat, in both the High Court and the Supreme Court, their arguments that the limits were so out of date that they constituted a breach of their right to earn a livelihood, one of the 'implied' rights recognised under Article 40.3 of the Constitution.

Resignation from the Labour Party finally gave Mary Robinson more time to apply herself to a range of cases, many of which ended up in the European courts and most of which she won. Excluding the Cafolla case, she handled almost as many major cases in this domain in the three years between 1986 and 1989 as she had done in the fourteen years between 1972 (the McGee case) and 1986. This is of course to some extent an over-simplification. Many of the cases took years to come to judgement and some overlapped the two periods. A case involving Aer Lingus cabin crew who were dismissed from the company under the old 'marriage bar' was not finalised until 1990. Overall, however, the impression is of a lawyer who was developing a rare capacity to take up the law and even on occasion the Constitution, and shake them until their teeth rattled; a lawyer who put flesh on the bare bones of constitutional rights until the resulting creation would have been almost unrecognisable to its draughtsmen (and, of course, they were all men); and above all a lawyer who was not afraid of unpopularity if she thought the cause was right. She was not always successful; but even the cases she lost were, in some respects, prophetic of future change. In this, at least, her Labour Party experience stood her in good stead: it had, as she said, taught her 'to learn the need for a hardening of my political tissues'.

It is important to distinguish the legal arenas in which she fought outside Ireland. These were the European Court of Justice, on the one hand, and the European Commission of Human Rights and the European Court of Human Rights on the other.[27] The European Court of Justice is the Court of the European Union (formerly the European Community and originally the EEC). It is now superior even to the Irish Supreme Court, where points of European law are involved. A case won here against the Irish government will change Irish law.

The European Commission of Human Rights and the European Court of Human Rights, on the other hand, are part of the Council of Europe's institutions and were set up in 1959 to enforce the Council's first major initiative, the Convention on Human Rights and Fundamental Freedoms, which was signed in 1950. The legal processes involved are lengthy: a plaintiff first has to exhaust all possible legal remedies in his or her own country and has then to satisfy the Commission that he or she has a good case before being allowed to present it at the Court of Human Rights. Even then, the court's decision is not legally binding although governments which lose cases there generally pass amending legislation after some years to bring their law into line with the court's decision.

In 1987, Mary Robinson was elected to the International Commission of Jurists (ICJ) on the recommendation of Seán MacBride, her former senior in a number of key cases at the Irish Bar, who was retiring from the forty-member body. The ICJ itself is simply an international group of lawyers which issues occasional reports on matters concerning international law and has for that reason some international prestige, but it has no formal function in relation to any other international agency or any international judicial body. What is of more interest in this connection is the relationship between Mary Robinson and MacBride. MacBride was a son of Maud Gonne. He was a radical republican in his youth, and at one stage Chief of Staff of the IRA. Later he became leader of the small Clann na Poblachta political party, a government minister (for Foreign Affairs) on his first day in parliament in 1948 and winner of both the Nobel and Lenin Peace Prizes. Outside politics, he was a barrister with an appetite for high-profile constitutional cases. As a young barrister Mary Robinson was to act as junior counsel in some of the cases on which he led, but their paths finally diverged in the run-up to the divorce referendum of 1986 when MacBride, to the astonishment of his admirers, announced that he would vote against the proposal.

In 1987, Mary Robinson brought the first of two of the most significant cases in which she was involved in the European Court of Justice. They were basically equality cases. The first, McDermott and Cotter v. Minister for Social Welfare,[28] was part of the long-running series of claims by married women against the government for late implementation of the 1978 Social Welfare Equality Directive. It should have been implemented in 1984 but was delayed by the Fine Gael/Labour coalition then in power, simply because it would cost too much money. In the Senate, Mary Robinson noted percipiently that this delay in paying the women what was owed to them would cause problems. Outside the Senate, she made certain that these 'problems' could not be easily ignored by being involved in all the cases.

The government's strategy was deeply conservative – and extremely expensive – in that it insisted on fighting each individual case all the way through the Irish courts and the European Court of Justice before arriving at a settlement. It would then turn around and wait for the next case, when it would do the same all over again. It was in one sense an eerie prefiguration of the way in which the Blood Transfusion Services Board handled the Brigid McCole and other cases in the 1990s, although here the government had belatedly taken the initiative in setting up a tribunal to award damages in a non-confrontational setting. The difference between the BTSB cases and the social welfare cases is that the compensation, including arrears due to each of the claimants in the social welfare cases could be almost worked out mathematically in advance, and the strategy of fighting them case by case seemed destined to do little except add enormously to the State's legal bills. Eventually, a large number of women joined together to fight a 'group action'. This did not even reach Europe. When the case reached the High Court in early 1995, Mary Robinson was in Áras an Uachtaráin, the rainbow coalition was in power and the State agreed to pay in arrears the full bill of about £265 million to the 70,000 women involved. It is difficult not to imagine that a discreet toast was raised to the decision in the Phoenix Park.

Mary Robinson's other major European Court of Justice success was in relation to the Murphy v. An Bord Telecom case. This was a case which blended injustice with farce in epic proportions. Under the Anti-Discrimination (Pay) Act of 1974, which had belatedly been brought in by the Irish government to bring it into line with European directives on equal pay, women could get equal pay if they could prove that men were doing the same work but being paid more for it. The anomaly in the Telecom case was that men were being paid more – but for doing *less* important work! The Irish courts held firm, arguing that because the men's work was of less value the women couldn't use them as a basis for comparison – even though the men were being paid more. This truly Alice in Wonderland situation was resolved in short order by the European Court of Justice which ruled that the Irish courts were required to interpret the 1974 Act in a way that gave full effect to the equality principle. In other words, it established that the Irish courts could not shelter behind casuistry and had to implement the Act in the fairest possible way.

Mary Robinson fought two critical cases before the European Court of Human Rights. The first involved a man named Roy Johnston, the former husband of the woman involved in one of her earliest cases, Mairín de Burca. Roy and his partner Janice had a daughter, Nessa, and sued the State on two grounds. The first was on the grounds that Article 12 of the Convention, which guarantees the right to marry and found a family, implicitly guaranteed either of them, as parents of Nessa, the right to a divorce from a first spouse. The second was that Nessa's position in Irish law, as a child who suffered certain disabilities because of her illegitimate status, was in breach of Article 8 of the Convention, which guaranteed a right of respect for privacy and family life.

This case had been initiated in the Commission of Human Rights in 1982 but the decision was not handed down until December 1986, after the failed divorce referendum. The judges found almost unanimously (by sixteen to one) that Article 12 of the Convention did not include a right to divorce. Had the case gone the other way, it would have left Ireland in a very anomalous situation and might even have put a question-mark over the country's membership of the Council of Europe. On the second front, however, the news was better: the Court was unanimous in its finding that Nessa's rights were infringed by the Irish law on illegitimacy and this was eventually put to rights by the Status of Children Act, 1987, which was being formulated at the time of the Court's decision and came into force in 1988. Mary Robinson also acted for plaintiffs called Stoutt in a related case, which was settled in 1987 after the passage of the Act.

The second case was no less than sixteen years in coming to a conclusion and illustrates the tensions between Irish and European law in a particularly vivid way. David Norris, a professed homosexual who was to be elected as a member of the Senate in the Trinity College constituency in 1987, brought an action against the State for the first time in 1977, arguing that the part of the 1861 Offences Against the Person Act which outlawed homosexual practices was unconstitutional. He lost in the High Court in 1980. In 1981 the European Court of Human Rights, hearing an identical case brought against the British government by a man living in Northern Ireland, held that the part of the Act concerned was in conflict with the right to privacy and family life. When the Norris case reached the Irish Supreme Court the following year, Mary Robinson argued strongly that it ought to follow the Dudgeon case, as the Northern case was called. The Chief Justice, Tom O'Higgins, administered a sharp rap on the knuckles. 'In my view', he said, 'acceptance of Mrs Robinson's submission would be contrary to the provisions of the Constitution itself and would accord to the Government the power, by an executive act, to change both the Constitution and the law. The Convention ... does not and cannot form part of our domestic law nor affect in any way questions which arise thereunder.'

It was whistling past the graveyard. The Supreme Court decision went against David Norris by 3-2 but one of the minority judges pointed out that the sections of the 1861 Act were in all probability 'doomed to extinction'. Norris and Robinson had to go back to the drawing board and begin the lengthy process of taking his case through the European Commission of Human Rights and the Court of Human Rights itself. Norris eventually won his case there in 1988 and, five years later, that Court's decision was implemented by the Oireachtas in the passage of the Criminal Law (Sexual Offences) Act 1993 which de-criminalised homosexual behaviour between consenting adults.

Pregnancy counselling, insofar as it involved access to information about abortion, was one of the most hotly contested areas of all. Mary Robinson appeared for the Well Woman Centre in a case brought against it (and against Open Door Counselling) by the Society for the Protection of the Unborn Child (SPUC) in the High Court in 1986 and in the Supreme Court in 1988, although it was not decided in the European Court of Human Rights until 1992, after she had become President. The Irish courts rejected Robinson's argument that there were European Community law questions involved, so that the Well Woman Centre had to travel the same route as David Norris via the European Commission of Human Rights and the European Court of Human Rights. Despite the objections of the Supreme Court (which gave SPUC the injunction it sought), the European Court of Human Rights held that the injunction infringed the guarantee of free speech and awarded the centre £25,000 damages for loss of income. Legal costs for both organisations came to about £170,000. The abortion issue was to dog Mary Robinson's steps, through her election campaign for the presidency and even into 1992 and what was to become known as the 'X' case. What, in a sense, was significant, was that at the end of the day her handling of the issues enhanced rather than impaired her status in a community in which abortion remains one of the most sensitive political issues ever discussed.

An unexpected defeat took place in 1989, when she took a case before the European Commission of Human Rights on behalf of a Radio Telefís Éireann producer, Betty Purcell, and the National Union of Journalists.[29] This fell at the first hurdle to the surprise of many commentators: the Commission declared as 'manifestly ill-founded' the claim that Section 31 of the Broadcasting Acts 1960-76 was in breach of the Convention's guarantee of freedom of speech. This section – or, more properly, the ministerial directives issued under the section by successive governments – acted to keep Sinn Féin and other organisations off the airwaves. The directives were allowed to lapse, i.e. were not re-issued as they had been annually for some two decades, in January 1994.

This defeat notwithstanding, the direction in which Mary Robinson was planning to go was already becoming clear. In 1988, she announced the creation of a new Centre for European Law in Trinity. Her husband, Nick, a qualified solicitor, was also involved in this initiative, which was designed to meet the growing need in Ireland for a source of expertise on European law and practice, capable of being tapped into by business, trade unions and the public service. It was funded by private subscriptions from individuals and (more frequently) by institutional subscribers and specialised in high-powered seminars and colloquia.

Mary Robinson still attended and spoke at the Senate. Almost her last major speech there – interestingly, in the light of her later appointment to the UN High Commissionership for Human Rights – was on 18 January 1989 on a motion which she herself tabled on China's human rights record in Tibet. She did not mince her words.

> The recent history of the Tibetan people is one of the saddest examples of a major violation of human rights and, indeed, of the right to self-determination itself. However, surprisingly, Tibet is not on the current political agenda and, despite earlier concern about the treatment of Tibetan people, Ireland has been silent in recent years and has not expressed any concern at international level. This is particularly strange because much of what has happened to Tibet should evoke deep chords in the Irish people. The suppression of a whole people, so that their independent religious, social and cultural ethos is denied and they are subjected to the humiliation of being colonised and indeed substantially planted upon to such an extent that the Tibetan people have become a minority in their own country, should evoke an immediate response from us.

On the other side of the debate was the man who was, a decade later, to be her opponent for the presidency: Brian Lenihan, then Minister for Foreign Affairs. Lenihan was as emollient as he could be, but did not offer any structured amendments to Mary Robinson's motion. This meant, in effect, that the Fianna Fáil majority in the Senate were going to vote it down and when the debate concluded on 1 February there was a distinct possibility that, had this happened, the Senate would have technically put itself into the position of approving of China's Tibetan policy. Noting that the 'reality of the situation ... is that there is a lot of common ground and there is a reluctance to have the matter, which is a very sensitive international issue, voted on in this manner', Mary Robinson withdrew her motion. She had been outflanked procedurally but she had still managed to get her views on the record, totally unconscious of a future in which she would be charged by the United Nations itself with the even more delicate task of attempting to put right what she had so forthrightly condemned.

Any lingering suspicion that she still hankered after political office was definitively dispelled when, on 23 May 1989, she declared that she would not be seeking re-election to the body which she had been a member of for almost twenty years. Her career as a legislator was drawing to a close and her decision was greeted with genuine regret in the Senate, whose members unusually engaged in a whole series of personal tributes to her record. One newspaper columnist probably summed up popular feeling fairly accurately when he declared that her decision 'marks the end of an impressive political career which never quite reached the heights which at one time looked likely'. The future, insofar as anyone could predict it at that stage, was law and Europe. Not even the most starry-eyed optimist, at this juncture, could have predicted the extraordinary diversion that was to take place, first towards the presidency and, ultimately, to the United Nations.

CHAPTER 7

The Presidential Election:
On the Way to the Park

IN THE POLITICAL DOG-DAYS between 1987 and 1990 Mary Robinson was easing herself out of politics. The Labour Party was in opposition. Its opponent was a Fianna Fáil minority government, led by Charles Haughey. Haughey, however, called an ill-advised snap election in 1989, lost his majority and had to rely on going into coalition with the Progressive Democrats – the first time Fianna Fáil had ever shared power with another party.

Despite its experience in government (some would say because of it), Labour was still a party with only sixteen TDs and intermittently fractious. The old coalition/no coalition arguments had never been entirely buried but Dick Spring's decision to lead the party out of government rather than support Garret FitzGerald's January 1987 budget – the first occasion on which a Labour leader had broken a coalition – showed that both party and leader had a new sense of political nerve.

Two other factors were going for the party. One was the poor image and performance of Fine Gael. When FitzGerald resigned in the wake of his party's 1987 defeat, his place was taken by Alan Dukes, who first of all went against the grain of Irish politics by supporting the set of conservative fiscal policies adopted by Haughey in 1987-89. This policy, known as the 'Tallaght strategy', after the location of the speech in which Dukes announced it, reflected Dukes's own economic thinking but did nothing for traditional Fine Gael morale.

It also left a gap in the political landscape which – and this was the second factor – Dick Spring moved rapidly to fill. As Fine Gael deputies sat in the Dáil with one hand figuratively tied behind their backs, he waded into the government on almost every issue, enhancing his personal profile and that of the party. At the same time, he was continuing to build his hold over a party which had in the past proved notoriously difficult to manage. It was a long and often slow process and his critics on the left of the party in particular were not going to cede the ground without a struggle.

One of these critics was Emmet Stagg, TD for Kildare and a prominent member of the 'Labour Left' ginger group within the party. Stagg was a staunch anti-coalitionist and at times fiercely critical of the leadership and, when Spring's campaign to achieve control over his divided party was gathering momentum after the 1987 party conference, he followed a path that had been trodden by other dissidents before him. What was at issue was the way in which members of the PLP would be appointed to the party's supreme governing body, the Administrative Council (AC). Up to now, these appointments had been made by the leader alone and had naturally strengthened the leader's position on the Council.

Stagg opposed Spring's suggested appointees, threatened to take the party to court and asked Mary Robinson to be his legal adviser. With the even-handedness which has sometimes astonished her friends as much as it has exasperated her foes, Mary Robinson agreed. Spring proposed a solution under which the PLP would elect its appointees to the AC; Mary Robinson countered that this would be unconstitutional since the system of election proposed was not by proportional representation. A compromise was eventually agreed and the court action never materialised, but if she had needed to put down a marker in relation to her independence she could hardly have chosen a more prominent one. The coincidence that Robinson, Spring and Spring's legal adviser, John Rogers, were all products of Trinity College's law school added a piquant flavour to the high-octane confrontation.

In this context, her decision to advise Stagg, after her resignation from the party, can hardly be portrayed as the result of a sudden rush of blood to the head, much less vindictiveness. She was also on the way out of politics for good. On 23 May 1989, two days after her forty-fifth birthday, she formally announced that she would not be standing again for the Senate: she was quitting while she was ahead.

Although Dick Spring, according to one biographer, is not quick to forget slights, the fact that within a very short period of time Mary Robinson was effectively being offered the Labour Party's nomination for the presidency speaks volumes for his ability to master the learning curve. The intermediary between them was the man – John Rogers – who had been appointed Attorney-General by Spring in 1984 instead of her.

Patrick Hillery was due to retire as President when the second of his two seven-year terms ended in late 1990. Apart from a slow-burning, almost subterranean Fianna Fáil whispering campaign in favour of Brian Lenihan, nobody appeared to have given the question of who might be his successor much consideration until the possibility of a contest was broached by Dick

Spring after a 1989 winter weekend's holiday in West Kerry. Spring went so far as to suggest that, if no-one else was available, he might stand himself – a proposal that caused amazement and not just within the Labour Party.

He subsequently wrote a newspaper article in which he fleshed out his views about a new vision for the presidency. These were the preliminaries to the meeting between John Rogers and Mary Robinson, which took place at Rogers's request on St Valentine's Day in 1990. The ostensible purpose of the meeting was only to discuss a position paper he had prepared on the presidency itself but the subtext of what he had to say was unmistakable. In a lightly coded fashion, he was inviting her to respond to the idea that she might be the Labour Party candidate. Initially she was astonished. The following day, she had a lengthy discussion about it with her close friend Bride Rosney. A few days later, the idea had fired her imagination. Within two months, she was on the campaign trail. In November, she was elected, the candidate of – although not from – a political party which at the time did not have a single woman TD.

To understand the reasons for, and the nature of, this apparent conversion it is necessary to look at the nature and politics of the presidency itself. The bald facts of the timetable just outlined conceal a scenario in which courage, imagination and luck combined to transform impossibility into improbability and improbability into inevitability. It was a scenario which was shaped powerfully, and in ways of which even her proposers were not at the time fully aware, by the preceding twenty years, just as the result was to transform one of Ireland's central political institutions in ways which its creator, Eamon de Valera, could never have envisaged.

The presidency itself was created by the 1937 Irish Constitution and replicated in some respects the office of its predecessor, the Governor-General of Ireland, which had been abolished. The Governor-General, appointed by the British government, was up to 1937 the official representative of the British crown in Ireland: a similar post continues to exist in many other former British colonies. In some it rapidly became a figurehead. In others – as in Australia when a governor-general dismissed a popularly-elected prime minister in the 1970s – it retained a constitutional significance and effectiveness out of all proportion to its political lineage.

The post was consciously downgraded by de Valera when he first attained power in 1932 and when he replaced it in 1937 with the presidency it was evident that the constitutional formula he devised was framed so as to remove it as far as possible from the political arena. However, nominations for the office would be tightly controlled by the major political parties – under the Constitution the right can be exercised only by a minimum of twenty members of the Oireachtas, four county councils or by a former or retiring President nominating himself or herself. Ireland's first President, Douglas Hyde, was a

Protestant and a scholar, characteristics which helped de Valera to secure the agreement of the other parties to his unopposed election. There was an election between three candidates for his successor, Sean T. O'Kelly in 1945 but O'Kelly's somewhat elfin charm secured his unopposed re-election seven years later so that by 1959, when Eamon de Valera was put forward as a Fianna Fáil candidate, there had been only one election for the post in the preceding twenty-two years.

The contest was clearly regarded as one between the two major political blocs. Labour had never put up a candidate at all, even on the few occasions when it could muster the twenty Oireachtas seats needed for a nomination. The only previous three-way contest had been in 1945, when the third candidate, Dr McCartan, was not formally associated with any party but had left-wing republican credentials. The idea that an independent candidate would be elected – let alone a women standing as an independent candidate – would have been regarded as unthinkable not only by the political elites but by the electorate as a whole.

In 1966 and 1969 a penniless barrister, broadcaster and genealogist, the late Eoin ('The Pope') O'Mahony, had made a quixotic attempt to secure a nomination for the contest but had barely got to first base. O'Mahony was a man of some personal charm who, in the words of one writer, 'combined paunch and panache', and made a voluble pilgrimage around the county councils seeking their nominations. As these, too, were controlled by the major parties, he could have spared his breath.

The presidency, although elected by universal adult suffrage, was effectively in the grip of the political machine and the pattern had already become clear: Fianna Fáil, which had since 1932 been the largest political party in the State, regarded the institution as peculiarly its own.

There were, nonetheless, elections to the presidency in both 1966 and 1973 but after that the political establishment had evidently grown weary of such costly and apparently fruitless exercises. When President Erskine Childers died in office in 1974, he was succeeded without an election by a former Chief Justice (and former Fianna Fáil election candidate) Cearbhall Ó Dálaigh. When he resigned in 1976, he was succeeded by the former Fianna Fáil Cabinet minister Patrick Hillery, who was also selected unopposed and who served two full terms. By 1990, therefore, the presidency had been uncontested during a seventeen-year period which had seen half a dozen changes of government and the retirement or defeat of a whole generation of senior Irish politicians. In fact, in the fifty-three years since the post was first established, there had been only four elections in all and all incumbents, with two exceptions, were former Fianna Fáil ministers. The exceptions were Hyde, the first president, and Ó Dálaigh.

The same period had also seen unprecedented changes in Irish society as the tide of emigration had been stemmed and finally reversed and a new generation of young Irish men and women challenged the assumptions of a past which had been more often romanticised than analysed. The presidency was untouched by all this change but it was not immune from controversy. Ó Dálaigh's resignation in 1976 was precipitated by an adverse comment from Patrick Donegan, the Fine Gael Minister for Defence, on the President's decision to refer a piece of security legislation to the Supreme Court to test its constitutionality. His successor, Patrick Hillery, had to cope with a series of rumours about his private life which he eventually scotched by adopting the expedient, unheard of up to then, of inviting media to Áras an Uachtaráin for a briefing on the matter.

The chief role of the President is to be the guardian of the Constitution, the fundamental law of the State. This was at the core of Ó Dálaigh's resignation: under the Constitution, the President was commander-in-chief of the armed forces. The offence caused by Donegan's criticism, which was made at a military function, could not be assuaged by the limp apology that was offered and resignation was the only option left – either that of the Minister or that of the President.

Like Ó Dálaigh, Mary Robinson was a lawyer and a constitutional lawyer to boot. She also possessed a number of key personal characteristics, notably an engaging (sometimes even uncomfortable) openness and honesty and an astonishing degree of physical resilience and strength. In a sense, therefore, her twenty years of experience had prepared her better for this post than almost anyone else who was likely to be nominated. Not that this had ever been an objective of hers: she had lectured on the presidency as part of the country's constitutional framework but the thought of actually running for that office had never entered her head.

The original suggestion of Mary Robinson's name had in fact been made almost as an afterthought, in the way that suggestions are made by people who never seriously expect that they will be taken up, by Denise Rogers, secretary to Ruairí Quinn. The suggestion eventually percolated to John Rogers, the former Attorney-General (no relation of Denise), who looked at it carefully from every angle before adopting it with a growing sense of enthusiasm.

There were, however, two potential problems. One was named Mary Robinson, the other Dick Spring. The relationship between the potential candidate and the party leader had been respectful but never close. Mary Robinson's politics were driven by issues and by a burning sense of injustice which was often impatient of other people's timetables and which placed a low priority on the wheeling and dealing which is often the necessary preliminary to political progress. In her early years in the Senate, Mary Robinson developed an almost unique capacity to annoy the leader of the Fianna Fáil majority there by her frontal assaults, to the point where she could not expect any political cooperation – and perhaps did not much want it from that quarter.

In 1982-87, during a period when Spring was fighting desperately to achieve control over the quarrelsome and factious party organisation, Mary Robinson's perceived pushiness on the issues – contraception and divorce among them – sometimes appeared as a distraction from the organisational and political challenge to which he had to give priority. This was all the more so if it had the effect, however unintended by Mary Robinson herself, of strengthening the position of his still numerous critics within the party. The irony was that there were few if any issues, apart from Northern Ireland, on which he and Mary Robinson would have disagreed. As Spring saw it, there was no point in speaking about issues if you did not have a united party behind you to push for political delivery of results. She was not, in his view, a good team player. It was a judgement with which Mary Robinson might at times have agreed; but she could not be anything other than what she was.

Rogers's job, therefore, was two-fold: to sell Robinson to Spring and to sell Spring to Robinson. It was a task he achieved with considerable skill and Spring came quickly on board. There was a series of meetings, all of them intensely private, at which key issues were resolved. But one issue became a major stumbling-block. This was whether Mary Robinson would re-join Labour or not.

Spring wanted her to rejoin, reasoning that this would make her candidacy easier to sell to the PLP and the AC and to the party organisation as a whole. In this he quite misjudged, as it turned out, the readiness with which both these bodies would greet her, even as a non-party member.

Mary Robinson and her adviser, Bride Rosney, were so strongly against re-joining the party that it became, especially for Mary herself, simply non-negotiable. It was not that she had anything against the party as such or that she would be unwilling to accept its nomination. It was that the price of a nomination in such circumstances would have been too high, in that it would imply that she had been wrong to resign from Labour. In addition, the electorate would easily be persuaded that if she was prepared to compromise her principles on this, she could compromise them on other things as well. There was also the danger that membership of the party might subsequently militate against attracting non-Labour voters to her standard. This led to a stand-off. For Spring, re-joining the party was essential; for Mary Robinson her refusal to do so was non-negotiable. Discussions between them then broke down – although amicably enough – for a period of about two weeks at the end of which Spring changed his mind and negotiations resumed.

The final hurdle to be cleared was Noel Browne. Like Mary Robinson, he was no longer a member of the party. Unlike her, he was to some extent still a totem of the Left and indeed would attract a wide cross-party vote, especially among the older voters, on the basis of his career as Minister for Health in 1948-51 (his autobiography, *Against The Tide*, sold an astonishing 80,000 copies). On the other hand, his shortcomings were also a matter of public record. He was unpredictable to a degree that made Mary Robinson's individualism look positively restrained and he could snatch defeat from the jaws of victory, even at Labour Party conferences, by abandoning reasoned political critique in favour of bitter personal invective. His capacity for personalising issues remained: almost his last public utterance, before his death in 1997, was a letter to the *Irish Times* in which he castigated President Mary Robinson's stance on emigration in waspish, wounding words.

Spring attempted a flanking manoeuvre by getting the PLP to endorse his invitation to Mary Robinson on 4 April before submitting it to a joint PLP-AC meeting later in the month. Browne's candidacy, however, was already up and running and his supporters claimed that Spring was attempting a coup. Mary Robinson felt that this was in effect a re-run of the 1985 situation on the basis of which she had left the party – the leadership committing the party to a certain course of action without consultation – and told Spring so, in no uncertain terms. It was not to be the last spat in the campaign but like the others it was smoothed over. Newspaper coverage concentrated on the disagreement between Spring and Browne's supporters in the party, to the extent that Mary Robinson's candidacy was virtually ignored and certainly downplayed. One brief news report in the *Irish Independent*, after the PLP meeting, did no more than lump her in with other potential female candidates.

In the event, the names of Browne and Robinson were both put to the joint meeting on 26 April, Mary Robinson, who had maintained a dignified silence during the pre-meeting manoeuvres, was chosen by a 4:1 majority. Supporters of Browne like Emmet Stagg and Michael D. Higgins moved back loyally behind her and were to expend huge energy in her campaign.

For the time being, however, that was all that anyone thought it would be – a campaign. The hurdles to be overcome were immense. The first was the size of the Labour vote. Although Spring had increased the number of Labour TDs to fifteen at the 1989 election, the party's national vote was still no higher than 9%.

Nomination was one thing, election another. Good candidates have been defeated before now and the conventional wisdom was that, for all her evident qualities, Mary Robinson was destined to be a gallant loser. There was little in the early months of the Robinson candidacy to suggest to the commentators and analysts that here was anything more than a campaign destined at best for honourable defeat. If they had been more familiar with her background and her track record they would have given her better odds from the start.

An election committee was set up, headed by Ruairí Quinn of Labour and including Bride Rosney, Mary Robinson's by now seasoned campaign adviser, and Brenda O'Hanlon. O'Hanlon was an experienced and skilful PR executive, who resigned from her job to join the campaign, handling press relations with skill and enthusiasm. Bride Rosney, whose role was sometimes resented by Labour campaigners because she (quite understandably) tended to put Mary Robinson's interests above those of the party, was to become special adviser to the President immediately after the election, an appointment which was itself innovative. But she was 'not just another activist, she was a part of the intimate family circle with an emotional, psychological link to the candidate that no-one else could match.'[30]

Bride Rosney's role during the campaign and throughout the presidency itself fascinated some observers. *Phoenix*, the fortnightly Irish magazine which mixes political and financial gossip, scandal and satire, continually dubs her 'Richelieu'. The inference is clear – and it is actually the same inference that others sought to draw from the differences between Mary Robinson the senator-lawyer and Mary Robinson the campaigner. It is that Mary Robinson is not much more than a well-groomed puppet, the creature of her media managers or – in this case – of a dark and mysterious force named Bride Rosney. The hidden grammar of this assertion is that Mary Robinson actually doesn't have a mind of her own, a proposition whose untruth is probably more evident to Bride Rosney than to anyone else.

Much was made, especially during the election, of the supposed changes in Mary Robinson's persona and presentation. Certainly, some things were altered. Her hair-style was changed but in order to reveal more of her features rather than to supply a spurious glamour; and her clothes were carefully chosen – in the final analysis, it must be said, by herself – to express a side of her personality that had always been there but that had to some extent been concealed behind the working uniforms of barrister and senator. The changes were most noticed by people who did not really know her well. To her intimates, what was happening was that a private person was learning – and she had to learn rapidly – to give the private qualities she had always possessed, but rarely exhibited, a new public dimension and expression. What was significant about the learning process was not just that it was so rapid and so effective but that it was essentially driven by something within the candidate rather than being externally imposed. She knew she had to do it but she could not have done it if she had not felt that it was worth doing, not just for the campaign but for herself.

The election committee was eventually to include representatives of the other parties, including the Workers Party. The participation of the Workers Party was especially problematic for Labour. The two parties were fighting for the allegiance of the Irish political left and for the past few years each had been trying to claim-jump the other. When one was in government, the other was in opposition, claiming greater ideological purity. And at the time of the presidential election, the Workers Party actually held more Dáil seats in Dublin – the great prize for any party claiming the allegiance of the working-class – than Labour. There were tensions from the beginning and it is a tribute to the management skills of the people involved that these tensions never surfaced in public and, more importantly, did not operate to undermine her growing public support.

At this stage Mary Robinson needed all the support she could get. Fianna Fáil had been in the field before her, in the sense that the candidature of Brian Lenihan had been an open secret for months. Lenihan was Tánaiste, one of the best-liked politicians outside as well as inside Fianna Fáil. He had been one of the bright young men hand-picked by Seán Lemass in the 1950s to rejuvenate a party which was beginning to resemble its even then antediluvian founder, Eamon de Valera, and had held a succession of ministerial offices, including most famously that of Minister for Fisheries, where his tendency to bluster earned him the opposition soubriquet of 'the Bismarck of the lobster-pots'. The level of popular sympathy for him can best be gauged from the fact that when he won his seat in the 1989 general election he was not even in the country: he was in an American hospital being treated for a serious liver complaint.

If Mary Robinson's prospects looked bleak *vis-à-vis* Fianna Fáil, however, Fine Gael's problems were worse. The perceived impossibility of beating Brian Lenihan would quite possibly have led that party to support his nomination if Mary Robinson had not already been entered in the lists by Labour. But now that Labour had a candidate, they had to have one too. There was not exactly a rush to the barricades. A number of potential high-profile candidates inside and outside the party were approached – some said as many as seventeen – but they all found that they had more urgent matters to attend to. The mantle eventually fell on Austin Currie, the Fine Gael TD for Dublin West.

Currie was as extraordinary in some ways as Mary Robinson. He was a Northerner and had been active in the old Nationalist Party as a young firebrand, squatting in a local authority house to draw attention to discriminatory housing policies and eventually helping to form the SDLP. He had even served as a minister in the power-sharing executive formed briefly with the Unionists in 1974, but in the late 1970s and 1980s his home was subjected to increasingly violent attacks and his wife Anita was the object of a particularly vicious sectarian assault. In 1989 he left the North and moved to Dublin, joined Fine Gael and stood successfully for that party in Dublin West: he was later to serve as a junior minister, thus becoming the only person ever to have served in administrations on both sides of the Border.

On paper, therefore, he was a challenging candidate. But even within Fine

Gael there were signs of deep unhappiness about the possible outcome. Some party members, sniffing the wind, suggested that it might be an idea to run two candidates, with Carmencita Hederman, the popular (and non-aligned) former Lord Mayor of Dublin, added to the ticket to neutralise Mary Robinson's growing appeal. This stratagem was abandoned when the party realised that Carmencita might beat their official candidate into fourth place. Currie was eventually chosen despite the evidence of private polls: one commentator said he might have some difficulty in coming third in a three-horse race.

There were four principal elements to the Robinson campaign. The first was that it was, organisationally, a successful, though often tension-filled, coalition between Robinson supporters and members of Labour and the Workers Party. The second was that it was, politically, the successful reaping of a harvest that had in fact been planted and tended by Mary Robinson, to a degree unconsciously, over twenty years of unremitting political and legal activity. The third was the ability to capitalise on the mistakes of her opponents. The fourth was that the election proved to be a period of extraordinary personal growth for Mary Robinson herself. She found, in an Ireland of which the political establishment is aware only at election time, a warmth and a response that awoke something in herself and gave her a public and private ease in campaigning which was as unforced as it was effective. The professorial hand movements and the sometimes slightly stilted public delivery remained; but they were now buttressed – supplanted, almost – by a quiet charisma and a sureness of touch which astonished people who had seen her lose political battles inside the Labour Party and for Dáil seats and who had come to assume that she would never be more than a classic liberal, hopelessly out of touch with the political realities of life.

The progress of the election committee is best summed up by one of its key members, Fergus Finlay, then as now Spring's closest adviser:

> For a long time, antagonism dominated the work of the committee. From the very first meeting, the atmosphere was tense and frequently carping. Two camps emerged, the Robinson camp and the Labour camp. The Robinson camp were anxious from an early stage to secure the endorsement of the Workers Party, the Progressive Democrats, the Green Party and as many other groups as possible, including independent senators and TDs. They suspected the Labour camp of dragging its heels. The Labour camp, on the other hand, was becoming more and more convinced that the Robinson camp was trying to play down its association with Labour all the time. These suspicions festered on both sides for months – but, unfortunately, a great deal of time was allowed to lapse before they were properly aired and dealt with.[31]

The suspicions were eventually aired but it is less certain that they were finally dealt with. Up to the end of the campaign tensions remained and only the victory applied necessary balm to the wounds that were still to some extent festering on both sides. The rawness of the experience is fully documented, not only by Fergus Finlay but by Emily O'Reilly:

> September saw endless squabbles between Labour and the Workers Party. Eamon Gilmore, Workers Party TD for Dun Laoghaire, made repeated attempts to get on the campaign committee, and Ruairí Quinn and others did their level best to keep him off ... Gilmore finally gained his committee seat on 10 October, less than a month before the election. When he did, Quinn set up a new core group that met apart from the main committee. Tensions were also running high between the Robinsons and the Labour Party ... What really maddened Rosney was when Robinson was tagged in the media as 'the candidate of the Left'.[32]

The management of the tensions involved fell principally to Ruairí Quinn, Fergus Finlay and, to an extent not generally observed, Nick Robinson, who was a quiet but solid and immensely skilful presence throughout the campaign. One of the few occasions when Robinson and Finlay fell out was during the bus tour, when a meal was ordered by mobile phone from a hotel in the next town on their itinerary. The wine, ordered by Robinson, came to considerably more than the cost of the food. Similar tensions were to re-emerge in the immediate aftermath of her election and to persist through the early years of her presidency.

For the time being all this was under wraps or in the future and the business of the election campaign absorbed everyone's attention. One of the central ironies of what was happening, however, was that many of her most experienced supporters not only did not expect her to win but were preparing to settle for a moral victory based on any substantial increase in the core Labour vote. Anything over the 9% that Labour had won in the last election would be cause for quiet satisfaction and public exaggeration. The real objective was not winning – for that was plainly out of the question – but beating Fine Gael into third place. The prospect of coming second had in fact occurred to Dick Spring even before Mary Robinson had emerged as the party's candidate, but the dominant assumption still was that Labour and Fine Gael, in whatever combination, would be incapable of overcoming Lenihan's appeal. There was a strong Labour Party view that the success of the campaign would ultimately be judged, not just by the percentage of the vote it garnered, but by the extent to which Lenihan would be forced to take up and respond to the issues raised. Increasing the vote and setting the agenda: these were the two key Labour objectives. For quite a long time, a win for Mary Robinson was pie in the sky.

Fergus Finlay was one of the first of the Labour Party people to realise that the election was actually winnable. 'What made her such a great candidate', he said later, 'was that she knew, as soon as it was suggested, that she would make a great president.' In the summer of 1990, he got odds of 10/1 at Paddy Power, the bookmakers, on a Robinson victory. So did Bride Rosney. The size of the odds they were given speaks for itself. The bookmakers were to make money out of the election itself, as they generally do. Paddy Power made £10,500 on Robinson's victory; had Brian Lenihan won, he would have lost £21,000. As late as August, on the other hand, a campaign group involving both Spring and Ruairí Quinn was enthusiastically speculating about the great speech an unsuccessful Mary Robinson would make after the count, riding on the crest of a wave generated by an anticipated 28% of the vote. Even the prospect of defeat at this level was exhilarating. Nor was there much support outside the confines of the Robinson camp, if this was measured by campaign contributions. A number of unpaid volunteers worked hard to raise funds but business was cool and 'company after company told the fund-raisers that "if this were a general election there'd be no problem – because then it would be in our interests to contribute".'[33] By the end of the campaign, the Robinson camp had raised £140,000 and spent £220,000. Fianna Fáil had probably spent £2 million, including an utterly wasted, last-minute advertising campaign. It was impossible to estimate what Fine Gael had spent.

The second element – the harvesting of political support – was in itself a tribute to Mary Robinson's dogged persistence over the years in pursuing causes that many others would have given up for lost. Not that she had won all of them; but many of those with or for whom she had worked had come to recognise in her qualities which the political establishment as a whole had discounted. Many of her causes were effectively minority ones but there were so many of them that, when they were all added together, they suggested another question: how many minorities do you need behind you to become a majority? She even had the gift of uniting groups in her support who would generally be antipathetic or even hostile to each other, simply because she had represented each of them in the legal system with equal vigour and commitment: prisoners and prison warders, for example. Her longer-term commitments were equally significant. She had been a founder member of the Women's Political Association; she had been closely involved with, and, since its foundation, president of, Cherish, the organisation for single parents; and she had always been a valuable legal, psychological and political back-up to the work of AIM, the family law and counselling service.

In all of this, her appeal to women was a trump card. Women, in a sense, were beginning to find themselves the focus of political attention in a way that they had never been before. And the process which focused on them also identified leaders: a new generation of women who emerged into their leadership roles on merit alone and because they represented an authentic response to a new historical phenomenon. This is not to say that all women thought alike on the question of Northern Ireland, on employment legislation, on contraception or on anything. Whatever they thought, though, they were finding voices in which to express it.

Mary Robinson's was one of those voices, from the beginning – although not always alone or uncontested. 'Away back in 1969, when young Mary Bourke first came on the scene, a lot of newly baptised feminists were disappointed that she wouldn't espouse the women's movement ideology wholeheartedly. She then proceeded to champion every cause from women on juries through contraception, divorce, abolition of illegitimacy, equal pay and pensions; and today, she's in court on equity in the social welfare code. No one has shouted less and achieved more.'[34]

It was a trump card because it cut across all the political boundaries. In Donegal, Kay McGlinchy, wife to one of the most prominent Fianna Fáil politicians in the country, declared for Mary Robinson and worked for her with a vigour and commitment common to the inheritors of that doughty political tradition. So did her two daughters, one of whom was to stand as a Labour Party candidate in the 1995 local elections. Mary O'Shea, a journalist in Cork, helped as did well-known chef, Darina Allen, in the same city. The activist Noreen Byrne, later to be chairperson of the Council for the Status of Women, was a staunch supporter. At the other end of the social spectrum, groups like the women's group in Coolock, a sprawl of Dublin working-class housing with far more than its fair share of social and economic problems, contributed to an energisation of female political support unknown for any candidate before, male or female.

By the time her election campaign took off, that heightened sense of consciousness was like a brush fire waiting for the spark of tinder. Women who had voted against every cause she had espoused were among those who turned out to vote for her. But even outside the narrow confines of the election itself, there was a sense of fresh green shoots appearing in the social undergrowth. 'In my travels around Ireland', Mary Robinson said in her inauguration speech, 'I have found local community groups thriving on a new sense of self-confidence and self-empowerment. Whether it was groups concerned with adult education, employment initiatives, women's support, local history and heritage, environmental concern or community culture, one of the most enriching discoveries was to witness the extent of this local empowerment at work.'

She did not add, although she might well have done, that women did not constitute just one of the groups in this list but played an unnoticed, substantial and increasing part in all of them. Equally significant was her realisation that the phenomenon of the self-development of women was not one which was limited to the area of sexual politics or which flourished only in urban areas: it permeated huge tracts of social, economic and community activity in rural as well as in urban Ireland. As she observed in a speech just before becoming

President: 'That is the beginning of a very real change in this country.'

Her election as President was accompanied by, and may well have stimulated, the creation of hundreds of women's groups all over Ireland. Networking became a buzz-word and many of the groups found that just as Mary Robinson had been ready to visit them on the campaign trail so the doors of Áras an Uachtaráin were open to them now.

The final MRBI opinion poll before the election showed women voters almost equally divided between the two leading candidates – 44% for Mary Robinson as against 43% for Brian Lenihan. In the circumstances, Lenihan's achievement in level pegging with Robinson in the battle for the woman's vote was almost miraculous; but it was not enough. On polling day, 7 November, experienced election workers from all parties noted, some with justifiable apprehension, one significant difference from recent elections. The common pattern up to then had been for married women voters to accompany their husbands to the polling stations and to vote at the same time. Now they were turning up before their husbands, alone or in the company of other women. Without a word being said, new territory was being staked out. One woman voter in Dun Laoghaire, who confessed to having been a Fianna Fáil voter all her life, thrust a Fianna Fáil canvasser angrily away with the words: 'I'm voting for a women who tells the truth, even if I don't agree with everything she says.'[35]

Party supporters in their different camps remained for quite some time unaware of the pulling power Mary Robinson's twenty-year career had generated. For some of them, the defining moment came relatively late in the campaign, when the Belgian-made battle-bus, vintage 1986, pulled into the tiny village of Kiltimagh for an election meeting. Kiltimagh is in Mayo, which would in itself partly account for an element of curiosity about a Mayo woman running for the presidency. But not even this could account for the enthusiasm generated by her visit to a community which had probably never even registered a Labour vote, let alone seen a Labour Party member, where even the name of the Workers Party was probably unknown and where the Greens were normally thought of only as vegetables.

The Kiltimagh meeting itself was part of the second phase of a carefully-planned strategy. According to one of her close advisers, it was effectively divided in two roughly equal periods. In the first period, she listened. She suggested to her audiences that the presidency did not need to be a fusty relic of the first half of the twentieth century and invited them to contribute their ideas to the process of re-making it. She had done 14,000 miles of this sort of campaigning before the other candidates were even in the field. In the second period, and after absorbing the messages she had heard and integrating them with her own ideas, she re-traced her steps, giving her by now rapidly growing audiences – at another Mayo venue five hundred people waited for her for half an hour in the winter rain when her schedule slipped – a potent mixture of what they had already told her they wanted and what in her bones she felt she could give.

Mary Robinson herself sensed in August that the battle was there for the winning, as she explained to the author. 'There was a moment, just before Nick and I took a week off in France in August, that I began to realise that this actually was winnable. I'd been getting an increasingly good reaction on the ground. I had been talking to community radio and local journalists and they had been giving me pages of publicity but at the end of it would be: "What a pity she won't make it" or, "Wouldn't she be a good candidate but there isn't a hope ..."

'Then, I went into a small meeting and suddenly I realised that everybody (a) knew who I was, (b) knew I was there as a presidential candidate, and (c) were there to meet me, believing that I would make a very good President. I remember feeling quite frightened and that this could be a very demanding change completely in my life. I said this to Nick, and Nick said, as only Nick could: "Sure, I've known that for a long time!" But I had a moment of what was actually a kind of fear: "This is for real, this is frightening, I've got to think about this," as opposed to "I've got to make a case for an elected President." I was always good at making the case as an advocate – I was really making the case up to that point. From the moment we came back from that holiday I was absolutely committed and pretty sure that we would win.'

The third element in the Robinson campaign was the ability to capitalise on the mistakes of her opponents. Initially, there was not much to seize on. Lenihan quickly developed and maintained a commanding lead in the opinion polls although it certainly seemed that the Mary Robinson/Austin Currie duel was more evenly matched than Fine Gael supporters would have liked.

In the first week of October things were looking well for Lenihan. He was registering in the opinion polls at 49%, six per cent over the core Fianna Fáil vote. The figures were a disaster for Currie who was showing at 19%. Mary Robinson at 32% was already 4% better than some of her supporters had in their wildest dreams hoped she would be. While Fianna Fáil were coasting, Fine Gael was in panic. Currie's party therefore seized on what it thought was a golden opportunity when, in the same week, *Hot Press* published an interview with her in which she appeared to indicate that she would, as President, be prepared to officially open a contraceptive stall in Dublin's Virgin Megastore. What had happened was that a Robinson mannerism – answering 'yes' at the beginning of what she had to say, not to signify assent to the question itself but to indicate that she had understood it and was prepared to answer – had been grotesquely, if understandably, misread.

Within the Robinson camp, there was something approaching dismay.

They moved swiftly into damage limitation mode, as her opponents tried to make the most of it. There were rumblings within Fine Gael of opposition to her 'liberal' views. Paradoxically, her misunderstood remark on contraception bulked considerably larger in the controversy than her quite unambiguous pledge, given in the same interview and accurately reported, to support the rights of gays if she were elected. As things turned out, her supporters' concern was to some extent misplaced. The voters who were already moving to her side were either uninterested in the controversy or decided that her opponents were going overboard in their attempt to make something of it.

On 22 October, barely a fortnight before polling day, the political landscape changed dramatically. In a statement that afternoon, and on the evening RTE television programme 'Questions and Answers', Garret FitzGerald raised an issue that had been lying around for months but that nobody had bothered to pick up or had seen the significance of at the time. A post-graduate politics student in UCD, Jim Duffy, had interviewed Brian Lenihan on tape as part of his research for a thesis on the presidency. In the course of the interview Lenihan had remarked, with the insouciance which was his stock in trade, that he had made a telephone call to President Hillery in 1982, when Charles Haughey had lost his Dáil majority; that he had urged the President to exercise his constitutional prerogative not to dissolve the Dáil; and that Hillery had told him to 'back off'. Duffy's report of the conversation had actually appeared as part of a series of articles he had written for the *Irish Times*, but had gone virtually unnoticed.

This suddenly became a major issue. Brian Lenihan charged Duffy with inaccuracy but a tape-recording of their conversation, played at a press conference organised by the *Irish Times*, proved that Duffy had incontrovertible evidence for his statement. Lenihan's only possible response was to argue, as he then did in an emotional television appearance, that on 'mature recollection' he now believed his statement to Duffy to have been erroneous. Lenihan's campaign had been deeply damaged but at the same time there was an astonishing burst of sympathy for a man who had returned to active political life in the wake of major surgery and for the evident strain which this series of events had caused for himself and his family. He was eventually dismissed from his ministerial post by Haughey on 31 October, nine days later, after the Progressive Democrats, Fianna Fáil's partner in government, had made their dissatisfaction clear, though this if anything gave added momentum to the Fianna Fáil fight-back. The Party's sense of urgency was increased by polls in which Robinson was now showing at more than 50% and Lenihan at 31%. In the Robinson camp, Mary Robinson herself was one of the few counselling caution, remarking, 'If he goes down, he can come up again.'[36]

As this fight-back gathered momentum, the Robinson campaign itself faltered. 'There's a perception that Brian Lenihan's problems helped,' Mary Robinson said many years later, with the total recall for the minutiae of campaigns that is the special preserve of elected politicians. 'But until that point Brian was getting no momentum. It was after he made his mistake on TV that he started to get the momentum and then we were terrified because the fightback had started and people were getting very enthusiastic.

'Paradoxically in Ireland, when you make a mistake in public people love you – they love you for the human element of it. Brian was getting huge crowds after that and all the opinion polls had him ahead of me on first preferences.'

In a television debate between the three contenders, a tired Mary Robinson, on the basis of advice from the broadcaster and journalist, Eoghan Harris, attacked Lenihan strongly instead of maintaining a distance from the controversy. It was a distinct blip in the campaign and although she pulled back some ground in a subsequent television appearance (in which her husband, Nick, also played a strong part) the two candidates were very closely matched going into the final week. Harris, for his part, was a strong influence in the campaign right from the start when he addressed a lengthy letter to Mary Robinson outlining his proposed strategy.[37] His advice in relation to the TV debate was misplaced, but in many other respects he had a knack for achieving a brilliant focus on issues of which the campaign might have been aware in a general way and which it had to address strategically. He also played a major part in the creation of a series of TV commercials for the candidate, the last one of which is universally acknowledged to have been a classic.

Not everyone who worked on the campaign saw Harris in the same light and his suggestions had sometimes to be moderated by the wise counsel of Nicholas Robinson, who in many respects admired him. One fellow campaigner suggested, many years afterwards, that Harris had been invaluable but that the best way of dealing with him would have been to have him in a locked room, provided with all the creature comforts he might desire and asked simply to generate opinions and advice – on the strict understanding that not all of it had to be accepted.

One final attack on the Robinson candidacy was made by a Fianna Fáil TD who asked in a speech: 'Is she going to have an abortion referral clinic in Áras an Uachtaráin?'[38] Paradoxically, this was so offensive that it gave Mary Robinson the energy, in what was the last week of the campaign, to lay to rest finally what Harris had earlier called the 'distortion issue'. In a television interview carried out almost immediately afterwards, she responded to the anticipated hard questions about her own views and about her role as a lawyer for the 'Right to Information' campaign waged by a number of student groups with a controlled anger, clarity and firmness that buried the issue for the rest of the campaign.

As the competition intensified, so did the commentary. Most Irish media maintained neutrality or at least did their best to conceal any editorial preferences they might have had until the very end. British media were not so inhibited. Just before polling day the *Sunday Telegraph*'s Stan Gebler Davies penned a diatribe against the person he described as 'this horrid woman' and reflected with undisguised alarm on the prospect of spending the next seven years 'giving out, as we say in Ireland, on such subjects as single-parent families, the plight of the homeless or jobless or itinerant, and the necessity of introducing into our comfortable if somewhat ramshackle society some element of the compassionate and caring society. Such is the pliability of the Irish people and so deep-seated the desire to please, at whatever cost to others, that some of what she advocates may well get enacted, if only to get her to shut up. The suffering which is the consequence of all liberal legislation would be widespread, devastating and almost entirely confined to the lower orders.'[39] At the other end of the spectrum, the Irish edition of the *Daily Mirror* published on its front page on polling day what was to all intents and purposes a political poster for the Robinson candidacy.

All this was in the last week of the campaign and there was a sense, difficult to pin down, that the Robinson campaign, which had come from nowhere suddenly to look like a winner, had faltered. The Lenihan one then tripped over its own bootlaces. The occasion was a widely-listened to radio programme, 'Saturday View', on which Pádraig Flynn, a Cabinet minister from Mary Robinson's own county of Mayo, took the pin out of a 'family values' hand grenade and lobbed it in her direction.

'She was pretty well constructed in this campaign by her handlers the Labour Party and the Workers Party,' he said. 'Of course, it doesn't always suit if you get labelled a socialist because that's a very narrow focus in this country – so she has to try and have it both ways. She has to have new clothes and her new look and her new hairdo and she has the new interest in family, being a mother and all that kind of thing. But you know, none of us who knew Mary Robinson very well in previous incarnations ever heard her claiming to be a great wife and mother.' He went on like a bull-dozer, through mounting protests and interruptions from fellow-panellists: 'Mary Robinson reconstructs herself to fit the fashion of the time, so we have this thing about how you can be substituted at will, whether it's the pro-socialist thing, or pro-contraception, or pro-abortion or whatever it is.'[40]

All that was necessary now was for Mary Robinson to lob the grenade back before it exploded. In a sense, she didn't even have to do that: an abject apology from Flynn within hours not only failed to undo the damage his remark had caused to Brian Lenihan but actually reinforced people's memory of what he had said. He might as well have carved it with a chisel on the heart of every woman in Ireland.

The fourth element in Mary Robinson's campaign was what was happening to the candidate herself. She was still focusing on issues, on the nature and potential of the presidency, in a way which set the intellectual pace of the debate. But something else was in the process of being liberated inside her – something buried deep in her youth and upbringing and which had been to some extent overlaid by the almost entirely male, even macho, world of the Senate, the Bar and Academe. Even to those who had known her well for years, there seemed to be a softening of the persona; she seemed to be turning into a different person – not better or worse, but different, more rounded. It was as if essentially private traits had suddenly found a public dimension, almost of a personality released from some confinement. To those who knew her best it was not a surprise; but there was surprise, nonetheless, at the seamless way in which the private Mary Robinson of old became the new and more public figure. People who had seen her at close quarters in her legal work – not in court, where argument, confrontation and quotation are the weapons of war, but in consultation with ordinary, often distressed and frequently all but helpless plaintiffs – knew that she did not lack a human touch. What was new was not that she had discovered it but that she had learned how to express it in public, in front of the cameras.

The point of Flynn's remark about 'handlers' was, of course, to imply that the 'real' Mary Robinson (whoever that might be – her critics were careful not to be too specific) was still there, hidden under a new hairdo, a changed voice-tone, new clothes and some smart PR advice. Don't trust the image, was the message: we know better.

The problem about this kind of analysis, however, is its central implication: that image is all, that mutton can be dressed as lamb, that you can fool all of the people all of the time. The truth, as seasoned practitioners of the black art of public relations know well, is that public relations techniques can help to solve image problems, insofar as the image that has to be changed is unfair to the reality of the person involved. Public relations cannot solve a reality problem. It cannot – except for very short periods and at a very high risk – turn black into white or even into grey. In more than six months of campaigning, any flaws in the Robinson reality quotient would have been ruthlessly exposed. Glitches there were and occasional maladroitness but basically, by November of 1990, what you saw in Mary Robinson was what you got.

Four years later, the poet Seamus Heaney put it with more elegance when he suggested that 'her endured life and her public life are the same thing. Whatever has been thought out and internalised is part and parcel of her personality. They are the same as her public discourse. The personality that's on view is the personality that's available in her home. That's very unusual in this world.'[41]

Pádraig Flynn was eventually appointed as Ireland's member of the European Commission. As further penance for his misdeeds, he had to face an angry European Parliament ratification hearing in January 1995, where female MEPs, well primed with the memory of his unsuccessful attempt to stymie Mary Robinson's candidature, did their level best to roast him alive. But he is in some respects a much underrated politician, quick to learn and to adapt and his tenure as Commissioner with responsibility for social affairs was marked by a number of important initiatives in favour of women's rights. Perhaps he, too, learned to adapt a public perception to a private persona.

There was one other area in which Mary Robinson's *bona fides* were sometimes questioned, usually behind the back of people's hands. This was her attitude to the Irish language. There is so much lip-service paid to the Irish language, especially by Irish politicians, that if someone who has previously shown little or no interest in it suddenly discovers an enthusiasm for it they run the risk of immediately being accused of opportunism.

Insofar as can be ascertained, Mary Robinson's views on Irish before the beginning of the campaign would, like those of many of her contemporaries, have been benevolently neutral. Mayo, her home county, still has a small area where Irish is habitually spoken; further to the west is the Connemara Gaeltacht, already at the time of her campaign the home of the Irish-language national radio service; to the North is the Donegal Gaeltacht. She could not ignore Irish, but neither would she, or could she, throw herself into it with a bogus fervour.

As it happened, it did not become an issue during the campaign. Even if it had, her opponents would have been on shaky ground had they chosen to criticise her because the homage paid by all political parties to the national language has generally been perfunctory. But there is evidence that, as part of her re-discovery of herself and of the country of which she was an integral part, she also re-discovered the Irish language. She did not rediscover it simply as a set of symbols, as a totem, or as a handy drum to beat but as a key which unlocked yet another part of Ireland for her and at the same time opened the door to an inner, more personal resource. She spoke in Irish in her acceptance speech, where her use of the phrase 'Mná na hÉireann' – women of Ireland – raised the rafters. She used it again, already more fluently, at her inauguration. She took pains as President to improve her Irish. And as she did so, she made it clear that this did not put her in anyone's camp: at a ceremony to celebrate the memory of Douglas Hyde, Ireland's first President and a passionate supporter of the Irish language, she made it clear that her own commitment to the language did not echo Hyde's vision of a 'de-Anglicised' Ireland and that her own vision was for a 'pluralist, open Ireland within Europe'.[42]

Polling day and the counting of votes was a crescendo of unutterable hopes realised, of joy quite unconfined. As one woman voter mused in disbelief: 'It's the first time in forty years I've voted for anyone who's actually been *elected* ...' The final opinion poll had shown Mary Robinson and Brian Lenihan on 43% each: in the event, her vote was slightly less than that, his slightly more.

Brian Lenihan, as had been widely expected, headed the poll with 694,484 votes (44.1% of the 64% of the electorate who voted). Mary Robinson, for whom Labour Party sources had been predicting 24% or 25% only months earlier, had 612,265 (38.9%). Austin Currie trailed in third place with 267,902 (17%).

Robinson came first in 25 of the 41 parliamentary constituencies, in every constituency in Dublin and in every constituency but one in Cork. Both she and Lenihan were short of the quota, which was 787,327, and the result would be determined by the distribution of Currie's votes. In the event, it was hardly in question from the moment of starting to count the transfers: 242,363 of Currie's votes were transferable and for every one that went to Lenihan Mary Robinson got more than five. She ended up with 817,830 (52.8%) against Lenihan's final total of 731,273 (47.2%).

It was all over bar the shouting and there was a fair amount of that. The fall-out went beyond what anyone could have expected and lasted for a full two years. One of the earliest casualties, almost immediately after the election, was the Fine Gael leader, Alan Dukes. His decision to step down was inevitably and directly related to the catastrophic performance by Austin Currie. The next casualty was the Taoiseach, Charles Haughey. Haughey had survived so many attempted putsches since becoming head of the party in 1979 that he had come to lead what seemed like a charmed life. However, the misjudged general election called in 1989 had weakened him, forcing him into reliance on a coalition with the Progressive Democrats. Mary Robinson's defeat of Brian Lenihan just pulled the bung out of the barrel. Within months, his Minister for Finance, Albert Reynolds, had moved against him, was defeated and resigned from his ministry. He was not destined to remain there for long. A second, better-planned attempt by what came to be described as the 'Country and Western' tendency in Fianna Fáil finally bore fruit in early February 1992 and Reynolds emerged phoenix-like from the back benches to take the increasingly embattled Haughey's place.

The final fruit of the campaign was the Labour Party's unexpectedly good showing in the 1991 local elections, which were themselves the foundation for the astonishing electoral performance by the Party in the 1992 general election. In 1992 it increased its number of seats from 16 to 32 and managed, for the first time in its history, to win two of the seats in two different constituencies. If the Robinson presidency was off to a good start, the Labour bandwagon seemed to be firmly hitched to it.

The newly elected President, Mary Robinson, steps up to the microphone on 9 November 1990 to begin her acceptance speech. (*Irish Times*)

ABOVE: Mary Robinson concludes her speech at her inauguration as President of Ireland. (*Reproduced courtesy of Derek Speirs/Report*)

BELOW: 'A Woman in a Man's World', a prize-winning photograph by Eric Luke of Mary Robinson inspecting the guard of honour. (*Irish Times*)

146

ABOVE: At Pavee Point Traveller's centre in December 1990. Pavee Point was set up as a social and cultural centre for travelling families, and throughout her presidency, Mary Robinson evinced a special regard for travellers, particularly for travelling women. (*Reproduced courtesy of Derek Speirs/Report*)

BELOW: President Robinson's first visit to Belfast on 5 February 1992. She is pictured here with, *left*, Inez McCormack, National Secretary of UNISON, and, *right*, the head of the North's Equal Opportunities Commission, Mary Clark-Glass. (*Associated Press/Irish Times*)

Among the many honorary degrees Mary Robinson has received, the award from Trinity College Dublin – the constituency which she represented for twenty years in the Senate – was of particular significance. The award ceremony in March 1992 took place in St Patrick's Cathedral, Dublin. (*Irish Times*)

President Mary Robinson at the Poor Clare Convent at Nun's Island in Galway in March 1992 –
her first visit to an enclosed order of nuns. She is pictured with the Mother Abbess.
(*Irish Times*)

ABOVE: Not quite in step, but on good terms: President Robinson and Taoiseach Albert Reynolds cross the tarmac at Dublin Airport on her way to Paris on 25 May 1992. (*Associated Press/Irish Times*)

BELOW: Mary Robinson's visit to Somalia in October 1992 led her to criticise the ineffectiveness of the United Nations' work for refugees in that war-devastated area: she was later to make a special plea for Somalia on a visit to the United Nations in New York. (*Irish Times*)

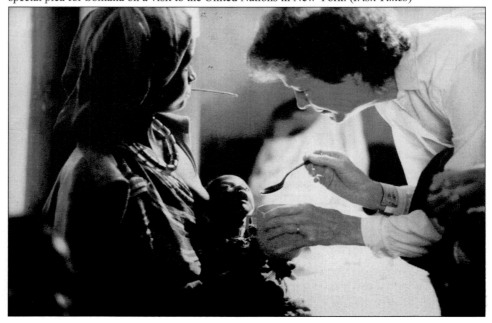

ABOVE: Susan Denham, the first woman to be appointed a judge of the Supreme Court, receives her warrant of appointment from Mary Robinson in December 1992. (*Reproduced courtesy of Derek Speirs/Report*)

BELOW: Mary Robinson's visit to the Rupert Stanley College in Belfast – she is seen here watching a display of Irish dancing – on 18 June 1993, was the setting for one of the most controversial gestures of her presidential career, the (unphotographed) handshake with Gerry Adams, president of Sinn Féin. Adams (bearded) can be seen in profile in the background, almost directly above Nicholas Robinson. (*Reproduced courtesy of Derek Speirs/Report*)

ABOVE: President Robinson and President Nelson Mandela in conversation in Pretoria on the occasion of his inauguration in May 1994. (*Irish Times*)

BELOW: President Robinson with Emperor Akihito of Japan at the beginning of her official visit in February 1995. The presidential visit to Japan was notable for an agenda that addressed both Japan's religious and cultural traditions and its modern, high-tech industrial base. (*Irish Times*)

ABOVE: Dr Patrick Hillery, Mr Justice Liam Hamilton (the Chief Justice) and President Robinson pictured before a meeting of the Council of State to discuss the constitutionality of the Abortion Referral Bill on 16 March 1995. In the background, *right*, is Dr T.K. Whitaker, former Secretary of the Department of Finance and later chairman of the Committee of Experts on the Constitution, who was also a member of the Council of State. (*Irish Times*)

BELOW: President Robinson and her husband, Nick, with Prince Charles, at Áras an Uachtaráin during his visit to Ireland in June 1995. (*Irish Times*)

Meeting Bridie Hyland, a resident of the Dublin Simon Community, in May 1995 after officially opening the Community's two residential houses in Sean MacDermott Street, Dublin.
(*Irish Times*)

Queen Elizabeth II and President Robinson meet for the second time in London in October 1995 –
the relationship between the two heads of state marked a new development in Anglo-Irish
relations. (*Irish Times*)

Seamus Heaney, who was on holiday in Greece when he heard that he had been awarded the Nobel Prize for Literature, was invited to drop in at Áras an Uachtaráin on his way home from Dublin Airport on 7 October 1995. (*Associated Press*)

ABOVE: The President with US President Bill Clinton, 1 December 1995. (*Irish Times*)

BELOW: Pictured with her husband and Gerry Adams, *left*, on a later, less controversial visit to Belfast on 12 September 1996. (*An Phoblacht*)

The British Labour Leader (but not yet Prime Minister) Tony Blair, pays a courtesy visit to Áras an Uachtaráin to meet President Robinson in December 1996. (*Irish Times*)

President Robinson meets Pope John Paul II in Rome in March 1997: the visit occasioned some controversy when an Irish priest studying in Rome published a newspaper article alleging that the presidential style of dress had been unsuitable for the occasion, and amounted to an insult to the papacy. *(Irish Times)*

Mary Robinson receives a standing ovation at the AGM of the Irish Refugee Council in June 1997, shortly after her appointment as UN High Commissioner is made public. (*Irish Times*)

But what kind of a presidency was it to be? Mary Robinson had put down quite a number of very specific markers on policy matters during the course of the campaign. She had a difficult course to steer, in that she had to promise something new and different, and yet the one area in which she was most talented and most eager for change – the area of the Constitution itself – had been put out of bounds by the very fact of her election. This was because, as already noted, the President is the guardian of the Constitution as it is, not as she would like it to be. Almost up to the eve of her election, she travelled with one foot firmly on each side of the demarcation line. She could no longer speak on the Constitution since she would be its guardian, she told one interviewer, but her personal opinion was that the guarantee to Northern unionists on their constitutional status, as it had found expression in the 1985 Anglo-Irish Agreement, should be case-hardened by having it inserted in the Constitution itself.[43] At the core of this argument is the question of 'consent'. The Irish Constitution declares that the national territory consists of the whole island of Ireland, thus finessing the question of the wishes of the Northern unionists, who emphatically want to remain part of the United Kingdom. An additional complication is created by the fact that the 1921 Treaty involved a recognition and acceptance – however unwilling – by the new government of the Irish Free State in Dublin of the border with Northern Ireland. Under Jack Lynch after 1969, increasing emphasis had been put by successive Dublin governments on winning over the unionists rather than compelling them (or getting the British government to compel them) to join in a united Ireland. The first article of the Anglo-Irish Agreement was historic in that it formally recognised and affirmed that 'any change in the status of Northern Ireland would only come about with the consent of a majority of the people in Northern Ireland'. The effect of this was to endorse the unionist veto on unity – not as a political principle but as a political fact of life. What Mary Robinson and others have argued is that a similar formula should now be formally inserted into the Republic's Constitution, not least as a reassurance to the unionists that they will not be coerced into unity. This, it need hardly be added, would present huge difficulties to any Dublin government led by Fianna Fáil, which has never accepted the right of the unionist population to opt out of a united Ireland. In opposition Fianna Fáil would effectively torpedo any attempt by another government to introduce it.

At the same time, Mary Robinson made it clear that if she were elected President, she would feel honour bound to support the Anglo-Irish Agreement which had been the occasion of her departure from the Labour Party five years earlier. She even suggested early on in the campaign that, in the wake of a recent high-profile case of extradition, the Constitution should be changed to allow extradition of suspects who had been charged with crimes of violence, as opposed to political refugees. This was a politically sensitive issue in that, while international law generally prevents the extradition of people who claim their actions were politically motivated, the extent of murder and mayhem in the Northern Ireland conflict was leading Mary Robinson – and eventually led the Irish legislature and the Supreme Court – to narrow the grounds on which suspects could legitimately claim protection from extradition to face charges in another jurisdiction. It was also an area in which Northern politicians frequently reproached the Dublin government – not often with just cause – of being 'soft on terrorism'.

Away from the confrontational area of Northern politics, Mary Robinson enumerated her friends in a way patently designed to leave people in no doubt about where her heart was to be found. Among them were Fr Peter McVerry, the Jesuit priest who has worked with homeless boys in some of the most deprived areas of Dublin; Sister Stanislaus Kennedy, who had in her own way become something of an ambassador for the voiceless in the interstices of the social welfare system; and Sister Colette Dwyer, who had pioneered traveller education.

Mary Robinson foresaw a concrete role for the presidency across a whole range of issues where the Constitution was not directly involved: gay people, emigrants, travellers. She foresaw a new role for the Council of State (later events were to make it clear that this was to be through a broadening of its membership rather than through any enlargement of its constitutional role). The role of the presidency, she said with deceptive simplicity, 'is to speak well of what is going on and to know why. It is to enhance the self-image of the people: the President must focus and focus in a positive way'. And she emphasised the under-valued resources of the presidency and the way in which they could be utilised to link voluntary organisations, to promote core values and to extend the hand of friendship to Northern Ireland. On any other lips, these ideas might have sounded trite or worse: the next seven years were to show exactly how innovative they could become.

As head of State, her personal opinions on a whole range of matters were now suddenly at best irrelevant or, at worst, risk-laden. The challenge to her was to identify areas in which change could take place within the parameters of the Constitution itself and it was a task which she set about with a deftness and a surefootedness that, like her campaign persona, was the product of intellectual mastery and not of any skin-deep 'image'. When she needed help, she went and asked for it: one Dublin academic was approached and asked for drafts for some of the many speeches she had to make. He took on board what he could and rounded up a number of equally talented journalistic friends to fill in the gaps he could not fill. She was more than a little pressed for time: in one twelve-day period prior to her inauguration, she gave thirty-eight interviews, mostly to foreign journalists. For all that, any Mary Robinson speech, including her acceptance and inaugural speeches, was, at the end of the day, precisely that: no matter where the draft came from, the overall thrust and the final shape were hers alone. At the end of her term of office, the practice remained the same: drafts were sought from government departments or from people she knew with an expertise in the field but the critical work was always done in the presidential study.

She kept her friends as she moved to the Phoenix Park. But there were problems in store with some of her erstwhile political opponents and even with some of her former political allies. The key to what was about to happen was in a little-noticed phrase which she insisted would form part of her acceptance speech in the Royal Dublin Society after the final votes had been counted.

'Today is a day of victory and valediction. Even as I salute my supporters as Mary Robinson, I must also bid them farewell as President-elect. They are not just partisans but patriots too. They know that as President of Ireland, I must be a President for all the people. More than that, I want to be a President for all the people because I was elected by men and women of all parties and none, by many with great moral courage who stepped out from the faded flags of the Civil War and voted for a new Ireland.'

She was, effectively, serving notice that although she had been elected to the presidency as the nominee of certain parties and independents, she was now, in the classic sense of the word, above politics and would remain so. Not everyone would see it that way and for some years afterwards there was a sense, among some of those who had campaigned vigorously for her election, that she had used a sharper knife than she had with anyone else when she cut her links with them. Towards the end of her presidency, she addressed the question directly in an interview with the author, saying that it was a necessary and important shaping of the presidential office to show that it was not owned by any political grouping, 'something that had not been sufficiently done by my distinguished predecessors. Now when I go around the country and meet elected representatives, nobody owns me at all and that is extremely important. Having said that, I went a very long way to make sure that I did thank people who should be thanked. The core committee were up at a very early stage for a dinner. There were a number of different groupings which came up at different times in those early days. It's not that I didn't thank my supporters here, from Áras an Uachtaráin.' Not all her supporters got the message; but by the end of her presidency all had to accept that she was, as she had always been, essentially her own woman.

CHAPTER 8

President and Politics:
A People's President

THE RELATIONSHIP BETWEEN the Irish presidency and the government has evolved slowly since the creation of the institution in 1937. Under Mary Robinson, that evolution was to change direction and pace with the re-definition of the presidency itself.

In 1937, as the sections on the presidency in the draft Constitution were being discussed, Eamon de Valera was accused by his political opponents in the Dáil of attempting to create a role for a political chief executive officer (generally assumed to be de Valera himself) who would be able to second-guess government decisions and generally make life difficult for everyone else. Constitutionally, however, the role traditionally foreseen for the Irish presidency was minimalist. The presidency has a number of powers which are generally limited in nature and a number of functions, most of which are ceremonial. It is not an executive position and does not operate in active politics to anything like the degree that, say, the US or French presidents do. It is not strictly speaking necessary for the Irish President to establish a close working relationship with government, since effectively there is no need for one.

Nor does it not particularly matter if the president of the day comes from a different political tradition from that of the administration, although it will not help matters if there is a conflict between them – as happened uniquely before 1990 in the incident which led to the resignation of President Ó Dálaigh. The Irish presidency, in fact, is closer to a constitutional monarchy – in terms of its powers and functions – than any of these later models. In the half a century or so that has elapsed since the establishment of the office in 1937, the civil service has learned to take a very restrictive view of the office and this view has been underlined by the minimalist way in which earlier incumbents have interpreted their own role.

This is not to say that the post is hermetically sealed from politics. The Constitution says that the Taoiseach 'shall keep the President generally informed on matters of domestic and international policy'. What this means in practice is up to individual taoisigh and presidents to decide. After Eamon de Valera was elected to the office for the first time in 1959, he found its remoteness from the realities of political life frustrating, even though he was then in his late seventies and almost completely blind. His successor, Seán Lemass, went to see him regularly every month, but this was not always enough: de Valera took to calling on his successor at home from time to time until Lemass had to remind him gently that he was no longer in charge. He was kept closely informed by one Cabinet minister, Erskine Childers, who was to be one of his successors in the presidency.

These visits were not entirely formal or perfunctory as far as de Valera was concerned. One senior civil servant who was closely involved in the drafting of the government's White Paper on the restoration of the Irish language in the mid-1960s, following the report of a special government commission set up to make recommendations on the matter, formed the distinct impression that de Valera made a direct input into the process. It is also possible that de Valera had an influence in the appointment of Dr C.S. Andrews as Chairman of the RTE Authority in 1966. And there were reports in 1972 of unsuccessful attempts to involve him in the crisis in Fianna Fáil engendered by the so-called 'arms trial' events.

The tempo of visits by the Taoiseach to the Park after Mary Robinson became President fluctuated according to need, rather than on the basis of any mechanically regular arrangement. The President could request a visit; the Taoiseach could suggest one. Throughout her period of office, visits by the Taoiseach of the day probably averaged one every six weeks or so.

The critical difference between the presidency and a constitutional monarchy, however, as Mary Robinson recognised and was to take full advantage of, is that it is the apex of a republican form of government, elected and not hereditary. Unlike the British or any other constitutional monarchy, the Irish presidency has a mandate, all the more so when the President has been elected by popular vote rather than emerging as an agreed choice of the major political parties.

Mary Robinson's position, in this context, was different from that of her predecessors in many respects. Like them, she was above party politics. Unlike them, she had become President in the wake of an extraordinary election campaign which had posed challenges not only for those who had lost but for those who had won. She had, in effect, been the candidate of the Opposition. She was now in power – although the parameters of that power were hazy and ill-defined – and some of the political forces which had supported her election perhaps looked forward to the possibility that she might, if only by living up to her campaign promises, make life difficult for the government. The government, for its part, still smarting from the result of the election, was determined not to allow the new President any more freedom than had traditionally been accorded her successors.

In a sense, the office had always been regarded as the possession of the political parties. As Opposition and government engaged in the early post-election skirmishes – the former in an attempt to take over the high moral ground, the latter in an attempt to ring-fence it – both sets of forces ignored what was to become a central, if implicit, theme of the Robinson presidency: the de-colonisation of the office of President and its effective return to the people who alone had the right to fill it by election. When Mary Robinson stood for election and indicated that she would be truly independent, she was not using independence as a cloak for any party allegiance. When she told her supporters, in her victory speech, that she was saying goodbye to them at the same time as thanking them, she was not engaging in facile rhetoric. She meant it and it cost: an active, independent presidency is, perforce, sometimes also a lonely one, calling on personal reserves of imagination and strength as well as diplomatic and political skills.

The skirmishing began early. At the end of November 1990, Dick Spring pressed the Taoiseach as to whether the government had any plans to confer additional powers on the President by law – a possibility envisaged by the Constitution itself. Charles Haughey played the straightest of bats: the role of the President in enhancing Ireland's international status, he said, could be achieved without additional legislation.

The Opposition were, in fact, keeping a close eye on what they anticipated might be a thorny relationship between government and President. It emerged early in 1991, for instance, that files relating to the President's office, the relationship of the President to the government and to the Taoiseach's office and to precedents going back over many years had been requisitioned by the Taoiseach's office from the National Archives during the presidential election campaign and after Mary Robinson's election. This came to light when a research student who had been studying the files was suddenly informed that they were no longer available. Challenged on this in the Dáil, Charles Haughey replied mildly that there was a perfectly innocent explanation: 'We had an incoming President and a change of regime. An additional official was assigned to the area who was not at all familiar with the situation and, to brief himself fully on all aspects of the job, he sent for these files to peruse them in the normal way.' The explanation, although it may not have been widely believed, was conveniently unchallengeable.

Any temptation to engage in an active presidency – with the partial exception of Erskine Childers no previous incumbent had seen this as an option – was however seriously limited by the resources available to the office, which underlined its purely nominal status. This was not a question of salary: the salary of the President has traditionally been set at a level 10% above that of the Chief Justice, and is currently £111,983. The staff and running costs of the presidential establishment are also borne out of public funds. What made the President effectively a prisoner in the Phoenix Park, however, was the extraordinarily low representation allowance – the funds set aside for travel and for the entertainment of visitors, distinguished or plebeian.

In 1973 this allowance had been set by law at £15,000 per year and had not been changed in the interim. If it had been adjusted upwards in line with inflation, it would, by the time Mary Robinson took office at the end of 1990, have been £86,000, so effectively there was an existing shortfall of at least £70,000 in real terms. In 1973, moreover, few people had foreseen the galloping inflation of the mid-1970s and, under the system set up at that time, increasing the allowance involved fresh legislation: it was not increased automatically nor could it be increased simply by a government order.

Haughey's government, for all that it was still in some sense in a state of shock following Mary Robinson's election, nonetheless met the situation rapidly and generously. Despite warnings from government sources about 'unrealistic expectations' from the Phoenix Park, Charles Haughey said that the new President would travel more frequently, and new legislation was introduced to increase the travel allowance for this purpose in February 1991.

There is a constitutional convention against discussing the presidency in the Dáil but the legislation which was now necessary to increase her allowance provided parliamentarians with a rare opportunity to discuss the office and, in the case of some of them, press home what they perceived as a political advantage. The legislation itself was non-controversial and indeed, in typical Haughey style, the amount provided was generous. Not only was the increase to be up to £100,000 – some £15,000 more than the necessary adjustment for inflation – but the law was being changed so that the allowance could be increased in the future by government order as and when necessary.

Despite the increasing unhappiness of the Ceann Comhairle, who had to remind speakers that it was not in order to discuss 'the personality, outlook or characteristics' of the presidency, a whole range of suggestions were made: that the President could chair an overseas development commission; that she could be given a consultative role in the appointment of judges; that she should chair the electoral commission (which revises electoral boundaries); or that she could chair an environmental commission. One speaker managed to evade the Chair's vigilance for long enough to draw attention to the refusal by many Irish organisations – notably golf clubs – to allow women to become members. The anomaly was all the more relevant in that a number of well-established golf clubs had in the past traditionally conferred honorary membership on Mary Robinson's male predecessors. Her election was to change all that and many other things besides.

In relation to government, however, the smoothness on the surface did not entirely conceal the fact that there was some energetic paddling going on underneath. The first difficulty to surface was in relation to staffing. The staffing situation at Áras an Uachtaráin had been preserved in aspic, as it were, for many years, and staff members who had been seconded there had become used to the idea that it was their permanent place of employment. Given to understand that there were no obstacles to redeployment, Mary Robinson and her adviser, the recently-appointed Bride Rosney, set about making changes, only to be confronted with a major industrial relations problem involving, in January 1991, even a threatened strike. The general secretary of the workers' trade union concerned, Kevin O'Driscoll – later to become programme manager to Labour's Michael D. Higgins when the latter became Minister for Arts, Culture and the Gaeltacht in 1992 – was particularly vocal in defence of the workers' rights. The staff concerned were gleefully christened by the media 'The Áras Eight' and by the time the inevitable solution had been found the presidential establishment was sporting a few bruises. In fact, the total number of household staff decreased during the Robinson presidency from 10.5 full-time equivalents to 10. On the other hand, four new secretariat positions were created: Bride Rosney's job as special adviser in 1990, a new clerical assistant position in June 1991, an additional higher executive officer post in 1993 and a new executive officer post in 1996.

What seems to have happened in 1990 is that the government, while reassuring those at the Áras that they would, of course, look after the interests of the presidency, in fact made little or no attempt to do so. Mary Robinson, as it happened, had remarked with uncharacteristic lack of subtlety in the controversial *Hot Press* interview during the campaign that she could 'stand up to Charlie Haughey and tell him to back off'. It was a remark that cut some people to the quick – one of the Taoiseach's advisers was overheard to remark grimly: 'We'll see who ——ing eyeballs whom!' It was not to be long before those who lived and worked in the Áras came to realise that, when it came to looking after their interests, nobody could do it better than they could themselves. It was a learning curve and a steep one at that.

The wounds went deep, initially at any rate. It would be easy to under-estimate the chagrin experienced, not just by Haughey but by Fianna Fáil Cabinet ministers and the party in general, at Mary Robinson's election. It was the first time in almost sixty years, after all, that the party had lost a presidential election or failed to have a controlling voice in the selection of an agreed candidate. People who are not members of political parties – in non-election years, the percentage of Irish people actively involved in politics can go as low as 2%, and even in election years is never higher than 7% or 8% – can easily under-estimate the centrality of political emotions to those most directly involved. The government had not only lost the presidential election – and the psychological blow of losing elections can never be fully understood by people to whom it has never happened – but Haughey had been forced to sack Brian Lenihan, one of his oldest friends, from the Cabinet and watch him go down to defeat in the presidential election. His own political position had been weakened as a result. If that was not enough, there was also the new phenomenon of an active president. In theory, there was nothing wrong with that. In practice, there were problems because the President, according to the Constitution, takes precedence over every other citizen in the state, and at functions to which both President and Taoiseach are invited, the Taoiseach must take second place. Under Haughey, the office of the Taoiseach had itself become more presidential than under previous incumbents: the building blocks for disagreement were lying around waiting to be picked up.

The relationship between President Patrick Hillery, a former Cabinet colleague of Haughey's, and the then Taoiseach was a smooth one, no doubt because the President was concerned not to upstage the Taoiseach and could decline invitations to functions which he knew Haughey planned to attend. President Robinson, anxious to live up to her pre-election commitments, was actually assuming an enormous number of public engagements and inevitably some of them conflicted with invitations to Haughey, who sometimes resolved the difficulty simply by staying away. There were plenty of opportunities for misunderstanding of motives on both sides and undoubtedly some occurred.

Apart from questions of protocol, however, there were other issues which on occasion stretched the relationship between Mary Robinson's new, active presidency and successive administrations to the limit of its elasticity. One of them was related to what the President could or could not say and where she could say it. For Mary Robinson, an active presidency did not merely signify an increase in the number of photo-opportunities: presidents should be heard as well as seen. Another involved the always difficult question of Northern Ireland. A third focused on the question of emigration, which was a permanent reminder of the failures of the Irish political and economic system and for that reason largely ignored by its politicians or smothered in pious platitudes.

The *Irish Times* noted, even as she was being inaugurated as President, that 'Mrs Robinson's biggest challenge is to break the government's stranglehold on the office and establish the right to freer speech'. Between 1937 and 1990, most Irish presidents were aptly described by the Fine Gael TD, Gay Mitchell, as 'political Trappists, silent on any matter that could be perceived as being political'. The political vow of silence which most presidents appeared to have taken was, however, based on what Mary Robinson, the constitutional lawyer, concluded was an unduly restrictive interpretation of a number of clauses in the Constitution.

Articles 13.1 and 13.2 provide that the President can, after consultation with the Council of State, communicate with the houses of the Oireachtas by message or address them on any matter of national or public importance and may also 'address a message to the Nation at any time on any such matter'. Article 13.3 qualifies that by providing that 'every such message or address must, however, have received the approval of the Government'.

The latter provision was plainly inserted to prevent a situation arising in which the President would come directly and publicly into conflict with the government of the day on a major issue. In practice, however, it seems to have been interpreted by most presidents as requiring them to receive prior government approval for all but the most innocuous of statements. In the end, this engendered a mood of quiet self-censorship which acted to make the presidency appear ever more remote and out of touch.

A commonsense reading of the Constitution, on the other hand, suggests strongly that the only presidential statements which need prior government approval fall into the precise categories of addresses to the nation or to the houses of the Oireachtas. For everything else, there is a blank cheque – not entirely blank, perhaps, because it is limited by the understanding that the President should never be involved in political controversy of any partisan kind and by a general sense of constitutional good manners. It was such a reading of the Constitution which, over the next seven years, was to enable Mary Robinson to speak not only to but for her fellow-citizens, to encapsulate popular moods and to respond to popular needs without ever running any serious risk of crossing that line in the sand. For both President and government, however, there was a learning process to be undergone and this was not without its period of adjustment.

The most public difference arose when she was invited by the BBC to give the highly-regarded Dimbleby lecture in 1991. Charles Haughey's government decided that she should not be permitted to accept the invitation. Even today, it is difficult to understand the reasons for this decision. It was certainly not because the government disapproved of what she planned to say: the decision was taken before any draft of the proposed speech had been prepared. It is possible that the government was apprehensive about what she might want to say and decided to launch a pre-emptive strike rather than wait until a speech had been prepared, thus opening itself to the accusation of censorship. This supposition, however, is problematic: much of the potential content of the Dimbleby lecture was to find a home in her Allen Lane Foundation lecture, which was delivered later in Dublin in 1992 without giving rise to any controversy. The government decided to act under Article 12.9 of the Constitution, which declares that 'the President shall not leave the State during his term of office save with the consent of the government'. This consent, it was understood, would be withheld because it was thought inappropriate for her to accept. Why exactly it was 'inappropriate' was not explained at the time.

Throughout 1991, Mary Robinson was a sort of super-charged President, fulfilling more than eight hundred engagements and making some seven hundred speeches. Although nothing could have been further from her own intentions, each one of her actions and speeches would have reminded the government of their defeat. She made six visits abroad; one each to Norway, Portugal and the United States and three to England. The most likely explanation of the refusal to allow her to accept the Dimbleby invitation was that there was a feeling within government generally that if sooner or later there had to be a mini-confrontation with the President, sooner was better than later. The eye-balling could start now. And the rationale for the refusal was just about as coherent and thought-out as that for any decision by a harassed parent faced with importunate demands from a child for yet another sweet before supper.

'No.'

'Why not?'

'Because I say so.'

Mary Robinson declined the invitation, as she had to, but the issue was raised in the Dáil by the Fine Gael leader, John Bruton, in February 1992. The new Taoiseach, Albert Reynolds, had resigned from government in November of the previous year after having been involved in an unsuccessful leadership challenge to Charles Haughey but had then found himself, after an extraordinary series of events, succeeding Haughey as Taoiseach. Reynolds gave the Dáil an account of the reasoning advanced for the government's decision but it hardly set headlines for clarity. The President, he suggested, 'as head of State, represents all citizens equally and she cannot by her acts or decisions unduly support any one group or special interest within the State'.

What was unclear was how, by accepting a BBC invitation, Mary Robinson would 'unduly support' anyone. The only possible clue is in the draft title for the speech which was to do with the role of women. If this was the straw at which the government clutched, it implied, astonishingly, that by supporting women the President would be 'unduly' supporting 'one group or special interest within the State'!

In fact it was not long before an issue surfaced which would be of particular relevance to Irish women. This was the legal quagmire which became known as the 'X' case, because the girl at the centre of it could not be named for legal reasons. She was fourteen and had become pregnant, and planned to travel to

England for an abortion. When this became known the Attorney-General, Harry Whelehan, took an injunction in the High Court to prevent her from travelling. The case rapidly reached the Supreme Court where, to the amazement of many – not least of those who had lobbied passionately for the Fianna Fáil amendment wording in the belief that it would make abortion impossible under any circumstances – the judges held that in the circumstances there was a real danger to the life of the young mother (who had apparently threatened suicide) which justified striking out the injunction.

Mary Robinson was on a visit to Waterford when the controversy was at its height. What could she say? As she noted later, it was neither appropriate nor indeed possible for her to be involved in any way in the process. But she had to say something. She said as little – and as much – as she could at the Waterford meeting. She had, she said, been in touch with people all over the country and knew that 'at the present time we are experiencing as a people a very deep crisis in ourselves. I cannot but say that this has been a very difficult week for women and girls in Ireland ... I hope that we have the courage we have not always had to face up to and look squarely and to say that this is a problem we have got to resolve.'

These very unspecific comments had two effects, both of them to some extent unexpected. Many Irish women apparently felt that Mary Robinson had, in some effective way, spoken for them and their concerns even though she had not proposed (indeed could not propose) any specific course of action. Just a year later, this was borne out by a major MRBI survey which showed that two out of three Irish women spontaneously mentioned Mary Robinson as the woman they most admired: the next most admired woman, and less than half as popular as Mary Robinson, was Mother Teresa of Calcutta. The same survey found that abortion and contraception were identified by women as two issues on which they felt that the government should pay particular attention to their views.

What Mary Robinson had done in her Waterford comments, however, was to indicate that the abortion issue was a political problem to be solved by politicians and this rang alarm bells in other quarters. Family Solidarity, one of the organisations which had helped to campaign for the initial anti-abortion amendment, charged her immediately with a 'partisan' attitude and alleged that she had, as part of the anti-amendment campaign in the early 1980s, 'campaigned to deny the unborn child's constitutional right to life'. This evoked a swift rejoinder from Bride Rosney, who pointed out that Mary Robinson had not – as had been alleged – been an executive member of the anti-amendment campaign but had been, in common with other members of the Oireachtas, one of its sponsors.

The controversy subsided, insofar as it involved Mary Robinson, but she returned to it in a radio interview in May – itself an unprecedented gesture by an Irish president to the media. She told the national audience that, rather than taking sides, she had tried to be a unifying force in very difficult, deep moral issues because in the past, when we had had these kind of difficult areas, they had divided us, and the language used had been redolent of hatred. Pluralism, on the other hand, meant having more understanding of a different point of view – even if it was a point of view which was diametrically opposed to one's own on a very deep moral issue.

Only four months before the 'X' case, Mary Robinson had told a meeting of American lawyers in Chicago: 'In a very few generations, we as lawyers and you as judges have been privileged to witness the progress of women from being recipients and objects of the law to being interpreters of it, and agents of change within it.' The 'X' case underlined both the truth of what she said – and, at the same time, the way in which the extreme sensitivity relating to issues of reproduction, in particular, operated to make that progress slow and fitful.

The moral issue and its political dimensions remain. The 1997 general election campaign was notable for a failed attempt by anti-abortion groups to secure political commitments from any party in relation to a new constitutional amendment and, in the aftermath of the election, the new Fianna Fáil government led by Bertie Ahern seemed to be inching towards a political resolution of the problems raised by the 'X' case and its implications.

President Robinson's strong implication in 1992 that the abortion problem was one which politicians alone – and not the President – had the power to solve was an unwelcome reminder to many of the self-same politicians that they could not evade this responsibility for ever. If anything, it increased the sense of wariness which had begun to characterise the relationships between the seat of government in Leinster House and Áras an Uachtaráin. There was a drip-feed of rumours about relationships between the presidency and the government. Nor, surprisingly, did it make much difference when the government changed. After the November 1992 election, Irish politics shifted dramatically when Dick Spring led the Labour Party, which had increased its number of seats to a total of thirty-three, into an unprecedented coalition with Fianna Fáil under Albert Reynolds. The relationship between Mary Robinson and Albert Reynolds had achieved a measure of warmth and stability but the rumours about misunderstandings and ill-feeling now increasingly focused on the Labour Party leader, Dick Spring, and on the issue of Northern Ireland.

Dick Spring, who was Tánaiste for five years from 1992-1997 and the person who had proposed Mary Robinson for the presidency, was in particular rumoured to be put out by the President's active role in areas which he felt were the prerogative of government or by actions of hers which, in his view, complicated the conduct of governmental policy.

In the eyes of the media, this was a clash of personalities and personal factors were undoubtedly involved to some extent. Mary Robinson and Dick Spring are not unlike each other in some ways: both are intensely private people, with strong personal loyalties and deep convictions. Each has a quirky sense of humour, which is very rarely on public view. Each has been accused of arrogance. Their relationship, while respectful, has never been close, certainly not close enough to obviate the problems caused by occasionally differing perspectives on policies or on the timing of particular statements. On the other hand, it has not been without warmth. On one occasion Dick Spring was taking the train to Dublin: as it happened, the presidential coach was part of the train. One of Mary Robinson's aides spotted the Labour leader boarding and she invited him to spend the rest of his journey in more comfortable surroundings.

There were, as it happened, important institutional and cultural contributory factors influencing their relationship. A new and highly active President who was already an internationalist would inevitably make more demands on the civil service machine. As has been noted, that machine in general had become accustomed to a minimalist view of the presidency. Both in Iveagh House, the headquarters of the Department of Foreign Affairs, and in the government secretariat, which had to be increased dramatically in size, the style and industriousness of the Robinson presidency involved not only an increased work-load but a different way of looking at things. In Iveagh House, the difficulties were less on the policy side than on the protocol side. Bride Rosney, the President's special adviser, has an eye for detail and a capacity for organisation that continually astonished and impressed those with whom she worked, but there were also occasions on which it could get on the wrong side of civil servants whose expertise contained a touch of officiousness.

Occasionally it got on the wrong side of others as well. Before the State visit to Spain in May 1993, Bride Rosney went out to Spain with the advance party. The locations for many of the functions were to be in Spain's ornate royal palaces and – among other more pressing concerns – she wanted to make sure that the clothes worn by the Irish party would not clash with the decor. When she got back, she sent details of the colour schemes of the principal rooms personally to Kristi Spring, Dick Spring's wife, who would be accompanying her husband as part of the Irish group. This well-meaning gesture blew up in newspaper headlines which implied that either Rosney or the President were, in effect, telling the Foreign Minister's wife what to wear – and at such short notice that the advice, as well as being insulting, was virtually useless. Offence was taken although none was intended: it was, in a sense, a function of the absence of any network or informal way of resolving differences or misunderstandings between the individuals and institutions concerned.

Of the three issues which were to occur after the November 1992 general election and were to involve both the President and Dick Spring in a particularly dramatic way, two related to the issue of Northern Ireland. Early in her presidency, Mary Robinson had asked someone from Northern Ireland how nationalists there viewed her. The reply was deeply unsettling. She was told that they regarded her basically as a unionist and could interpret in only one way her action in resigning from the Labour Party in protest against the Anglo-Irish Agreement which they had seen as a historic breakthrough. In her inaugural speech, too, her section on the North was careful; she had spoken of her desire to reach out to both communities there 'with no strings attached, no hidden agenda'. Events were to show that, of all the paths she walked this was the one most strewn with thorns.

In the 1980s, political and diplomatic offensives by the Irish government had succeeded in giving Dublin a greater consultative role than ever before in relation to the North. The corollary of this was that Northern unionists felt increasingly embattled and defensive, as Mary Robinson herself had predicted they would when she resigned from the Labour Party in 1985. The paradox was that Northern nationalists were not proportionately reassured. Insofar as they supported Sinn Féin, they were in a situation of double isolation: isolated both from the centre of political power within Northern Ireland at Stormont, home of the old Northern Ireland parliament and now seat of the British administration of the province, and isolated from Dublin, which regarded Sinn Féin as unhelpful at best, dangerously disruptive of the peace process at worst.

This sense of isolation among a substantial minority of Northern nationalists had been addressed by Mary Robinson's predecessors as president in only the most superficial of ways. Such visits as de Valera and others had made to the North were few and far between and were always on religious occasions to Armagh, where the head of the Roman Catholic Church in Ireland lives. By the time she had ended her seven-year presidency, Mary Robinson had visited Northern Ireland eighteen times, more than all her predecessors put together.

Her first visit to Belfast was in February 1992. Given the politics of the situation, it was essential that it should avoid being categorised as one which favoured one side or the other in this deeply divided society. Characteristically, therefore, the visit took place to organisations which had strong cross-community dimensions and which were focused on women rather than on political organisations as such. She went to Belfast as the guest of the Women's Support Network and the Women's European Platform and while she was there she attended a reception hosted by an organisation whose agenda mirrored that of her own pre-presidential career: the Equal Opportunities Commission, dedicated to achieving fairness in employment. Although it was unconnected with her visit, violence flared while she was there, claiming four lives in the space of an afternoon. In a deliberately low-key sort of way, the visit was a success, paving the way for a more daring initiative: this would be an attempt to reach out to the embattled West Belfast nationalist community. It was scheduled for June of the next year.

There was no IRA cease-fire nor, so it seemed, any prospect of one. What was worse, an IRA bomb had gone off only three months earlier, on 20 March, in the British market town of Warrington, killing two boys, and giving rise to a wave of revulsion right across the two islands. Mary Robinson had attended a memorial service in Warrington for the two children on 7 April, attracting extraordinary attention from the British media. It hardly seemed the best time to be reaching out to West Belfast, much less if it involved a meeting, however superficial, with a prominent member of Sinn Féin.

For these and other reasons, mainstream political opinion in Dublin and London was extremely jittery about her next proposed visit to West Belfast, fearful in particular that it would be seen as a propaganda coup for the IRA. West Belfast in particular has for years been a nationalist mini-ghetto, signalling its defiance of the established power structures by dividing its political allegiance between the mainstream nationalist party, the SDLP, and Sinn Féin. It is a community which has elected Gerry Adams, the President of Sinn Féin, to the Westminster parliament (as an abstentionist MP, he refused to take his seat there) on two occasions, most recently at the 1997 British general election.

At the time of Mary Robinson's June 1993 visit to West Belfast, her fifth visit to Northern Ireland, Adams was not an MP, but the critical question was: would the two meet and shake hands, where, under what circumstances and what would happen next? In the event, she met Adams as one of a large number of community leaders at a function in an educational establishment in West Belfast. A handshake was exchanged but without any special emphasis and nothing of any political significance was said. The significance was in the symbolism of the event, a symbolism which was not lost on any of the many, often opposed groups which had an interest in the occasion, from the British government to the wilder shores of Irish republicanism.

To understand the politics of the situation, it is important to look at the context and not just at the handshake alone. And one of the most significant – and under-estimated – parts of that context was Mary Robinson's meeting with Queen Elizabeth II in May, only a matter of weeks before her visit to West Belfast. The visit attracted little attention in the British media although it was dutifully noted, much as a visit by the President of one of the other small European countries might be. The main evening BBC news on the day of the visit ignored it completely, giving pride of place in its news agenda to a Cabinet re-shuffle. Nobody echoed the paean of praise contributed by a writer in the left-wing *New Statesman* only a few months earlier: 'I find it almost painful to contemplate Mary Robinson. She is radical, literate, a woman, and she's in power. Couldn't she be President of us as well?'

In Ireland North and South, on the other hand, the visit had an immense significance, difficult to evaluate but indisputable. For an Irish audience, seeing the Irish President in Buckingham Palace was an especially potent symbol. In more ways than one, it broke – as Mary Robinson said later – a psychological barrier. In retrospect, moreover, the timing of the two visits appears to be intimately or, at the very least, fortuitously related. Because the visit to Queen Elizabeth was the first of its kind ever to take place, it stirred unfamiliar emotions. And it is worthwhile remembering that although Queen Elizabeth is personally well-regarded in Ireland (the exhaustive coverage of the British Royal Family's activities in the UK tabloid newspapers is, along with sport, one of the main reasons for these papers' strong circulation in the Republic), the symbol she embodies in the North is more contentious.

The Robinson visit to Queen Elizabeth, while it did not fireproof her against the anticipated criticism by unionists of her meeting with Adams, undoubtedly helped to draw the teeth of much of that criticism. It would have been difficult, if not impossible, to arrange things in the reverse order – for Mary Robinson to have a meeting with the Queen in the immediate aftermath of her Adams handshake. Indeed, had things happened in this order unionists would have been incensed. And it was easier, paradoxically, for her to shake Adams's hand precisely because she had already shaken the hand of the political symbol he and his organisation so defiantly reject.

Perhaps it is significant, therefore, that in all the controversy which subsequently developed, the talk was solely about the potential embarrassment for the President and the two governments directly involved. A potential embarrassment for the Sinn Féin leader was not so much as mentioned: that he should shake the hand of an Irish head of State who had, only a month earlier, shaken the hand of the Queen of Great Britain and Northern Ireland!

Before the handshake itself, many other factors caused concern. Once the news of the impending visit to West Belfast entered the public domain, the Fianna Fáil/Labour government under Albert Reynolds came under quite astonishing pressure from the British government, aimed at having the visit cancelled if at all possible. There were even hints from the British side that they might not be able to guarantee the President's security if the visit went ahead – as substantial a threat as it is possible to imagine in inter-governmental negotiations.

The Reynolds government was in a double dilemma. On one visit by both Reynolds and Spring to London in June, the President's projected Belfast visit was practically the only topic of conversation, The consensus was that the planned visit was too risky, at least from the political point of view. This was a view arrived at quite independently of the British pressure. The emergence of this consensus did not, however, make things easier. If anything, it made them more difficult.

There were two major problems and an anomaly. The first problem is simply stated: if the visit was cancelled, even if the real reason was because the Irish government independently disapproved of it, it would appear as if Dublin had bowed to British pressure. Nor would the British government have been slow to claim the credit, with incalculable political consequences not only for Irish-British relationships but for the morale of Northern nationalists and for the prospects of peace in the North itself.

The second problem was more complex. Article 12.9 of the Constitution lays down that 'The President shall not leave the State during his term of office save with the consent of the Government.' This raised the extremely difficult question: would a visit by the President to Northern Ireland involve her leaving 'the State' and, if it did, should the government prevent her from travelling North by invoking Article 12.9 of the Constitution?

The Constitution itself is not much help on the issue. Article 4 says that 'the name of the State is Éire or, in the English language, Ireland'. This would seem to imply that Northern Ireland, whatever arrangements for its governance were currently in force, was in fact part of 'the State'. Indeed, Eamon de Valera, when he drafted the Constitution, expressly intended it to be applicable with as few modifications as possible to the united Ireland he hoped to see emerging. Nowhere in the Constitution, for example, is the twenty-six county area described as a Republic. Article 5, on the other hand, says bluntly that 'Ireland is a sovereign, independent, democratic State'. It is difficult, to put it mildly, to incorporate Northern Ireland into this definition, no matter how it is stretched. And, just to make matters more difficult, Article 2 declares that 'the national territory consists of the whole island of Ireland, its islands and the territorial seas'.

If the government had decided to instruct the President not to travel North, this would have involved defining Northern Ireland as being outside the State. The consequences of this can be readily imagined. So the government decided not to address the issue but simply to express its concerns to the President and to act as a kind of *porte-parole* for the similar concerns of the British government.

This is where the anomaly came into play. Article 28.5.2 of the Constitution states plainly that 'the Taoiseach shall keep the President generally informed on matters of domestic and international policy'. The man who came to see the President with the government's message, however, was not the Taoiseach, Albert Reynolds, but the Tánaiste, the man who had helped to put her in the Park – Dick Spring. At one level, this was simply nifty footwork by Reynolds.

He had, as a back-bencher after being sacked by Haughey for taking part in a failed coup against him in late 1989, watched from the sidelines as the Robinson presidential campaign had all but dismantled Haughey's political credibility. He was not going to make the same mistake himself.

Reynolds, his press secretary noted, 'viewed the President with a mixture of mild awe and wariness. He might privately share some of Spring's reservations about her peripatetic tendencies but he was also pleased that he got on well with her at a personal level and he assiduously avoided unnecessary friction between Merrion Street and Áras an Uachtaráin. He would regularly draw my attention to the latest public opinion poll showing overwhelming support, in whatever issue, for the President. This comment after one such poll was typical: "No arguing with that. We walk around that. Let her off."'[44]

The rationale for sending Spring was partly that the whole business was essentially in the territory of the Department of Foreign Affairs. But the Reynolds sub-text was not hard to discern. Spring was the man who had helped to put this difficult woman into the Park and he was the man who was going to have to sort her out. This decision solved Reynolds's problem, but it was plainly not as the Constitution envisaged and it had the additional effect of immediately raising the temperature to a level at which misunderstandings, if they occurred, could have an explosive effect.

Spring went to see the President *en route* from a government meeting to the airport where he was to take a plane to an inter-governmental meeting with Sir Patrick Mayhew in London. Mayhew, the British government's Secretary of State for Northern Ireland, was a Tory whose patrician manner masked the fact that he actually had extensive family connections in Co. Cork. He was, in the end, one of a long succession of holders of this position who found that it signposted the way to a political graveyard rather than to preferment and high honours.

Spring explained the concerns of the government to her and passed on those of the British but, for the reasons outlined above, stopped short of intimating that the government would instruct her not to travel. As he understood the matter, she then promised to consider her decision overnight.

In London before the meeting, Spring was suddenly told that Downtown Radio, the Northern Ireland independent radio station, had just broadcast a statement to the effect that a spokesperson for the President had confirmed to them that the visit would be going ahead. The timing was extraordinary. If it was true, it meant that the decision to go ahead had been taken between the time that Spring left Áras an Uachtaráin and the time he arrived in London whereas he had understood that it would not be taken until the following morning. The statement, if true, seriously compromised his position in negotiations with the British. At the inter-governmental meeting the atmosphere was sulphurous: the British side had heard the same news, and were adamant that the visit should not go ahead.

Spring was now in the different but equally difficult position of having to defend the President, even though he and his own government were deeply concerned about the proposed visit. In the event the British side was told, in no uncertain terms, that what the President of Ireland did was not a matter for them. It was, by some accounts, one of the most heated meetings ever between the two sides and it ended in a stand-off.

Back in Dublin, Spring made enquiries and was assured by Áras an Uachtaráin that as no such statement had been issued by them to Downtown Radio there had been no breach of trust. The denial was accepted, as of course it had to be. Wherever the story came from, or however it had been formulated, it wasn't from the President. But the temperature was still at or near boiling point, and bridges that had been demolished were to be a long time being rebuilt. It is difficult to imagine that anyone will ever know the full details of what happened. Downtown Radio might have made a mistake or misunderstood what was happening; there might have been a hoax call for political purposes or even for a prank. Whatever the reason, the incident seriously damaged the basis of trust between the presidency and the government at a critical period and certainly harmed the relationship between Mary Robinson and Dick Spring. (After she had returned from Belfast, one of Spring's advisers told the government press secretary, Sean Duignan, that 'she shouldn't be given permission to go to Disneyland'.)[45]

In the absence of a formal instruction from the government not to go ahead, Mary Robinson decided that the visit would take place. Last-minute attempts were made to persuade her otherwise, including visits to the Park by both Spring and, eventually, Reynolds. Reynolds's response to her conviction that she should go was terse: 'Some woman'. Spring's 'furious' comment was 'She is determined to make history'.[46] They were both right.

The full story of the negotiations with the people whom Mary Robinson was to meet in Belfast has yet to be told but it is already clear that it was deliberately organised in such a way as to minimise any possibility that Sinn Féin could extract undue political mileage from it. Photographers were not allowed to record the Robinson/Adams handshake; there were to be no protests by nationalist groups, such as the parents of children killed by plastic bullets fired by the police or relatives of prisoners in Northern Ireland jails. The venue was also deliberately chosen to be as far as possible from West Belfast's Falls Road, an area of the city where nationalist feelings ran high and where almost anything could spark violent confrontations between residents and the security forces. If she had been caught in the middle of such a confrontation, Mary Robinson's Northern initiative would have been in ruins.

Taking the risk – and it was plainly a major risk – paid off. Mary Robinson's relationships with unionists had received, in the words of unionist Chris McGimpsey, 'significant, but not necessarily irreparable' damage. What was equally significant was that she had and retains among unionists, a reputation capable of surviving such damage. After a while, they even gave up attending some of her visits North in order to stage protests. Two years later, in October 1994, she was to meet six of Northern Ireland's leading loyalist politicians on an informal occasion in Washington: her willingness to make this gesture, in contrast to the Adams handshake, was widely applauded.

Her visit and the handshake also prompted criticism in the Republic, largely from Fine Gael. The party leader, John Bruton, confined his objections to the careful statement that the President should not have met someone the government was not prepared to meet. One of his most vocal TDs, however, Alan Shatter, came closer than any public representative to overt criticism of the President when he charged that in the previous two years Irish people had 'lived in a world of coded messages delivered in a script of political blancmange, carefully crafted in soothing words of verbal levitation'. The handshake, he warned, was 'open to serious misrepresentation and could prove to be a tragic miscalculation by a President who up to now has done us proud'. Some journalistic commentators, particularly Eamon Dunphy in the *Sunday Independent*, could not find words that were critical enough to condemn what they felt to be a sustaining hand held out to terrorism. In the same group's newspapers, Conor Cruise O'Brien, whose relationship to Mary Robinson's views had twice gone through 360 degrees, was by turns saddened and dismayed.

The public reaction to the Adams meeting, on the other hand, was almost entirely positive. This did not, Robinson's critics would argue, make it right. But·one of its main side-effects, according to one of the most perceptive commentators on Northern affairs, was on the government which had been most anxious about its possibly deleterious consequences. It may even have been crucial in convincing the Taoiseach, Albert Reynolds, that 'there would be huge popular support for a political leader willing to take risks to bring Sinn Féin in from the wilderness'.[47] The cease-fire, as it turned out, was not far off.

In 1994, the government changed without an intervening general election. This procedure is not unprecedented – during a number of Fianna Fáil administrations governments changed when the party leadership changed – but it was the first time in which the new taoiseach came from a different party, in this case from Fine Gael rather than Fianna Fáil. Labour remained in government as junior coalition partners after an extraordinary series of events in which Mary Robinson was peripherally involved. The issue which eventually sank the government turned on the role of the Attorney-General and the responsibility of Albert Reynolds's government in a complex case of child abuse involving legal precedents. The Attorney-General, in particular, was accused of having mismanaged the administration of his office in such a way as to allow a suspected child molester to escape prosecution. Reynolds was determined to appoint his Attorney-General, Harry Whelehan, to the presidency of the High Court and eventually did so, despite the objections of Dick Spring. That appointment was made formally and 'glacially' by Mary Robinson, as she was required to do by the Constitution.[48]

The Northern Ireland issue surfaced dramatically again in 1995 when, in the course of a presidential visit to Japan, Mary Robinson was interviewed by Joe Carroll, the diplomatic correspondent of the *Irish Times*, who asked her for a comment on the Framework Document – a document that had been agreed by the previous Fianna Fáil/Labour government and the British government, with the intention of bringing about an all-inclusive talks process in Northern Ireland. Mary Robinson said she thought the Framework Document might give rise to 'genuine fears' among unionists in that it could undermine their sense of identity. Shortly afterwards Dick Spring, who was giving an off-the-record briefing to journalists on quite a number of other matters, was asked to comment on what the President had said in Japan.

Spring told journalists – or so it was reported – that her comments had gone beyond the bounds of acceptability. It was inevitable, in the circumstances, that such a high-profile response should escape from the off-the-record enclosure and be found wandering abroad in the public gaze, as immediately happened. It was published first in the *Irish Independent* where it was attributed, not to Spring personally but to an unnamed 'Labour minister'. A statement from Áras an Uachtaráin raised the stakes: if the unnamed 'Labour minister' who was reported as having made these comments was prepared to make them again on the record there would be an on-the-record response from the Park.

This long-range exchange underlined one of the key factors of the Robinson presidency. If the President finds herself at odds with the government, she has one extremely potent weapon: the ability to go public. It derived, in Mary Robinson's case, from her electoral mandate and at the end of the day governments simply had to learn, by and large, to put up with it. The government also has a weapon but it is so big that it can only be fired once and if it is used it has to have fatal consequences: impeachment. This is why – in the sort of circumstances under discussion – it is, paradoxically, hardly a weapon at all.

Spring's office, after an initial attempt to transfer responsibility for the problem by blaming the journalists who had (undoubtedly) broken confidence on the issue, had to retreat into a wounded silence, broken only by a spirited defence from Fergus Finlay, Spring's programme manager. Finlay, who had also been at the briefing, described the main thrust of the newspaper reports as 'total rubbish' and an 'entirely spurious' controversy and went on to castigate the newspaper which had broken the story for subsequently commissioning an opinion poll to find out whether people thought that Spring had been right to attack the President. 'If I had been polled', Finlay commented acidly, 'I would have said that Dick Spring was wrong to attack the President. But I know he didn't.'

None of the two dozen or so reporters present subsequently intervened to contradict Finlay's version of events and one or two confirmed it. But one anonymous politician commented, more than ten days after Finlay's article: 'It is a pity that Dick is so petty and he cannot give the President his support when she is such an obvious success in terms of foreign relations.'

The circumstances of the two controversies are replete with ironies. For one thing, a large part of Spring's briefing was devoted to a defence of the President's recent visit to South America, some of which had come in for ill-informed journalistic comment. Two other factors, however, were more significant. Firstly, Dick Spring has been generally considered, particularly during the period of the rainbow coalition in 1994-97, to be on the hawkish side of the arguments with Northern unionists and the British government in relation to the claims of Northern nationalists. He has become, for this very reason, a hate-figure for many unionists, who regard him as more treacherous than any taoiseach with whom they have had to deal. Secondly, Mary Robinson, having left the Labour Party precisely because she believed that the Anglo-Irish Agreement was unfair to unionists (to put it no more strongly), had – at least until the famous handshake – the reputation of being someone who was, in a sense, soft on unionism.

The political logic of the two events is difficult to unscramble, implying as it does that she was criticised twice by the same person, once for an action which would be unwelcome to unionists, and the second time for remarks that seemed to endorse a unionist position. Either one or both of the protagonists were being inconsistent or there is some other explanation which fits the facts.

There may be such an explanation but until both participants are in a position to speak openly about the events concerned, something which is demonstrably not yet the case, it must remain in the realm of speculation. If there is, it may well be that Mary Robinson has seen her role in relation to Northern Ireland as a role to both communities: it has certainly been understood as such by many unionists, such as John Taylor, who praised her 'unique understanding' of unionist concerns. This can explain her desire to reach out to each of these communities at times when they are particularly beleaguered, politically speaking.

The exigencies of political timing can explain ministerial concern in relation to the same events. If unionists are feeling beleaguered, it is usually precisely because a Dublin political offensive on the North appears to be bearing fruit. If nationalists are feeling beleaguered, it is precisely because they are concerned at events which highlight their isolation from Dublin as well as from Stormont. In politics, which has strong resemblances to drama at some levels, timing is critical and if there is a feeling that all the actors are not reading from the same script the director gets anxious.

In such circumstances, it is not only possible for governmental policy and presidential initiatives to be sometimes out of sync: it is virtually inevitable. The argument could well be put the other way – given strong personalities in government and in the presidency, what is significant is not that differences occurred but that they did not occur more often and that when they did occur they were dealt with by mature political figures reacting coolly to situations as they develop.

At the root of it all is a central paradox: the presidency, although it is above party politics, is a political office and its holder is elected by universal suffrage to fulfil certain key public functions. To pretend that there are never tensions between government and presidency at times of political movement, growth and development is to adopt a hopelessly idealised view of both institutions; to ascribe such difficulties to personality clashes or to thwarted personal ambition is to reduce a complex reality to the level of individual pettiness.

The personal aspect of the differences between Dick Spring and Mary Robinson was not entirely irrelevant, insofar as their relationship was always characterised by respect rather than closeness. Especially after Mary Robinson's election, there were really no opportunities for sorting out problems on a personal basis and there was always the risk that each would misinterpret the motives of the other. The 1993 controversy was smoothed over and the 1995 one eventually evaporated but the best indication that these differences, although significant, were not deep-rooted and were essentially political rather than personal in origin came in 1997 when the Department of Foreign Affairs under Spring was the most energetic supporter of the campaign to secure her nomination as UN High Commissioner for Human Rights. A special three-man committee under a former Irish ambassador to the UN was set up to co-ordinate the international lobbying activity which finally produced a positive result on 12 June 1997. As Mary Robinson was to discover and acknowledge, the powerful Iveagh House culture could work for you as well as against you.

Another of Mary Robinson's initiatives was equally remarkable but in an entirely different way. This was her address to both houses of the Oireachtas on the subject of the Irish diaspora, or emigration, as it is still more colloquially known. During her election campaign, she had enumerated emigrants among the forgotten groups in Irish society and, immediately after her election, she had made a symbolic gesture indicative of her commitment when she ensured that there would be a light permanently shining in the kitchen window of the apartment she and her family occupy on the top floor of Áras an Uachtaráin. The window is situated just under the pediment of the imposing portico; the continual presence of the light is unmistakable.

Initial reactions to this gesture were mixed. While it struck a chord for many people, especially those only a generation or two removed from rural life, it appeared to others sentimental and even trite. After she had announced that she would not seek a second term as President, one newspaper correspondent, a friend of Noel Browne's, urged her to 'take the ostentatious, meaningless object with her'.

'I shall', she said in her inaugural speech, 'rely on symbols.' It is a measure of the continuing power of symbols that this particular gesture has, in its own way, seeped into the national consciousness in a positive and even reassuring way. On visitors, it has had an effect that is even more dramatic. One day towards the end of her presidency, an Irishman living in Canada came to Áras an Uachtaráin by arrangement with a group of friends specially organised for this purpose. As the President explained to the group the symbolism of the light, perhaps the thousandth time she had done it for similar groups, they listened attentively and politely. A staff member accompanying the President noticed that the young Irishman who had organised the visit was standing a little apart from his companions. Tears were streaming down his face.

Her visits to the United States were, of course, replete with resonances and recollections of emigration but it was a visit to Canada in August 1994 that, almost unexpectedly, stirred the blood in strange ways. Her visit focused on two things – her meetings with Commonwealth leaders at the Commonwealth Games was one of them but it paled into insignificance beside the symbolism of her visit to Grosse Isle, the small island in the St Lawrence estuary which was established as a quarantine station for immigrants arriving in Canada from 1832 onwards. In 1847 alone, more than 5,000 Irish people died on the island and were buried there in a mass grave: the total number of Irish emigrants to have died there is estimated at 15,000.

In all her trips abroad, President Robinson made a special point of arranging meetings with groups representing the Irish diaspora. On her Australian visit in October/November 1992, these meetings had an especial resonance for the seven million (out of seventeen million) Australians of Irish origin – so much so that the visit attracted extraordinary media coverage in spite of the fact that Australia was then experiencing a major domestic crisis.

The subject of emigration was the theme for her second formal address to the Oireachtas, on 2 February 1995. The first, on 8 July 1992, was a reflection on Irish identity in Europe, a thoughtful, almost low-key reflection which left many of its audience puzzled rather than enthused. In the words of newspaper columnist Nuala O'Faolain, it evoked 'a certain polite bewilderment'. The parliamentarians did not yet know what they needed her for, or what she could do for them. 'Perhaps', she added, 'yesterday broke ground they don't even know is there.' It was not that her meaning was unclear: what she had to say was strong, and positive. What the parliamentarians were unclear about was why she had chosen that particular subject, and that particular time.

Her address on the diaspora, however, was in a different category. The facts of emigration have been a feature of Irish politics, economics and demography for more than two centuries. Until 1922, responsibility for that phenomenon could, fairly enough, be laid at the door of successive English administrations. After 1922 and the creation of the Free State, however, there were fewer excuses: native governments themselves had to accept responsibility for continuing emigration and attempt to devise measures to end it. In this they were, at least until the 1960s, both powerless and ineffective. While emigration to the United States had been choked off to a large extent in the late 1920s, Ireland, although politically independent of Great Britain, effectively operated a common labour market with the larger island. When there was economic growth in Britain, Irish emigration accelerated dramatically (and, with it, the inflow from emigrants' remittances). British recessions were accompanied by a diminution of emigration but by a consequent and equally dramatic rise in privation and hardship at home, as those leaving the land swelled the ranks of the urban unemployed because they both had nowhere else to go. Caught between the devil and the deep blue sea, the Irish worker faced the impossible choice between dislocation and exile on the one hand and domestic penury on the other.

The Irish political response to this phenomenon had always been partial and inadequate. Some politicians, indeed, may have recognised its advantages: the continuing outflow of young, able-bodied workers, many of them male (although women were also emigrating in striking numbers), took the kettle of social discontent off the fire. This did not stop opposition politicians at every election from berating the government for its failure to solve the problem. When oppositions took over the levers of power they were, for the most part, as incapable of doing anything to stop it as their predecessors had been.

Watching the President speak to an assembly of Irish politicians about emigration was, therefore, a little like watching a cat have its fur rubbed the wrong way. Nothing was said but the animal stirred uneasily on its haunches. What gave the whole occasion added point was the fact that the politicians were at that time beginning to confront the question of political representation for emigrants, a question raised with increasing urgency by emigrants' groups, notably in Britain and in the United States.

Ireland is in fact the only country in the European Union which does not allow at least some of its emigrants to vote in domestic elections. The Irish problem, of course, is that there are so many of them and there is a fear among Irish politicians that – no matter where the cut-off line is drawn – the 'emigrant vote', which is by definition almost unreachable and therefore incapable of being influenced by traditional electoral politics, could determine the shape of governments.

In its programme for government in 1994, the new Fine Gael-led 'rainbow coalition' proposed that emigrants should be allowed to vote for three seats in the Senate (where all voting is postal). This, described by one commentator as an 'ill-considered political sop', was as far as it was prepared to go. Any further and the delicate, largely predictable arithmetic of power would be changed.

In the partly oblique but actually unmistakable language which she had made peculiarly her own since her inauguration, Mary Robinson made her own position clear. She quoted the lines of her friend, the poet Eavan Boland, in her poem 'The Emigrant Irish':

> Like oil lamps we put them out the back
> Of our houses, of our minds.

And she went on: 'To cherish means that we are ready to accept new dimensions of the diaspora. But if cherishing the diaspora is to be more than a sentimental regard for those who leave our shores, we should not only listen to their voices and their viewpoint. We have a responsibility to respond warmly to their expressed desire for appropriate fora for dialogue and interaction with us by examining in an open and generous way the possible linkages. We should accept that such a challenge is an education in diversity which can only benefit our society.'

Newspaper readers were told, almost simultaneously with Mary Robinson's address, that the government was now considering as a matter of urgency the possibility of allowing emigrants to vote for seats in the Senate. By 1997, almost three years later, nothing had been done except to prepare a civil service study of the problems involved which, as might have been predicted, were discovered to be numerous and tangled. In the meantime, the light continued to shine in the Áras kitchen window up to the end of the presidency.

CHAPTER 9

From the Phoenix Park to Geneva: The UN Trajectory

MARY ROBINSON'S INTEREST in human rights, already amply evidenced in the course of her legal career, was moving onto a new plane. She had already signalled in her inaugural address her desire to contribute on behalf of the people of Ireland 'to the international protection and promotion of human rights'. In her travels and in her speeches over the next seven years she was to put down marker after marker in this field.

Initially, it was travel. She was the first head of State to visit Rwanda in the wake of the genocidal conflict there and the first to visit the International Criminal Tribunal for the former Yugoslavia, established in The Hague. Of all the countries she was to visit, however, Somalia, in the midst of a bitter and horrifically destructive civil war, provided experiences of an extraordinary intensity. During that civil war, an estimated million Somalis left their own country as refugees, while tens of thousands died of starvation. In the autumn of 1992, when the Irish Foreign Minister David Andrews first visited the country, it was estimated that 1.5 million of the country's 7.8 million population were in immediate danger of death by starvation and that a further 2.5 million were seriously at risk.

The Somalis have been described by their original British colonisers as 'the Irish of Africa' and Irish relief agencies and workers were involved in many areas of that country when Mary Robinson visited it in October 1992. A *Voice for Somalia*, the book that she wrote after her return, is remarkable for many reasons but perhaps principally because of the rawness of the emotion, of the powerful sense it conveys of a highly articulate and politically sophisticated European stateswoman knocked off her feet by a tidal wave of moral indignation and reduced almost to incoherence by the sight of so much hunger and suffering in a world of potential plenty.

'I find', she told a press conference at the end of her visit in Nairobi, as her voice broke and her eyes filled, 'that I cannot be entirely calm speaking to you because I have such a sense of what the world must take responsibility for.' Later, she wrote in her diary: 'Because I was hit by a wall of frustration, of emotion and of anger as I tried to convey what I had seen, I thought I had blown the opportunity. That part of me that was a barrister – with the training and discipline of my profession, based on the ability to take a briefing and to advocate a case – knew it was not appropriate to let emotions break through. However, I wasn't just a barrister pleading a case. I was the President of Ireland giving a personal witness and responding to the people of Somalia. Above all, I was a human being devastated by what I had seen. In that context it was impossible not to show emotion.'

She went on to New York to make a personal report to the Secretary-General on the situation in Somalia, not least about the failures and weaknesses of the United Nations operation there. It was a highly unusual and a self-appointed role, certainly, but it was driven by something more fundamental than politics: the sense of injustice and wanting to put right what is wrong that had burned within her from childhood. On the long flight from Nairobi to Paris on her way to the UN, she closed her eyes and wept quietly for a long time.

From this point on, although her destination was still uncertain, the route was being mapped out with increasing clarity. And her increasing interface with the UN had two important dimensions. It helped in the rapidly accelerating process which might loosely be described as the internationalisation of Ireland; and it helped to give the problems of the wider world an immediacy and relevance to Irish people which made them, in turn, less self-absorbed and more conscious of their comparative good fortune in a world scarred by misery and want.

President Robinson was invited to be the general rapporteur at an inter-regional meeting on 'Human Rights at the Dawn of the 21st century' organised by the Council of Europe in Strasbourg in January 1993. This was significant for two reasons. In the first place and most obviously, it involved a recognition of her human rights record at the highest level. Second and in the long term even more important for Mary Robinson, the work of the meeting was in fact part of the whole process of re-thinking the role of the UN.

The Strasbourg conference was effectively also part of the preparation for the second World Conference on Human Rights being organised by the UN in Vienna in June 1993. It was a short conference, only two days in length, but remarkably intense; some Irish civil servants who accompanied the President were astonished to find her at one point munching sandwiches for lunch at her desk as she drafted and re-drafted her conclusions. These, encapsulated in ten pages in the official conference report, noted her role as a listener but also made it clear that she was prepared to endorse statements which posed a challenge to the status quo.

The idea was proposed, she emphasised, that the time had come to create a High or Special Commissioner for Human Rights. But merely creating a new job and appointing someone to do it would not, of itself, be enough. 'Clearly the financial and human resources made available must be significantly boosted. In particular, the UN Centre for Human Rights must be placed in a position where it can offer advisory services and technical assistance programmes without impinging on effective human rights monitoring.'

Her summation of the conference was notable for two other emphases. One was her call for further consideration to be given to the creation of an international criminal tribunal at regional or global level 'with powers not only to punish but also to grant reparation to victims'. The other was her expressed conviction that 'at the end of the road it is our capacity as individuals to be concerned and moved by injustice that is the real driving force behind the human rights movement'.

Striking a balance – the theme of her 1992 Allen Lane lecture on the relationships between men and women and the institutions of political power – was also, in a sense, at the core of her thinking on human rights problems. Personal involvement and commitment at one end of the scale, institutional innovation and executive power at the other.

By now, as it happened, her future career was already beginning to take shape. In response to the Vienna Conference, the UN had decided to appoint a Commissioner on Human Rights and the first incumbent of the office in January 1994 was from Ecuador, Jose Ayalo-Lasso. The primary task of the office was to secure a more widespread implementation of the UN Declaration on Human Rights adopted in 1948. The Vienna Conference itself had taken a lead not only from the declaration, but from the first International Conference on Human Rights in Teheran in 1968. Strictly speaking, its parent was the UN Committee on Economic, Social and Cultural Rights. The new office was to have many teething problems. Its budget was limited, as were its functions. According to the UN resolution establishing it, these are:

> To promote and protect the effective enjoyment by all of civil, cultural, economic, political and social rights, including the right to development; to provide advisory services, technical and financial assistance in the field of human rights to States that request them; to coordinate United Nations education and public information programmes in the field of human rights; to play an active role in removing the obstacles to the full realisation of human rights and in preventing the continuation of human rights violations throughout the world; to engage in a dialogue with governments in order to secure respect for human rights; to enhance international cooperation for the promotion and protection of human rights; to coordinate

human rights promotion and protection activities throughout the United Nations system; to rationalise, adapt, strengthen and streamline the United Nations machinery in the field of human rights in order to improve its efficiency and effectiveness.

This 148-word menu is of a type which will be familiar to connoisseurs of international organisations and the resolutions they pass. It makes no mention of resources; it skates over the undeniable problem that, as many human rights abuses are committed by governments, the self-same governments will rarely seek UN help to extirpate them; and it accepts that it cannot operate any sanctions against any offending governments, organisations or individuals. Even more relevantly, it ignores the central definitional problems which have plagued human rights campaigns wherever and by whomsoever they have been inaugurated: Western nations see human rights problems as existing only, or at the very least primarily, in developing countries, whereas the latter countries defend themselves against such charges by arguing that the price of security for all is a loss of rights for some, and pointing unavailingly to Western myopia in the same area. As a menu, it is very much *à la carte*, and what appears on the plate will, at the end of the day, reflect the characteristics and political skills of the High Commissioner above everything else. In the circumstances of its institution, it was hardly a recipe for dramatic executive action and indeed in its beginnings the office operated with little fanfare.

By March 1994, when Mary Robinson delivered a major speech at the Harvard University's John F. Kennedy School of Government on the future role of the UN, she was striking a positive note. There had been achievements in human rights in the past fifty years, she said, and it was important to hold onto them. For the future, connectedness, listening, sharing and participation were fundamental ways of structuring international relationships.

This was the context in which, about half-way through Mary Robinson's term of office as President of Ireland, there was a contretemps involving President and government in an issue which was, seen in retrospect, of considerable significance for what was to come. It also involved Dick Spring in a way which re-opened the wounds of the previous encounter on both sides. It related to the UN.

For years, the usefulness and effectiveness of the United Nations had been increasingly questioned. It had had some modest successes in peace-keeping operations but had been continually handicapped by the unwillingness of member governments to allow it to make more than a marginal input into national policies in contested areas. The United States, in protest against some decisions by third-world dominated UN committees or agencies, was refusing to pay its appropriate financial contributions, adding to the recurrent resource crisis within the organisation.

In 1994, a proposal emerged for a new committee outside the UN itself and funded by the Ford Foundation to examine the future role and function of that organisation. Mary Robinson was one of those invited to be a member and, in a sense, her track record made her an ideal candidate. There was a likelihood that, because of her seniority, she would become co-chair of the Committee and that the Committee would become known, in the way of these things, as the 'Robinson Committee'.

At one level, this invitation was another honour for the Irish presidency and by extension for Ireland itself and signalled the extent to which Mary Robinson had raised the country's profile. The Department of Foreign Affairs was asked for its view and indicated to the government that, despite some reservations, it had no objection to the President accepting the invitation. The government as a whole, however, decided otherwise and yet again the stage was set for a difficult and perhaps dangerous confrontation.

Unwittingly, the situation had been exacerbated by the terms of the letter which was initially sent to the President indicating the government's unwillingness to allow her to accept a position on the committee in that it implied that there were constitutional obstacles in the way of her acceptance. This was dangerous territory to stray into when dealing with a constitutional lawyer but Mary Robinson did not rely on her own expertise alone. She took legal advice, not on a personal basis but on behalf of the office of the President, from two senior members of the Bar. One of them was Frank Clarke, the Chairman of the Bar Council; the other was Gerry Durcan, who had been junior counsel on a number of Mary Robinson's constitutional cases. As might have been expected, this legal advice was that the invitation from the Ford Foundation had no relevance to her constitutional position as President and that she therefore was perfectly free to accept it. She told the government as much.

The matter was now back on the government agenda, in capital letters this time. In the course of reviewing the situation, it emerged that the government's view was misrepresented in the wording of the original letter sent to her. Effectively, the problem did not relate to her constitutional rights but to the possibility that the Committee might adopt a policy position or positions which would be at variance with those of the Irish government. The same problem could arise even if she did not chair the Committee: membership of the committee itself could create the same problems if the Committee as a whole made policy recommendations with which the Irish government would have to disagree.

If this were the case, there would then be the highly awkward situation in which the Irish government, for its own good geo-political reasons, would find itself in opposition to the conclusions of a committee chaired by the President of Ireland. In these circumstances, talk about Mary Robinson's constitutional rights would not bridge the political gap easily, or perhaps at all, and the inevitable outcome would be considerable political embarrassment on all sides and perhaps worse.

This argument made much more sense than one based on a challenge to the President's constitutional rights and for that reason was accepted as such, no doubt with some reluctance but with a sense of inevitability. Mary Robinson's legal training and experience, in the end, was a powerful offset to her personal inclinations in the matter. It might all have ended there but for the fact that the presence of independent legal advisers in Áras an Uachtaráin somehow leaked to the media shortly afterwards.

The President believed – and wrote to the Taoiseach to express her belief – that the Tánaiste or someone in his office had been responsible for the leak. Albert Reynolds, with, one suspects, a sense of relief, passed the letter on to Dick Spring who was furious at what he believed was a totally unwarranted reflection on himself and his officials. He had not leaked the information; he was personally satisfied that none of his officials had done so either; and he made his views clear in no uncertain terms. A frosty stand-off rapidly developed and it was quite some time before the temperature cooled on both sides.

The incident is, however, one which needs to be considered in the light of Mary Robinson's earlier involvement in UN-sponsored human rights activities, and in the context of two specific later instances in which Dick Spring and the Department of Foreign Affairs played a crucial and positive role in the interface between the President and the UN. In the meantime, her interest in human rights waxed rather than waned, and she was not slow to avail of other opportunites as they were presented to her.

The following year, for example, she was to return to the theme of human rights, but in a much more specific context when she gave the keynote speech in Strasbourg to another Council of Europe conference on 'Equality and Democracy: Utopia or Challenge?' Here she addressed, without specifically endorsing it, but with evident warmth, the vexed question of parity democracy – the idea that because there are two equal sexes, almost like constituencies, each should be entitled to equal representation on democratically elected bodies, and that positive action, including quotas, could be applied to ensure this.

'What is society losing by not having that parity?' she asked with a not totally convincing air of innocent enquiry. 'What contribution would it bring to the broader debate on the malaise and scepticism about modern representative government and parliament? What differences would it make to have a balance between men and women at every level? Would the views of women, their way of organising and their interpretation of social priorities have an impact on the structure of modern societies? What kind of adjustments would men need to make, both in their involvement within the home and in the structures of society as a whole?'

As she was making speeches like these, opinions were being canvassed internationally about possible successors to the Secretary-General of the UN, Dr Boutros Boutros Ghali, who was due to retire in 1997. Partly because of the earlier incident, Mary Robinson was repeatedly rumoured to be interested in the position. There were, however, a number of problems. One of them was that the Secretary-General might, in normal circumstances, have a reasonable expectation that his tenure of the office would be renewed for a second term. But circumstances were not normal, insofar as the United States and a number of other countries had become increasingly dissatisfied with what they saw as his inadequacy and were anxious to see him replaced.

While these powerful Western nations could block his re-appointment they could not, however, have a central role in the nomination of his successor. The biggest problem was that those nations, mostly from the developing world, who had played a key role in the choice of Dr Boutros Boutros Ghali might have been prepared to accept *force majeure* in the matter of his re-appointment but they would not lie down under a new appointment proposed by the United States.

Mary Robinson's early denials that she was interested in the post were not sufficiently strenuous to put people off the scent and indeed there was a time when the possibility that she might throw her hat in the ring was not entirely discounted. The obstacles to her appointment were substantial. The first of them was the geo-political situation already mentioned. The second was that it would be difficult to be considered as a serious applicant for the job without declaring one's candidacy publicly. In 1996, with two years of her presidency still to run, this would have undoubtedly been a high-risk option.

Here again the Department of Foreign Affairs would be a key player. Accordingly, a meeting took place early in 1996, involving the Department and a representative of the Tánaiste, to assess the situation. The inference was clear: if Mary Robinson was interested, the Department would play its part to the full in organising an intensive campaign at the UN and elsewhere to maximise her chances. In one sense, the contrast with 1994 could not have been more marked. Now the Department, presumably with the implicit approval of the government, was offering to back her all the way. But Mary Robinson was genuinely not interested.

The rumours of the President's candidacy for the top UN job waned, although they never entirely disappeared. However, the scene was now set, although the participants did not know it at the time, for the big push that took place in the early months of 1997 to help secure the UN High Commissionership on Human Rights for the President.

Jose Ayalo-Lasso, the first High Commissioner, succeeded in increasing its budget substantially, largely by securing subventions from private charitable and other organisations, and by 1997 he oversaw an annual budget of some £30 million, a staff of some 250 people in the organisation's head office in Geneva and approximately 250 other staff at various locations around the world. The rest of the track record, however, was not good. An attempt to make the UN's human rights presence felt in Rwanda was a lamentable failure, earning a scathing report from Amnesty International.

Domestic political exigencies then intervened and Ayalo-Lasso was summoned back to Ecuador to take up the position as his country's foreign minister. Quite unexpectedly, a succession race was open. It was just after that, on 12 March 1997, that Mary Robinson announced formally that she would not be seeking a second term. She indicated as she made it that the decision had been taken some time earlier, presumably to reduce (because she could not eliminate) speculation that in fact she had waited until the vacancy at the UN arose before making up her mind about the presidency.

'It's very hard to take a decision like that,' she explained just before she left Áras an Uachtaráin. 'We went away to Malta for a week to take a decision and came back without one. But while I had taken no decision, I knew that I had shifted. Now I needed a context. The letters were coming in and the pressures were piling up, not least from the sectors that I most care about.'

Almost immediately it became widely understood that she was passionately interested in filling the position at the end of her term of office in December 1997. The government as a whole and the Department of Foreign Affairs in particular immediately launched a major lobbying campaign, kicked off by the Taoiseach, John Bruton, who lobbied President Clinton privately during a St Patrick's Day visit to Washington. In Iveagh House a special three-person committee, headed by a former Irish ambassador to the UN, coordinated a network of contacts and put pressure on anyone they thought could help.

Although the groundswell of support for Mary Robinson was immediate and substantial, there were several obstacles, real or potential, to be confronted. The first was the opposition. The other major contender in the field was the Costa Rican ambassador to the US, Sonia Picardo-Sotela, with Elizabeth Rehn, the former Finnish defence minister, as an outsider. Although the Costa Rican candidate was fervently supported by the Latin American countries, her chances were never highly rated and by the beginning of June it was already being intimated that she had been told that the post was not hers. Later, her country's ambassador to the UN was the only speaker at the UN General Assembly to query the ratification of Mary Robinson's appointment.

The two other potential problems were geo-political. One was that Mary Robinson should not be seen too openly as the candidate of the highly-developed Western nations, although this was evidently the case. There was no point, in the circumstances, in countries like the US and Britain pretending that they did not support her: what had to be done was to widen the base of her support and this was the chief objective of the Irish diplomatic and political campaign. Suggestions were made at the time that her eventual success owed much to her membership of the Trilateral Commission, an elite group of people which its critics believe embodies a subtle, non-governmental and malign form of international influence. It is not a secret organisation, insofar as it has prestigious addresses in Manhattan, Paris and Tokyo and publishes occasional papers. Its meetings, however, are private, and its funding obscure. That, together with a membership that includes or has included such notables as Henry Kissinger and George Bush, is not calculated to reassure doubters.

Mary Robinson was a member of the Commission for many years, and served on its executive from 1973 until 1980. The former Taoiseach, Garret FitzGerald, has also been a member as have the former Labour Cabinet minister, Justin Keating, and the former Irish EC Commissioner, Peter Sutherland. Mary Robinson's membership, although widely known, has barely been commented on, and its effect, if any, on her candidature for the UN appointment must remain unknown. All that can be said with any certainty is that it would not have endeared her to at least some UN member states. As far as Mary Robinson herself is concerned, it does not pose any problems. 'It has never impinged on me as it has impinged, I know, on the conspiracy theory theorists. My overall impression is that it is a further illustration of how small the club world of power is. If you don't know that, you don't know much about how power is exercised in the world. It was a learning curve – it was the other end of the stream from the Dublin City Council: I didn't achieve anything in *it* either! I did learn. Not that the Trilateral Commission itself did *anything*. It was the excuse for people to be together, have a context to be together and to talk about whatever they talked about privately. I was out of that loop so I didn't know what the hell they were talking about. But if you want to have a conspiracy theory, that's it.'

The other factor worth commenting on is her attitude to China, which has traditionally regarded UN-based human rights criticism of her actions as a thinly-veiled excuse for interference in her internal affairs. Mary Robinson, in her active political years, was never slow to condemn human rights abuses by China, particularly in Tibet. She even took part in a protest outside the Chinese Embassy on Dublin in 1990, during her presidential election campaign. And the Irish government's position on China was, if anything, harder by 1997, when the government backed an EU resolution critical of China at a meeting of the Commission on Human Rights in Geneva.

Nonetheless, the Chinese appear not to have signalled disapproval during the behind-the-scenes negotiating that preceded her appointment or, if they did, they indicated that they were not prepared to push it to the point of open criticism. On 12 June 1997, a bare three months after the vacancy had been announced, the new UN Secretary-General, Kofi Annan, announced that he would be proposing her to the General Assembly as the new UN High Commissioner for Human Rights, and the appointment was finally ratified on 17 June.

Mary Robinson was to leave the presidency with a sense of achievement but also with some considerable regret. 'I was certainly conscious that coming into this position was entirely different from what I had done before. Previously it was all about effecting change through using law. As President, I had a total commitment to remain within the constitutional framework and I had then to see what I could try to do. One of the very evident things was to be in touch with what mattered to people and what they were doing and to try to represent that. I have learned – and it has been very enriching – that what people are doing is not captured by the formal structures of society and actually finds them a barrier. Power does not reside where it should.'

What is unexpected, she feels, is the way the presidency prepared her for her next assignment. 'I feel, curiously, that I'm more prepared to take on the daunting task of being High Commissioner for Human Rights because I know more after six and a half years of being President about real human rights, human endeavour, human aspirations, poverty and deprivation. It's because I have had to forget the tools of the doing and learn the skills of the listening and the linking.'

Above all this remains her commitment to women and to a woman's way of doing things. Her view of the role and potential of women does not limit itself to the often vexed question of whether women should benefit from quotas in politics, in employment or in other areas. It goes beyond that to argue that there should be a greater role for women, not just because they are equal, but because they are different.

In a speech to a Council of Europe Conference in 1995, she put it this way: 'In contrast to many of the formal structures of organised society, which are based on precedent and are hierarchical, women seem to devise instinctively structures which are open, enabling, consultative and flexible. I have observed a similar *modus operandi* in women's groups and networks in the developing world. Is there not a strong case for thinking that those formal structures and decision-making processes of society – whether political, business, trade union, public service or whatever – could benefit greatly from the style of decision-making and leadership operating in such women's groups? Perhaps they provide the best evidence of the benefits of parity democracy.'

At times she has emphasised the common humanity of women and men and at other times she emphasised women's different (and by implication better) ways of doing things. The balance was neatly struck in two major addresses in the United States. The cause of women was 'inseparable from the cause of humanity itself', she told a University of California audience at Berkeley in October 1991. Three years later, she was arguing to the UN Forum on Women's Leadership in New York that women were not the only potential beneficiaries of equality. 'Equality in the workplace, in public life and in the home has to stress the wider benefits for men and society as a whole,' she said.

Her credo on equality, however, was embodied in her 1992 Allen Lane lecture. Up-beat and optimistic, she reflected again on the experience of her election campaign and how it had revealed to her 'the new energies and real creative forces which still remain outside the power structures of the established order.' She was not arguing for the replacement of one set of power structures by another but for willingness on the part of each to learn from the other, 'so that men and women have an equal chance to make their contribution and find their creativity in a society which neither owns and both share.'

In her seven years as President, Mary Robinson used these insights, the insights of a feminism which escapes from the stereotypes, in a number of ways. She used them as a counterweight to the tendency of all the professions, not least the profession of politics, to colonise and dominate areas of human experience and power, and served notice on all of them that they have to learn to be partners in a more complex relationship with all the different groups and individuals who make up society as a whole. She used them to give the language of human rights and law – language in which she was already devastatingly proficient even before she became President – a human and community context which would be irrelevant in a court of law but which would evoke a strong and direct response from all her listeners. And she listened before she spoke, an approach which has been the key to achieving moral leadership without direct power – a role for the presidency that she knew was achievable as she campaigned for it, although she did not know precisely what form it would take, or how it could be implemented.

She did more, though, than change the presidency. She was the symbol of, and reflected to many audiences abroad, a new sense of Irish maturity and self-confidence in which everyone Irish, men as well as women, could participate. It is a self-confidence which did not exclude self-criticism: even after she had been confirmed as High Commissioner, but before taking up office, she warned one of her Irish audiences of the dangers of racism close to home. Her years in Áras an Uachtaráin, instead of isolating her from social reality, sharpened her focus on the many things in Irish society which still need to be put right, and on the inequalities and injustices which still exist. But she also became symbolic of a renewed and in many ways deepened set of relationships between Ireland and other countries – relationships based on mutual respect rather than on ancient or not-so-ancient stereotypes.

Like her own presidency, this is the subject, not of image but of reality. Ireland is no longer the picturesque backwater beloved of Hollywood, or the supplicant with the begging bowl at the door of its richer European neighbours. It is a country where economic growth is increasing at an unprecedented rate, even as the political problems connected with the distribution of that wealth remain. It is a country to which former emigrants are returning in increasing numbers to take up jobs in expanding new industries and services. It is a country in which political decisions have increased the percentage of its GDP devoted to foreign aid and at an unprecedented if still inadequate rate. And it is a country which, for these and many other reasons, has a real significance in the relationship between the Northern and Southern hemispheres.

The new note she struck still resonates, and there is no doubt that the new challenges she has undertaken will deepen, rather than sever, the links between Mary Robinson and the people of Ireland.

NOTES

Chapter 1

1   Michael O'Sullivan, *Mary Robinson: The Life and Times of an Irish Liberal*, Blackwater, Dublin, 1993. I am grateful to Michael O'Sullivan for many of the details used in *passim*.

2   'Family Positions and the Attainment of Eminence', by R.S. Albert, *Gifted Child Quarterly* (1980), 24, pp. 87-95.

3   *Irish Times*, 13 November 1993.

4   'Cherishing the Irish Diaspora', Address to the houses of the Oireachtas by President Mary Robinson, 2 February 1995.

Chapter 2

5   *National Action: Plan for the National Recovery of Ireland*, by Josephus Anelius, GAA, 1943, pp 119-120.

6   Information from Enda McDonagh.

7   For full text see *The Furrow*, Maynooth, Vol. 23, No. 6, June 1972.

Chapter 3

8   Garret FitzGerald, *All in a Life*, Gill & Macmillan, Dublin, 1991, p. 146.

9   Quoted in *Masterminds of the Right*, by Emily O'Reilly, Attic Press, Dublin, 1988, p. 35.

10   *Irish Times*, 28 October 1974.

11   Profile by Mary Maher, *Irish Times*, 26 March 1982.

Chapter 4

12   Maurice Hickey, *Evening Herald*, 7 June 1977.

13   *Viking Dublin Exposed: the Wood Quay Saga*, edited by John Bradley, O'Brien Press, Dublin, 1984.

14   *Wood Quay: the Clash over Dublin's Viking Past*, University of Texas Press, Austin, 1988, p. 111.

15   Speech to Women's Studies Forum, UCD, 2 May 1986.

16   Interview with Geraldine Kennedy, *Irish Times*, 28 July 1979.

Chapter 5

17   Much of the chronology in this section is drawn from Tom Hesketh's invaluable and extraordinarily detailed study, *The Second Partitioning of Ireland: the Abortion Referendum of 1983*, Brandsma Books, Dublin, 1990.

18   Hesketh, p. 2.

19   Hesketh, p. 71.

20   Hesketh, p. 132.

Chapter 6

21   Archbishop (later Cardinal) Cahal Daly of Armagh, Primate of All Ireland.

22   Speech to Merriman Summer School, 24 August 1985.

23   Stephen Collins, Spring and the Labour Story, O'Brien Press, Dublin, 1993, p. 133.

24   Mary Maher interview, *Irish Times*, 26 March 1982.

25   Fergus Finlay, *Mary Robinson: A President with a Purpose*, O'Brien Press, Dublin, 1990, p. 89.

26   Interview with Nicholas Robinson, *Irish Times*, 22 October 1990.

27   I am indebted to my Dublin City University colleague, Ray Byrne BL, for much of the information in this section.

28   [1987] E.C.R. 1453.

29   Application No. 15404/89.

Chapter 7

30   Emily O'Reilly, *Candidate: The Truth behind the Presidential Campaign*, p. 38.

31   Finlay, p. 47.

32   O'Reilly, p. 61.

33   Finlay, p. 55.

34   Mary Maher, *Irish Times*, 26 March 1982.

35   Finlay, p. 119.

36   Finlay, p. 126.

37   See O'Reilly, *passim*.

38   Finlay, p. 129. The TD, John Browne, was speaking at Wexford in support of Brian Lenihan, who was present at the meeting.

39   *Sunday Telegraph*, 4 November 1990.

40   Finlay, p. 135.

41   Quoted in Deirdre McQuillan, *Mary Robinson: A President in Progress, Gill & Macmillan*, 1994, p. 97.

42   *Irish Times*, 12 May 1992.

43   Interview with Maol Muire Tynan, *Irish Times*, 16 October 1990.

Chapter 8

44   *Irish Press*, 13 September 1991.

45   Seán Duignan, *One Spin on the Merry-Go-Round*, Blackwater Press, Dublin, p. 108.

46   Duignan, p. 107.

47   Duignan, p. 107.

48   Mary Holland, *Irish Times*, 13 April 1995.

49   Duignan, p. 7.

GLOSSARY

AC – The Administrative Council of the Labour Party, was the party's executive authority during the period of Mary Robinson's membership.

Anglo-Irish Agreement – signed in 1985 between the Garret FitzGerald-led coalition government and Prime Minister Margaret Thatcher's administration in Britain, this agreement was widely rejected by unionists because it gave the Irish government a consultative role in the internal affairs of Northern Ireland.

Áras an Uachtaráin – the name of the former Vice-Regal Lodge in Dublin's Phoenix Park, since 1937 the official residence of the President of Ireland.

Bar, The – the shorthand term for those members of the Irish legal profession who are barristers, rather than solicitors, and plead cases in court; also applies to barristers' place of practice.

Council of Europe – a consultative assembly of nineteen European states, in which the various countries are proportionately represented by members of their national parliaments.

Dáil Eireann – the directly elected legislative assembly, comprising 166 members, which elects the Taoiseach and the government.

EEC – the name under which the entity formerly known as the 'Common Market' became known in 1958.

EU – or European Union, the name by which the EEC became known after the Maastricht Treaty in 1993, and its current designation.

European Commission of Human Rights – one of the Council of Europe institutions, set up in 1959 to enforce the Council's first major initiative, the Convention on Human Rights and Fundamental Freedoms, signed in 1950. The Commission acts as a screen for applications which, if successful, proceed to the European Court of Human Rights

European Court of Human Rights – one of the Council of Europe institutions, set up in 1959 to enforce the Council's first major initiative, the Convention on Human Rights and Fundamental Freedoms, signed in 1950. The Court's decisions are not legally binding on member states, but usually national governments embody court decisions in later domestic legislation.

European Court of Justice – the shorthand term for the Court of Justice of the European Communities, which sits in Luxembourg, and has been established under the Treaties of the European Communities.

Falls Road – in West Belfast, the epicentre of the city's nationalist population, housing – among other services – the Sinn Féin headquarters.

Fianna Fáil – Ireland's largest political party, founded by Eamon de Valera in 1926. It has been in power on many occasions since the creation of the State, including two unbroken sixteen year periods (1932-48 and 1957-73).

Fine Gael – Ireland's second-largest political party, it was formed out of Cumann na nGael, the party which provided the first government of the Irish Free State in 1922. Its fortunes have fluctuated considerably, and since 1932 it has never governed other than as part of a coalition.

Framework Document – negotiated by Albert Reynolds with British prime minister John Major, this was a document which laid part of the groundwork for the IRA cease-fire.

Hot Press – A rock magazine published in Dublin which specialises in unbuttoned interviews with major political and artistic figures.

Inghinidhe na hÉireann – a women's organisation formed in 1900 as a result of a protest against Queen Victoria's visit. Later subsumed into Cumann na mBan, the women's arm of the Irish Volunteers.

Iveagh House – former townhouse of the Guinness family, and presented by them to the State. For many years the administrative headquarters of Ireland's Department of Foreign Affairs.

International Commission of Jurists – an international body limited to some forty lawyers of acknowledged international standing. Mary Robinson succeeded Seán MacBride on this body, on his proposal, when he retired from it in 1987.

Labour Party – the oldest political party in the State, founded in 1912. It has gone through many vicissitudes in a political culture dominated by two larger parties – Fianna Fáil and Fine Gael – which owe their origins to the Civil War split in 1921. From 1954-73 it was strongly anti-coalition.

MRBI – Market Research Bureau of Ireland, one of Ireland's premier polling organisations.

New Ireland Forum – created in 1984 to help fill the political vacuum caused by the breakdown of political activity in Northern Ireland and designed, with indifferent success, to achieve a consensus between all political parties on the island committed to democratic methods.

Oireachtas (The) – the technical collective term for the three institutions which, together, form the governance of the Irish Republic: the Dáil, the Senate, and the presidency.

PLP – the Parliamentary Labour Party, comprising that party's TDs and senators.

Progressive Democrats – a party formed in 1980, largely but not entirely from a split within Fianna Fáil, and driven by liberal economic and social policies and by a rejection of some elements of nationalist thinking on the Northern Ireland issue.

Proportional representation – the Irish electoral system, based on the single transferable vote in multi-member (three, four or five seat) constituencies, designed to achieve a close relationship between the percentage of votes cast nationally for each party, and that party's representation in the Dáil.

Rainbow Coalition – a three-party government comprising Fine Gael, Labour and Democratic

Left, formed after the deposition of Albert Reynolds as Taoiseach in 1994.

Seanad Éireann, The Senate – the upper house of the Irish parliamentary system, whose sixty members are partly indirectly elected (forty-three), partly elected by university graduates (six) and partly nominated by the incoming Taoiseach (eleven). It has a limited power to amend or delay legislation.

SDLP – the Social Democratic and Labour Party, formed in Northern Ireland in 1970 as a coalition of former Nationalist Party members and civil rights activists.

Sinn Féin – the party that regards itself as the most authentic inheritor of the Irish Republican political tradition, and has survived numerous splits and defections. It has a close relationship of an unspecified kind with the IRA, and currently has three members of parliament – two at Westminster, where they do not take their seats, and one in the Dáil (1997).

Stormont – Stormont Castle, seat of the unionist-dominated administration which governed Northern Ireland, with frequently deleterious consequences for the nationalist minority, from 1922-72.

Unionist – the political tradition in Northern Ireland, represented by various parties, which rejects the idea of Irish unity in favour of continuing attachment to Britain and a measure of self-government.

'X' Case – case involving a fourteen year old schoolgirl who had become pregnant, was initially prevented from travelling to Britain for a legal abortion there after the then Attorney-General took out an injunction, based on the constitutional prohibition of abortion. The Irish Supreme Court later interpreted that prohibition as not excluding the right to travel for an abortion in certain circumstances, and the girl involved travelled to Britain, where she had a spontaneous abortion in hospital.

BIOGRAPHIES

Adams, Gerry – president of Sinn Féin, and an elected member of the British parliament for the West Belfast constituency, although he does not take his seat.

Ahern, Bertie – since 1994, the leader of Fianna Fáil (q.v.), head of the Irish government since June 1997.

Airey, Josey – separated from her husband in the early 1980s and subsequently waged a legal battle for legal representation in costly separation proceedings. Her advocate in a number of Irish and European courts was Mary Robinson.

Asmal, Kadar – former lecturer in law in Trinity College, Dublin, and a contemporary there of Mary Robinson. He is currently a minister in the South African government.

Browne, Dr Noel – died in 1997 after a lifetime in Irish politics. He became a government minister on his first day in parliament in 1948, and subsequently established a reputation as a radical left-wing politician, especially on health policy and on Church-State relationships.

Bruton, John – elected leader of the Fine Gael Party in 1990. He was Taoiseach 1994-97, and is currently leader of the Opposition in Dáil Éireann.

Childers, Erskine – Fianna Fáil TD, government minister, and eventually President, the second Protestant holder of that office. His presidential term – he was elected in 1973 – ended prematurely with his death in 1974.

Cluskey, Frank – Dublin trade unionist who led the Labour Party from 1977-81, died in 1988.

Connolly, Niall – Dublin solicitor and a college contemporary of Mary Robinson's who acted as director of elections during her failed bid to win a seat in the Dáil in the 1977 general election.

Corish, Brendan – leader of the Labour Party (1960-1977) when Mary Robinson joined it in 1976, and Minister for Health 1973-77.

Cosgrave, Liam – leader of Fine Gael 1965-1977, and Taoiseach from 1973-77. His government was the first to sponsor an attempt to reform the contraception laws, although he himself voted against the measure.

Cruise O'Brien, Conor – writer and historian who has also been various a diplomat, TD, Senator and government minister. In all of these roles he has been controversial; close to Mary Robinson's views on some issues, he opposed her on others.

Currie, Austin – former member of the Nationalist Party and SDLP, who later joined the Fine

Gael Party in the Republic and became their presidential candidate, standing against Mary Robinson, in 1990. When he was eliminated from the contest, the substantial proportion of his votes that transferred to Mary Robinson ensured her election.

Daly, Cardinal Cahal – former Archbishop of Armagh, who played an active role in community relations in the North, and in Church-State relations generally, during the 1980s and 1990s.

de Valera, Eamon – leader of Fianna Fáil, 1926-1959, and President of Ireland, 1959-73, one of the pre-eminent Irish politicians of the century and the principal architect of the country's 1937 Constitution.

Duignan, Sean – journalist who acted as government press secretary to Taoiseach Albert Reynolds from 1992-94. His book, *One More Spin on the Merry-Go-Round*, is an unvarnished account of political intrigue and tension during that period.

Dukes, Alan – leader of Fine Gael from 1987-1990, when he resigned in the wake of the dismal performance by his party's candidate, Austin Currie, in the presidential election.

FitzGerald, Garret – Garret FitzGerald was leader of Fine Gael 1977-87, and Taoiseach from 1982-87. A friend of Mary Robinson's, he also believed in the need to reform the Irish Constitution, but his efforts in that regard were not crowned with success.

Flynn, Pádraig – former TD, government minister and EC Commissioner from Co. Mayo. His ill-judged attack on Mary Robinson during the last week of the presidential campaign swung many votes in her favour.

Gonne, Maud – early twentieth-century nationalist revolutionary, active particularly in women's movements and in the journalism of the era.

Fennell, Nuala – journalist and consultant who was, as a TD, appointed to the newly-created junior post of Minister for Women's Affairs, 1982-87.

Finlay, Fergus – former trade union official who has been a close adviser to Labour leader Dick Spring for many years. His book *Mary Robinson: A President with a Purpose* is a pacy account of the 1990 election campaign.

Halligan, Brendan – general secretary of the Labour Party when Mary Robinson joined in 1976. A former TD, he is now associated with the Institute of European Affairs in Dublin.

Harris, Eoghan – former Radio Telefís Eireann producer, now a journalist and political consultant. Originally associated with the Workers Party, he now has no political affiliations. He gave considerable advice to the Robinson 1990 campaign, and has also advised former Taoiseach John Bruton.

Harte, Paddy – until 1997 a TD for Donegal, the only Fine Gael representative in his constituency.

Haughey, Charles – former leader of Fianna Fáil, and Taoiseach on a number of occasions. He was replaced as Taoiseach and leader of his party by Albert Reynolds in 1991, after the defeat of his party's candidate, Brian Lenihan, in the 1990 presidential election.

Hederman, Carmencita – Independent member of Dublin City Council, active particularly in liberal and conservationist causes.

Higgins, Michael D. – a strong supporter of Mary Robinson during her years in the Labour Party. He is a TD and was a government minister, 1992-97.

Hillery, Patrick – a doctor who became successively a TD, government minister, EEC Commissioner, and President of Ireland. He served two unopposed terms in the latter post and retired in 1990.

Hume, John – leader of the Social Democratic and Labour Party (SDLP), and closely involved with attempts to resolve community tension in Northern Ireland and with the peace process in particular, since 1968.

Hussey, Gemma – Fine Gael Minister for Education in 1982-87, after a period in the Senate, where she represented the National University of Ireland.

Keating, Justin – an academic and journalist. He is also a former Labour TD and government minister, 1973-77.

Lane, Ann – working as a secretary in insurance when she became Mary Robinson's first part-time, and later full-time secretary.

Lemass, Seán – leader of Fianna Fáil and Taoiseach, 1959-66. He is credited with having contributed substantially to the modernisation of Ireland, and sponsored an early attempt (in 1966) to reform the Constitution.

Lenihan, Brian – a former senator, TD, government minister and Tánaiste who died in 1995. Renowned for his amiability, he was a key figure in Fianna Fáil for many years, but was defeated as their presidential candidate in 1990.

Lynch, Jack – Taoiseach and leader of Fianna Fáil from 1966-79. A cautious moderniser, he was the last Fianna Fáil Taoiseach to win an overall majority in the Dáil.

MacBride, Seán – son of Maud Gonne, and at various times a revolutionary (he was once chief of staff of the IRA), TD, government minister and leader of the small Clann na Poblachta party. A prominent jurist and a winner of both the Lenin and Nobel Peace Prizes, he specialised in high-profile constitutional cases, on some of which he had Mary Robinson as his junior.

Markievicz, Countess – born Constance Gore-Booth of a Sligo Anglo-Irish family. She married a member of the Polish aristocracy, and was intensely involved in revolutionary and social activities in Dublin at the beginning of the twentieth century. She was Ireland's first woman minister (for Labour) in the 1919 Dáil. She died in 1927.

Martin, Fr F.X., OSA – Augustinian priest and historian who was closely involved in – and acted as one of the key representatives of – the campaign to save the Wood Quay archaeological site in Dublin in the late 1970s and early 1980s.

McDonagh, Dr Enda – for many years professor of Moral Theology at St Patrick's College, Maynooth, a Mayo-born theologian who has exercised unparalleled influence, through his writing and teaching, on several generations of Irishmen and women, both lay and clerical.

McQuaid, Dr John Charles – Catholic Archbishop of Dublin 1940-72, during which period he became virtually an icon of religious conservatism, and defended with particular vigour the Republic's civil laws which embodied or echoed Catholic Church doctrine.

Norris, David – Trinity College lecturer and Senator, and a campaigner for gay rights. Mary Robinson was his counsel in the proceedings which eventually, in 1988, produced a ruling in the European Court that Ireland's domestic legislation in this field was in contravention of the European Convention on Human Rights.

O'Reilly, Emily – journalist and author. Formerly on the staff of the *Irish Press* (which closed in 1995), she now works for the *Sunday Business Post* and Radio Ireland. Her book on Mary Robinson, *Candidate: The Truth behind the Presidential Campaign*, was published in 1991.

Owens, Evelyn – now chairperson of the Labour Court, was a long-time member of the Labour Party and a former senator for that party, and one of only two women members of the Parliamentary Labour Party when Mary Robinson joined it in 1976.

Quinn, Ruairí – student leader of the late 1960s and an architect, active in the Labour Party (of which he is now deputy leader) at an early age, and has held a number of important ministerial positions. He was chairman of, and a key figure in, the broadly-based committee that ran Mary Robinson's election campaign in 1990.

Reynolds, Albert – succeeded Charles Haughey as leader of Fianna Fáil and Taoiseach in 1992, himself succumbing to political adversity in 1994, when he lost the leadership. During his period in office, he was closely involved in the negotiations that brought about the IRA cease-fire.

Rogers, Denise – a long-time Labour Party activist and secretary to Ruairí Quinn since the 1970s. Without electoral ambition herself, she nonetheless typifies a critical core element in the party's organisation.

Rogers, John – a Trinity College contemporary of Dick Spring's, and a close friend. Appointed Attorney-General in 1984 in preference to Mary Robinson.

Rosney, Bride – a close friend of Mary Robinson and her family since the late 1970s, when they met on the Wood Quay protest. She is godmother to Mary's youngest child, Aubrey, and was the first-ever appointee – in 1990 – as special adviser to a President of Ireland.

Spring, Dick – leader of the Labour Party since 1982, and the longest-serving leader of any Irish political party. A lawyer, he performs particularly effectively in Opposition, and led his party to an unprecedented thirty-three seat total in 1992, falling back to seventeen seats in 1997 after five years in government.

Stagg, Emmet – Emmet Stagg is a left-wing member of the Labour Party who led opposition within the party to coalition in the 1980s, but secured appointment as a government minister in two coalitions in the 1990s.

Sutherland, Peter – Fine Gael lawyer who was Attorney-General from 1982-84, when he became Ireland's EEC Commissioner. His ability has been recognised in a wide range of business appointments since that date, including that of Director-General of GATT.

Thornley, David – a brilliant Trinity College academic and broadcaster who was one of the new wave of intellectual recruits to the Labour Party in the late 1960s. His parliamentary career never matched his early promise, and he died, aged forty-three, in 1978.

West, Trevor – an academic on the staff of Trinity College since the late 1960s. A keen sportsman and superb organiser, he was director of elections for Mary Robinson's first Senate campaign, and subsequently served for several terms in the same Senate constituency.

Whelehan, Harry – a barrister who was appointed Attorney-General by Charles Haughey and continued in that role under Albert Reynolds. Several of the decisions made by that office during his incumbency became controversial, leading eventually to the defeat of the Reynolds-led government and its replacement by the 'rainbow coalition'.

CHRONOLOGY

1944
21 May: Born Ballina, Co. Mayo, 1944, third child and first daughter of Aubrey and Tessa Bourke

1949-54
             Private education at Miss Ruddy's School, Ballina

1954-61
             Boarding school: Mount Anville, Dublin

1961-62
             Finishing school: Mlle Anita's, Paris

1963
             University: Trinity College, Dublin (Dublin University) – entrance scholarship

1965
             Scholarship in Legal Science

1967
             BA (Mod.), TCD, 1st class
             LL.B 1st class.
             Barrister-at-Law 1st class
             Fellowship, Harvard Law School

1968
             LL.M Harvard Law School, 1st class

1969
July: Appointed Reid Professor of Constitutional and Criminal Law, TCD
Sep: Elected to Senate (Dublin University constituency)
Nov: Attends first meeting of Senate

1970
May: Speaks in Senate on censorship
Dec: Marries Nicholas Robinson
             First president, Women's Progressive Association (later Women's Political Association)

1971
Feb: Circulates text of a bill to change laws on family planning
March: Senate refuses, by majority vote, to add Family Planning Bill to order paper
May: Senate refuses, by majority vote, to add Family Planning Bill to order paper

211

July: Senate votes to refuse Family Planning Bill on first reading, i.e. permission to be printed. Introduces Adoption Bill

Dec: Joins Working Party of Irish Theological Association on the Irish Constitution; appointed Irish member of the EEC Vedel Committee to report on the future of the European Parliament

1972

Feb: Labour Party TDs introduce Family Planning Bill in Dáil, identical to that introduced by Mary Robinson in Senate and it is defeated

April: Mary Robinson's Adoption Bill is withdrawn, with the agreement of the House, after the government gives a commitment to introduce its own legislation

May: Irish Theological Association's Working Party Committee issues report

June: Mary McGee case challenging constitutionality of ban on contraceptives opens in the High Court; Mary Robinson appears for the plaintiff

Oct: First child (Tessa) born

            Mary Robinson publishes text of Family Planning Bill without permission of Senate Member, Executive Committee, Trinity College Dublin Trust

1973

Jan: Appears in court to challenge the decision to hold the general election in February, thus disenfranchising thousands of eighteen year olds who would have been entitled to vote if the election had been postponed for two months

Feb: General election

March: Dr Tessa Bourke, Mary Robinson's mother, dies

May: Re-elected to Senate

May: Presidential election: Erskine Childers (Fianna Fáil) defeats Tom O'Higgins (Fine Gael)

Dec: Supreme Court declares ban on contraception unconstitutional (McGee case)

            Becomes president of Cherish, the association of single parents, on its foundation Member, Joint Oireachtas Committee on EEC legislation

1974

Jan: Second child (William) born

March: Senate refuses second reading to Family Planning Bill

May: Dublin couple have section of 1952 Adoption Act declared unconstitutional; Mary Robinson appears for them in court

July: Government legislation on Family Planning Bill defeated in Dáil

Nov: President Erskine Childers dies

Dec: Cearbhall Ó Dálaigh elected unopposed as President

1975

April: Free Legal Advice Centres opens its first centre in the Dublin working-class estate of Coolock

            Raises, with others, the danger to archaeological heritage caused by excavations at Dublin's Wood Quay

Dec: Supreme Court declares that the rules applying to women on juries are unconstitutional Mary Robinson appears for the plaintiff, Mairín de Burca

            Appointed lecturer in European Community Law, Trinity College, Dublin

1976

March:	Government changes laws on juries in response to de Burca case
April:	Joins Friends of Mediaeval Dublin, organisation launched to defend Wood Quay archaeological site
July:	Government changes adoption laws in response to 1974 legal challenge
	Joins Labour Party
Aug:	Josey Airey, an Irish woman separated from her husband, gets legal aid from Strasbourg to pursue her case in the Irish courts; Mary Robinson acts for her
Oct:	Cearbhall Ó Dálaigh resigns as President
	Accepted as member of Parliamentary Labour Party
	Member of the Advisory Committee, Common Market Law Review
	Joins Irish Transport and General Workers Union
Nov:	Patrick Hillery elected unopposed as President

1977

	Fails to win selection for the Labour Party in the Rathmines Dáil constituency; added to ticket by Labour Administrative Council
May:	Dáil dissolved
June:	General election: fails to win Rathmines seat by 400 votes; Fianna Fáil forms government
July:	Appears before European Commission of Human Rights in Strasbourg for Josey Airey
Aug:	Re-elected to Senate (Dublin University constituency)
Nov:	Appears in first of many court battles to save Wood Quay site
	Chair, Social Affairs Sub-Committee, Oireachtas Joint Committee on EC legislation
	Norris case (on gay rights) begins in Dublin

1978

	Wood Quay controversy continues
Dec:	Loses preliminary hearing in Labour Court on issue of whether Oireachtas pension scheme, by failing to make provision for widowers, is discriminatory

1979

Jan:	Speaks to 10th Congress of Confederation of Socialist parties of EC
March:	Selected to contest Rathmines in elections to Dublin City Council as candidate for the Labour Party
May:	Labour Court reverses equality officer finding on pension scheme case
June:	Elected to Dublin City Council
July:	Appears for plaintiffs in case alleging unconstitutionality of income tax legislation (Murphy case)
	Government passes new law allowing access to family planning methods for married couples only, on doctor's prescription
Oct:	Josey Airey wins case in Europe

1980

March:	Called to Inner Bar
April:	Divorce Action Group formed
	Murphys win tax case in Supreme Court
May:	Calls for end to Special Criminal Court

1981

Feb:	Josey Airey awarded damages in Strasbourg
April:	Expelled from Senate in controversy over woman usher's job
May:	Third child (Aubrey) born
June:	General election; fails to win seat for Labour Party in Dublin West constituency
Sep:	Re-elected to Senate; announces that she will not stand again for Dáil
Nov:	Threatens to vote against government on primary school entry age

1982

Feb:	General election
April:	Anti-Amendment Campaign on abortion is formed
May:	Re-elected to Senate
	Ireland elected to UN Commission on Human Rights
Nov:	General election
	Norris loses case in Supreme Court

1983

Jan:	Resigns from Dublin City Council
Feb:	Re-elected to Senate
March:	Helps to launch Labour Committee Against the Amendment
Sep:	Constitutional referendum on abortion
Oct:	Government legislates to abolish concept of the 'illegitimate child'
	Appointed as member of New Ireland Forum
	Appointed member of Oireachtas Joint Committee on Marriage Breakdown

1984

Jan/Feb:	New Ireland Forum meets
	Patron, Liam Maguire Trust for the Disabled
	Member of the International Centre for the Legal Protection of Human Rights, London
	Fails to secure appointment as Attorney-General

1985

Nov:	Anglo-Irish agreement signed at Hillsborough
	Resigns from Labour Party
	Patron of the Marriage and Family Institute

1986

April:	Introduces bill to change Constitution on divorce
May:	Divorce Action Group campaign starts
June:	Calls for revision of Anglo-Irish Agreement
	Referendum to introduce divorce is defeated

1987

Feb:	General election
March:	Elected to International Commission of Jurists
May:	Re-elected to Senate
Dec:	Calls Anglo-Irish Agreement 'fatally flawed'

1988

Appears for Well Woman Centre in abortion information case in Dublin
Hyland case; equal social welfare benefits
Norris case succeeds in Europe
Opens European Law Centre with husband, Nicholas Robinson

1989

Feb: Withdraws Senate motion on human rights in China 'to avoid misunderstanding'
May: Announces that she will not stand again for election to Senate
        Tributes in Senate to Mary Robinson
        Joins legal chambers in London and Brussels

1990

Jan: Dick Spring announces that he may be a candidate for the presidency
Feb: John Rogers proposes to Mary Robinson, with Spring's approval, that she be the Labour Party's presidential candidate
April: Mary Robinson's candidacy is officially endorsed by the party, although she has declined to re-join and will run as an independent backed by Labour and other political groups
May: Campaign is launched
June: Brian Lenihan is nominated as Fianna Fáil candidate
Sep: Austin Currie is nominated as Fine Gael candidate
Nov: Robinson elected
Dec: Robinson inaugurated

1991

Jan: President is refused permission to give BBC Dimbleby lecture
Feb: New Council of State is appointed; President's appointees include five women, a representative of people with disabilities, and a person from the voluntary sector in Northern Ireland
June: First State visit abroad (to Portugal)
Oct: First meeting of Council of State

1992

Feb: First visit to Belfast
May: State visit to France
July: Address to joint houses of Oireachtas on Irish identity
Oct: Visit to Somalia, followed by visit to UN, and visit to Australia
Nov: General election
Dec: Meets members of GLEN (Gay and Lesbian Equality Network) at Áras an Uachtaráin

1993

Jan: Acts as general rapporteur at Council of Europe meeting on human rights, Strasbourg; Visit to Scotland, the first by an Irish president
May: Visit to US; meets President Clinton; unveils statue to Irish emigrants on Ellis Island
        Visit to London: meets Queen Elizabeth II – the first visit by an Irish head of State to a British monarch
June: Visits West Belfast, where she meets Gerry Adams
Oct: Prince Charles visits President in Dublin
Dec: UN establishes post of High Commissioner for Human Rights

1994

Feb:	Controversy over invitation to Ford Foundation Committee on future of UN
March:	Speaks on future of United Nations at JFK School of Government, Harvard
	Speaks at UN Forum on Women's Leadership in New York
May:	Attends inauguration of President Nelson Mandela in Pretoria
	Opens Ireland's first Famine Museum in Strokestown, Co. Roscommon
Aug:	Visit to Canada; commemorates Irish emigrants at Grosse Isle
Oct:	Visit to Rwanda and other Central African countries

1995

Feb:	Address on emigration to joint houses of the Oireachtas
	President visits Japan; informal comments on Framework Document create controversy
March:	Visit to Latin America

1996

Feb:	Working visit to US
June:	Second visit to Queen Elizabeth II at Buckingham Palace
	State visit to US

1997

Feb:	Visits to England and Wales
March:	Visits Rwanda for the third time
March:	Announces that she would not be seeking a second term in office
April:	Visit to Pope John Paul II in Rome
June:	UN ratifies appointment as High Commissioner for Human Rights
	Addresses Irish Refugee Council on racism
Sept:	Leaves office to take up appointment to United Nations

INDEX